Y0-BZA-784

"The finest book ever written for small and medium-sized manufacturers."

Advance Praise for **Saving American Manufacturing**

"Mike Collins has it right. U.S. manufacturers must now look outside their businesses for new customers, markets, and opportunities. His 'how to's' and real-life methods are must-read and do for small and medium-sized manufacturers. Saving American Manufacturing is a hands-on recipe for turnarounds and developing profitable growth strategies."

Charles France
Manager of Strategic Services, Enterprise Innovation Institute

"A practical, employable resource … for identifying target customers."

Phil Dickie
Sales and Industrial Marketing Consultant

"Book stores have shelves full of business books with catchy titles. What they lack is an answer to the most important question, 'What can I do today to be in business 10 years from now in the face of crushing competition?' Collins has finally written a book that gives you practical direction on how to get started facing a global economy. It is one of the few books you will re-read every year to mine it again for answers to challenges that keep coming."

Richard Armstrong
General Manager, Columbia Machine

"Mike Collins's outstanding book identifies, interprets, and poignantly presents the key external factors and internal/operational imperatives that must be addressed in order for a manufacturing company to remain viable and continue on an improvement path. Without question, this is the finest book ever written for small and medium-sized manufacturers. It will remain the authoritative work on the subject for years to come."

Yurij Wowczuk
VP Sexton Can, Division of ITW

Saving American Manufacturing

Growth Planning for Small and Midsized Manufacturers

Michael P. Collins

© Michael P. Collins, 2006

All rights reserved. No part of this publication may be reproduced or transmitted, in any form or by any means, electronic, mechanical, photocopying, recording, or otherwise, without the prior written permission of the publisher.

This publication is designed to provide accurate and authoritative information in regard to the subject matter covered. It is sold with the understanding that neither the author nor the publisher is engaged in rendering legal, accounting, or other professional service. If legal advice or other expert assistance is required, the services of a competent professional should be sought.

Cover Design: Greg Paus
Publisher: Lorelei Davis Bendinger
Supervising Editor: Bruce Bendinger
Production Editor: Patrick Aylward
Photographer: Steve Ewert
Printer: McNaughton-Gunn, Inc.

ISBN: 0-9763675-1-3

Published by First Flight Books
A Division of Bruce Bendinger Creative Communications, Inc.
2144 N Hudson
Chicago, IL 60614
773.871.1179
www.firstflightbooks.com
firstflightbooks@aol.com

Michael P. Collins
MPC Management, LLC
503.661.1156
www.savingamericanmanufacturing.com
mpcmgt@att.net

*This book is dedicated to America's
small and midsize manufacturers,
whose survival will determine the
long-term growth of the economy.*

Contents

Preface
The American Manufacturing Crisis   xi

Chapter 1
Introduction: Success through Transformation   1
Who Are These Manufacturers We Need to Save?   2
How to Read this Book   4
Success through Transformation in Five Stages   5
Companion Handbook   12
Conclusion   13

Chapter 2
Finding New Customers and Markets   15
New and Growing Industries   16
The Six Essential Questions   20
Sales Prospecting by Phone   37
Conclusion   56
Transition and Transformation   57

Chapter 3
Developing New Products: Transformation through Innovation   59
The Difference between R&D and New Product Development   60
Why New Products Fail   61
Types of New Products   65
Three Other Approaches to Developing New Products   74
A 7-step Approach to New Product Development   80
Advantages and Disadvantages of the 7-Step Process   90
The New Product Challenge   103

Chapter 4
Selecting the Best Industrial Distribution Channels   107
Sales Channel Alternatives   108

Primary Factors to Consider in Selecting Channels   111
Getting Ready to Interview: How to Profile the Sales Channel   124
Phase II – How to Find General Reps and Distributors   130
Conclusion   131

Chapter 5
Adding Specialized Services   **135**
EBC Industries – A Job Shop Example   136
Ashland Inc. – A Product Manufacturer Example   141
How to Get Started Adding Services   146
Conclusions   149

Chapter 6
Changing the Organization to Compete   **151**
A Job Shop Example   152
Product Manufacturer Example   153
Four Organization Types   155
What Is Driving Organizational Change?   159
Strategic Renewal: Getting Started   163
Strategic Renewal: Evaluation   164
The Special Case of the Family Manufacturing Business   171
Team Concepts   174
Case #1 – Prime/Sub Alliance   175
Case #2 – Outsourcing Business Alliance   182
Case #3 – Exploring Foreign Markets   188
Conclusion   193

Chapter 7
Cost Reduction and Continuous Improvement   **195**
Reducing Costs and Maintaining Margins   196
Costs and Margins   210
How to Get Started   214
Subcontracting   222
Keeping the Work in the U.S.   235
The Bottom Line on Offshoring   239
Conclusion   244

Chapter 8
Workforce Education and Training   **247**
"The Skills Gap"   247
Problems and Challenges   248
Service Industry Jobs   251
Automation and Technology   254
Apprentice Programs   255
The Crisis in Education   257
Large Manufacturers and Globalization   264
Solutions to the Skills Gap   267
Apprentice Training   272
Education – K-12   275
Vocational Schools and Colleges   277
Universities and Four-Year Colleges   279
Conclusion   280

Chapter 9
Developing a Growth Plan or a Turnaround Plan   **285**
What about Strategic Plans?   286
A Growth Plan for Small and Midsize Manufacturers   291
Step A: Internal Information – Show Me the Money   293
Step B: External Analysis – Where Will We Grow   298
Step C: Analysis – Putting It All Together   301
Step D: Implementation – The Magical Step   305
Step E: Strategic Renewal – Changing the Organization   308
Conclusions – Investing for the Long Term   313

Chapter 10
Conclusions – We Can Compete   **317**
The New Stars of Manufacturing   318
Wanted: New Types of Leaders   331
Discovering Opportunities in Change   337

Preface

The original title of this book was *How to Save American Manufacturing*. Well, let's get the bad news out of the way first. There's no way that we'll save *all* American manufacturers. If you make large quantities of a relatively simple product, with suppliers that are squeezing you on price – well, it's going to be tough to survive.

But, if you become closer to your customers, innovate, and make things that are hard to make in quantity half way around the world – well, your future might be a lot brighter than you think. And, our revised title delivers on the promise – *Saving American Manufacturing*.

With energy, innovation, and a transformation into a company that understands all the opportunities offered by your markets and your customers – you can succeed. The innovative American spirit and our capacity for hard work and hustle can make it a productive and prosperous future. It's a new world. You may have to learn some new ways of working, but it's a world where Americans who make things can still play a large, vital, and important role.

The American Manufacturing Crisis

Today, there is a problem of massive proportions in our economy. It is a crisis so great that ignoring it could pull the whole U.S. into permanent stagnation. That problem is the decline of American manufacturing – a problem whose ramifications are barely understood by much of the American public and largely ignored by politicians. Moreover, it is a problem that does not lend itself to easy solutions.

That problem is the slow but relentless decline of the manufacturing sector, which will have far-reaching consequences on the economy in terms of exports, the trade deficit, job creation, state economies, strategic industries, defense, and the research and development that has powered American innovation.

Manufacturing has traditionally supplied the family wage jobs for a significant portion of the middle class. It can continue to supply a good share of good jobs if we make saving the manufacturing base as important as the war against terrorism.

Am I being overly dramatic? Actually, I'm not. Terrorism can destroy lives, infrastructure, and our feelings of being secure in our own country. The destruction of this important part of our economy could have a similar – and even more widespread – effect. While the answers may be difficult, the mission is clear: we can't allow manufacturing to decline below the critical mass it will take for manufacturing to continue to play its vital role in the rest of the economy.

The Changes that Led to the Crisis

They started in the 1980s. Everyone likes to blame Wal-Mart or the Chinese or recent economic changes for the decline of manufacturing, but the forces that led to this new stage of globalization are not new. These changes began more than 20 years ago and the results were predicted in a 1987 report "Technology and the American Economic Transition" from the Office of Technology Assessment.

Here's what that report predicted:

> "During the next two decades, new technologies, rapid increases in foreign trade, and the tastes and values of a new generation of Americans are likely to reshape virtually every product, every service, and every job in the U.S. These forces will shake the foundations of the most secure American businesses."[1]

This was the very first report in my research. It predicted the potential problems associated with the start of a transition to the "Post Industrial" economy. The report went on to say that "Certainly, it is now possible that the U.S. will find its living standards in decline with respect to its competitors, and discover its role as an economic and military leader of the free world called into question in the next two decades."

Well, it has now been eighteen years since that report and all evidence seems to support the conclusions. The report made four fundamental predictions that are worthy of review. They are as follows:

1. **"Change can lead to wrenching dislocation and pain for workers with obsolete skills, for management unable to recognize opportunity, and for communities where traditional businesses have failed."**

Figure P-1

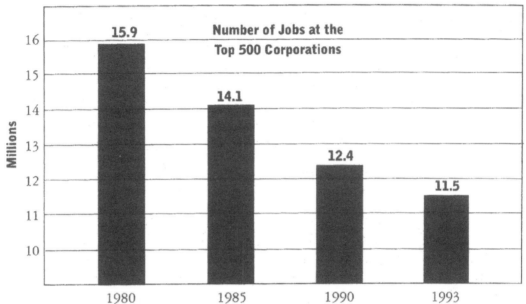

Declining Employment at the Top 500 U.S. Industrial Corporations

Source: U.S. Department of Commerce, Bureau of the Census, *U.S. Statistical Abstract*, various years, and "The Fortune 500. The Largest U.S. Industrial Corporations," *Fortune*, April 18, 1994.

Clearly, this prediction was correct. It is particularly true when you examine the losses in manufacturing and related industries,

- More than 2.3 million manufacturing jobs have been lost just since the year 2000. Over 6 million manufacturing jobs have been lost since 1979.
- The wrenching pain of job loss is not limited to blue-collar workers. Figure P-1 shows the number of corporate jobs lost in Fortune 500 corporations. Between 1980 and 1993 the top 500 industrial corporations cut 4.5 million jobs, both blue collar and white collar.
- In addition, the information jobs that were supposed to be the answer in the post-industrial society – jobs such as financial services, and software – are also slowly moving to lower cost countries.

Figure P-2

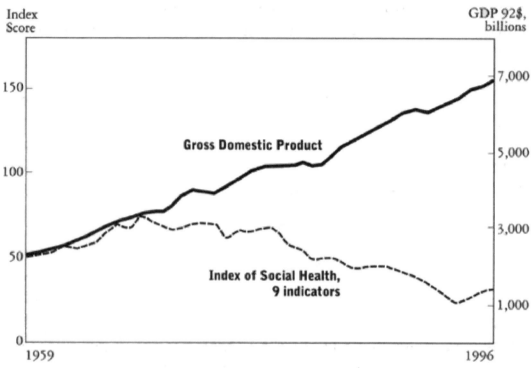

Index of Social Health and Gross Domestic Product, 1959-1996

Source: Fordham Institute of Innovation on Social Policy

So the first prediction that the transformation could affect every product, service, and job is proving correct; and the dislocation and pain seems to be spread over a wide range of industries and jobs. But wrenching dislocation and pain are turning out to be more than just loss of jobs.

The Index of Social Health and Gross Domestic Product (Figure P-2) was created by the Fordham Institute of Innovation on Social Policy to measure 9 social indicators in relation to economic growth. Since the 1970s the Index of Social Health has shown a disturbing downward trend in measurements like child poverty, healthcare coverage, youth homicide, food assistance, housing assistance, and employee benefits, as well as other key measures of social health.

Certainly, the decline of manufacturing is not responsible for all of this, but, just as clearly, it has been a significant contributing factor.

Figure P-2 shows that the long-term trend line for social problems is worsening as compared to GDP growth. This trend is closely associated with the decline of working class and middle class income. This is an important chart regardless of whether you are a liberal or conservative. History shows us that eventually we pay for social problems one way or another. Usually it is the government that is forced to step in and attempt to provide the programs and answers. However, government answers are often expensive and inefficient compared to our market economy. One part of the answer is to have an economy that provides the family wage jobs that help support families and keep them together.

Now let's look at prediction #2.

2. **"Change can create an America in graceless decline – its living standards falling behind those of other world powers."**

The answer again, for much of America, is YES. Even with the inarguable growth in wealth in the top tier, U.S. living standards have fallen for most of the middle and working class.

Figure P-3

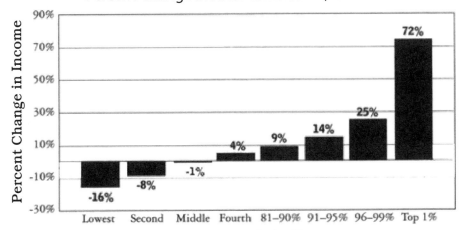

Percent Change in After-Tax Income, 1977-1994

Source: Congressional Budget Office

Figure P-3 shows that since 1977, the after tax income of 60% of American households have been declining and another 20% have made a small gain. The data in this report clearly shows that the shift to the "Post Industrial Economy" is now lowering the living standards of the majority of Americans. Whether our living standards will fall behind the other world powers is still in question, but an "America in graceless decline" is, sad to say, an appropriate prediction.

We are approaching degrees of inequality we usually associate with corrupt and inefficient countries – a disturbing trend.

3. **"Change can result in a gap between those fortunate enough to have the talents, education, and connections needed to seize the emerging opportunities and those forced into narrowly defined, heavily monitored, temporary positions."**

The gap adds another dimension to this inequality. For one of the strengths of our country and our economy has been the possibility of improving the life of you and your family through hard work and opportunity.

Clearly, the gap between the haves and have-nots is widening at an accelerating pace. Moreover, many windows of opportunity seem to be closing. This has been documented by many economic studies. It is shown graphically in Figure P-4, The Economic Polarization of America, 1967-1997. The chart shows that the after-tax income of the poor and middle class has not gained in 30 years, while the richest 6% of our population has enjoyed an unprecedented increase in income – a much worse problem than the 1987 prediction.

4. **"Will people be able to find a variety of attractive opportunities for work, or will only the credentialed elite enjoy such opportunities?"**

All evidence points to the fact that "the credentialed elite" (the top 20% of the working population in income) will enjoy the opportunities. This group includes those with technical or professional degrees. It is not just about getting a college education. You probably buy your Starbucks from a college grad. To be credentialed enough to command high incomes depends on getting the right education and training.

Figure P-4: The Economic Polarization of America, 1967-1997

Average Inflation-Adjusted Annual After-Tax Income of
Poor, Middle-Class and Rich Households

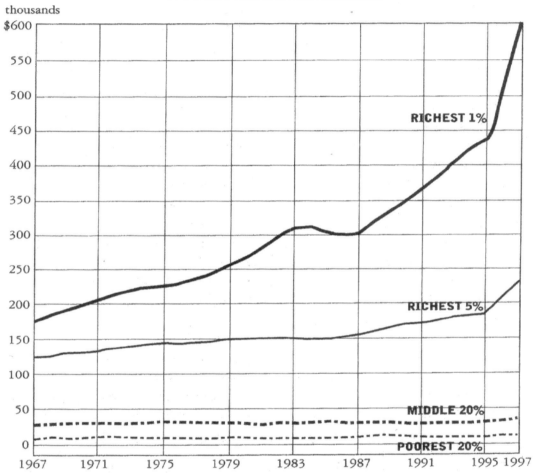

Source: Doug Henwood, *The Nation*, March 29, 1999, modified to include the top 1% and
to include 1997 figures based on Table 1-1C of the Congressional Budget Office study
"Effective Federal Tax Rates," October, 2001, p. 128.

But, a related question that few people ask is "if more people invest in advanced education and expensive training will there be enough non-manufacturing jobs to go around. The U.S. Department of Labor lists the following jobs as the "fastest growing occupations" covered in the 2003 "Occupational Outlook from 2000–2010."

	% **Employment Growth** **2000-2010**

Computer Jobs

Computer software engineers, applications	100
Computer support specialists	97
Computer software engineers, systems software	90
Network and computer systems administrators	82
Network systems and data communications analyst	77
Computer database administrators	66
Desk top publishers	67
Computer and information systems managers	60
Computer systems analysts	57
Computer and information scientists	40

Health Care Jobs

Medical assistants	57
Social and human service assistants	55
Physician assistants	53
Medical records technicians	49
Home health aides	47
Physical therapists aids	46
Physical therapist assistants	45
Audiologists	45
Mental health and substance abuse social workers	39
Dental assistants	37
Dental hygienists	37
Pharmacy technicians	36
Occupational therapist assistants	34

Other

Special education teachers	37
Speech language pathologists	39
Fitness trainers and aerobics instructors	40
Veterinary assistants and lab animal caretakers	40

The two biggest job categories are computers and health care. But a recent question has emerged. Are these projections going to be accurate? Consider the following factors and issues:

1. The McKinsey Quarterly in November 2003 estimated that the number of U.S. service jobs lost to offshoring will accelerate at a rate of 30-40% per year during the next five years
2. More than 50% of the banking and financial service firms are sourcing work offshore.
3. It's even happening in health care. 32% of health care and medical companies are doing some outsourcing. And some countries, like the Philippines, do a very good job of exporting qualified health personnel.
4. General Electric's 70-70-70 credo is: Outsourcing 70% of its headcount: Pushing 70% of that outsourcing offshore: Locating 70% of such workers in India
5. More than 28% of the U.S.-China trade deficit is now in computers and electronics.

It isn't just the computer and health care service jobs that are in danger of leaving. The Internet has eliminated many of the routine tasks of travel agents, real estate brokers, accountants, engineers, actuaries, legal and consulting activities, and, of course, telephone-based services. Do you know where your help desk is?

I am continuously amazed that more politicians, parents, teachers, and students aren't more concerned about what is going to happen in the service economy. There seems to be a general assumption that the economy will transition into a non-manufacturing (post industrial) economy and there will still be plenty of good paying jobs for everyone – if you just get a college degree. But if you carefully examine the jobs that are now being lost against those being gained and the degrees being issued there is a huge mismatch.

The obvious conclusion is that nobody really knows what is going to happen in the service part of the economy. At present, there is no evidence that our post-industrial economy can produce enough high paying jobs to replace the lost manufacturing jobs or that living standards will be maintained in the post industrial economy.

Why is Manufacturing So Important?

Americans build things. We build big things (like airplanes, cars, and earth-moving equipment) and we make little things (like faucets, fountain pens, and non-stick frying pans).

More important, we build industries that power our economy and those industries make the jobs that support our families and help pay our health insurance. Let's take a deeper look at why manufacturing is so important

- **THERE ARE MILLIONS OF MANUFACTURING JOBS:** The Bureau of Labor shows that manufacturing reached a peak of about 21 million workers in 1979. As of 2003 manufacturing employment was 14,305,000 workers. More than 2.3 million jobs have been lost since year 2000. Where did those millions of jobs go? According to a study by the National Association of Manufacturers 50%-60% of manufacturing job loss from 1993 to 2001 was caused by plant closures.

- **MANUFACTURING JOBS PAY MORE THAN SERVICE JOBS:** In 2003 the Bureau of Economic Analysis of the U.S. Department of Commerce showed that wages and benefits of a job in the manufacturing sector averaged $54,000 per year, compared to the average of $45,600 for the overall private sector. The average wages and benefits of the typical service job is $29,000. That's why the loss of manufacturing jobs contributes to lower living standards.

- **MANUFACTURING CREATES SECONDARY JOBS:** Manufacturing stimulates employment in other sectors at a greater pace than other industries. On the average, each $1 million in final sales of manufactured products supports 8 jobs in the manufacturing sector and six jobs in other sectors of the economy. That's "the multiplier effect" at work. The point is that manufacturing jobs help create many other jobs in the economy.

- **MANUFACTURERS PERFORM THE LARGEST SHARE OF R&D:** In 2002, manufacturers performed 60% of the $291 billion invested in R&D in the U.S. Innovation and R&D has been a traditional strength of the U.S. for decades. It comes from manufacturing companies as large as General Electric and as small as companies with fewer than 15 employees. But, with the reduction in manufacturing companies, workers, and industries, we're beginning to see a reduction in R&D expenditures. If the U.S. is going to have a chance for continued economic growth based on innovation and new products, it will be extremely important to keep investing in R&D – a manufacturing strong point.

- **MANUFACTURING GENERATES EXPORTS:** Despite continuing trade deficits, manufacturing contributed more than 62% of American export earnings. But, with the continued decline of manufacturing, the U.S. is beginning to lose its place as "exporter to the world." U.S. exports have fallen from 13.5% of world exports in 2001 to 11% in 2002. The U.S cannot rely on service exports to close up the gap. As we know, services, from call centers to computer programming to financial services, are being taken over by foreign companies. For a healthier balance of payments, we still need to make things other people want.

- **MANUFACTURING ADDS VALUE:** For example, let's look at parts suppliers. Many of these are SMMs (Small to Midsize Manufacturers). SMMs supply parts and equipment that account for 55% of the value-added content of finished products. Value added is the difference between the value of goods produced and the equipment and supplies used to produce them. OEMs in the auto, electronics, and aerospace industry particularly are sourcing more and more parts from foreign suppliers. In 2001 the Commerce Department estimated that $526 billion or 47% of all merchandise imports fell under this kind of trade category. This has been obvious in consumer goods for a long time, but now it includes precision machine parts, moulds, plastic injection parts, and many other job shop parts. Reducing the 55% of the parts supplied by the SMMs would only make our trade deficit worse.

- **MANUFACTURING SUPPORTS STATE ECONOMIES:** In terms of percentage of Gross State Product, manufacturing is a huge part of many state economies such as: Ohio ($92 billion), Pennsylvania ($68 billion), California ($128 billion), Texas ($89 billion), and Illinois ($73 billion). In terms of tax receipts, manufacturers are also huge contributors to the state revenue budgets. The Bureau of Economic Analysis notes that "During the last 10 years, manufacturing corporations have paid 30%-34% of all corporate tax payments for state and local taxes, social security and payroll taxes, excise taxes, import and tariff duties, environmental taxes and license taxes."[2] In light of the current crisis in state budgets, states cannot afford continued loss of manufacturing. In fact, we can eventually expect increased help from the states because they don't want to see decreased tax receipts.

- **THE SUPPLY CHAIN BRAIN DRAIN:** As noted, we are losing many high skilled jobs in both blue collar and the white-collar ranks. As part of that, there are very few "journeyman" programs left in the U.S. – training the skilled people who are the backbone of manufacturing. Jobs and the training programs that created some of these "master workers" – high skilled jobs such as machinists, mould makers, tool and die, and fabricators – are declining rapidly in the U.S. At the same time, many Asian countries are funding massive programs to create these skilled manufacturing jobs.

  In 2001, a study conducted by NAM (National Association of Manufacturers), "The Skills Gap 2001," reported that 80% of existing manufacturers reported a moderate to serious shortage of qualified applicants. The study notes that "what manufacturing is facing is not a lack of employees, but a shortfall of highly qualified employees with specific educational backgrounds and skills." One of the reasons large companies are moving offshore is that they cannot find skilled workers. This is not an easy problem, but it is within our power to fix.

- **HIGH SKILL MANUFACTURING JOBS CAN PAY AS MUCH AS PROFESSIONAL JOBS:** Entry-level pay for machinists with a two-year degree is $20,000 to $30,000 per year. Journeymen can make from $40,000 to $100,000 per year. Yes, these are people who work with their hands and they can earn as much or more than professional engineers. In fact, between 1980 and 2000 tool and die workers made 20% more than engineers. This trend has the potential to make manufacturing more attractive to our best and brightest students.

- **MANUFACTURING IS KEY TO OUR NATIONAL DEFENSE:** Many industries, like aerospace, high technology, software, and others build the products that allow America to have the world's most powerful arsenal. Basic industries like the chemical, petroleum, mining, and electronics industries are part of our strategic and defensive reserves. Maintaining these industries and the suppliers and skilled workers in them is also a matter of national security.

- **MANUFACTURING AFFECTS OUR INFRASTRUCTURE:** We need to maintain all of the interconnecting links for distribution networks, communications, transportation, utilities, and trade. For example, 80% of all goods hauled by trucks and 80% of all goods hauled by railroads are manufactured goods. The decline of manufacturing will automatically force a reduction in the railroads, trucking, utility, and communications industries as well as all of the OEMs that supply the equipment for building and maintaining these industries. All of these interconnected industries also generate good paying jobs. Many will decline as manufacturing declines.

Why aren't more people concerned?

I have asked myself this question over and over in recent years. Certainly, when there's a big layoff it makes the local news for a day or two, but most of my business friends don't seem to be very worried. Very few politicians seem very concerned unless it's election time and one can blame the other for job losses. But then the election is over and it's business as usual. And most citizens don't even discuss manufacturing much less worry about how it might affect them.

Furthermore, most economists seem to believe that we are in a natural economic transition to some kind of "post industrial" economy and that will keep America on top somehow.

Some of this is understandable. After all, only one in ten workers now works in manufacturing. Consequently, most have no real knowledge or appreciation of the overall value and importance of manufacturing (much less what it has to do with them).

Politicians (particularly congressmen) are not manufacturers – they are lawyers. They have many other issues on their plates right now and very few from either party want to touch the tar baby that is manufacturing. In fact, very few of them, just like most citizens, know anything about manufacturing. They may agree we need more of it. But then what?

What about economists? Shouldn't they know the big economic picture? Why don't they seem to be worried? The prestigious journal *Economist* ran a recent article on manufacturing employment that eloquently summarizes what most economists think about manufacturing and manufacturing employment. The article's sub-title was "Factory Jobs are becoming scarce. It's nothing to worry about."

After this reassuring title the article goes on to say the following.

> "Since contrary to conventional wisdom, manufacturing output has been growing strongly not declining, the fall in employment in America and elsewhere should be seen as a good thing. It does not represent a wholesale shift of production from developed economies to China. Instead, it largely reflects rapid productivity growth. And because unemployment rates in most developed economies have not increased during the past decade, even though manufacturing jobs have been lost, it would appear that most laid-off factory workers have found new jobs."

Well, I'm not so sure. Let's look at some of the facts. Since 1979, the Census of Manufacturing shows that U.S. manufacturing employment has declined by 6 million jobs. Since the early 1990s, 22,000 manufacturing companies have been closed. At the same time the 500 largest industrial corporations have eliminated 4.4 million workers. There is no evidence to support the notion that all of these workers, particularly laid off factory workers, have found new jobs – much less new jobs that paid anywhere near the same as those eliminated factory jobs.

Nothing to worry about? Perhaps if you are not one of those millions of laid off workers. For each of these displaced workers and their families this has been, in most cases, a painful loss. The only way to understand the true loss is from experience. I wonder if the authors of the *Economist* article would be so cavalier in their observations if they were suddenly told that they were going to be paid $10 per hour with no benefits – if they were among the people not laid off.

But it was ever thus: If you get laid off, it's a recession; If I get laid off, it's a depression.

The Decline of Living Standards

In my view, the *Economist* missed the real truth in their discussion about manufacturing employment. The issue isn't about just finding another job in the service economy. It is about the decline of living standards for individuals and overall economic health for our nation. Chart P-1, at the beginning of this preface, shows that for 60% of us, middle class living standards have been declining since 1977. There is no economic evidence that this trend will be reversed. But there is a lot of evidence to support the notion that the middle class living standards could worsen for many with the decline of manufacturing. So when the *Economist* says there is nothing to worry about, it depends on whether you are in the middle class or part of the credentialed elite.

The "Post Industrial" Economy

There's a third big question about manufacturing's effect on the rest of the economy – deindustrialization. I think the *Economist* speaks for most economists and politicians when they state that "Deindustrial-ization – the shrinkage of industrial jobs – is popularly perceived as a symptom of economic decline. On the contrary, it is a natural stage of economic development."

In my view, this is another sweeping generalization that is not supported by the facts. It does not take into consideration declining R&D budgets, loss of skilled workers, the trade deficit, pressure on defense industries, declining tax revenues, manufacturing infrastructure links, or other factors described in this Preface. Even if deindustrialization is the "natural stage of economic development," there is no evidence that it won't lead to economic decline.

The *Economist* and others make the case that we can transition to a "post-industrial" service economy with continued economic growth. They say: "Neither manufacturing nor services is inherently better than the other; they are interdependent. Computers are worthless without software writers; a television has no value without programs. The issue is not whether people work in factories or not, but whether they are creating wealth. Manufacturing once delivered the highest value-added; high-tech industries, such as drugs and aerospace, still do. But in developed economies today, telecom, software, banking and so on can create more wealth than making jeans or trainers. Writing a computer program creates more value than producing a computer disc."

The report continues, "Before long no one will much care whether firms are classified under manufacturing or services. Future prosperity will depend not on how economic activity is labeled, but on economies' ability to innovate and their capacity to adjust."

I think this argument does a good job of capturing what 90% of our citizens have been led to believe. That is, that we really don't need a manufacturing base and our country – or any country – can transition to the service economy as long as we are innovative.

It says that we don't need factories to create wealth; that service industries like software, banking, and telecom can create the wealth we need on their own. It suggests that we don't need to manufacture things to remain a world economic power. There is no sense of danger that we may become a nation of lawyers, software designers, and contractors looking for someone to invoice.

I would like to offer a dramatically different perspective.

Consequences of a Declining Manufacturing Sector

A research report from economists at the National Association of Manufacturers suggests that the reality could be much different than the view offered by such as the *Economist*.

It notes that "U.S. manufacturing is the heart of a significant process that generates economic growth and has produced the highest living standards in history. But today this complex process faces serious domestic and international challenges which, if not overcome, will lead to reduced economic growth and, ultimately, a decline in living standards for future generations of Americans." The report's Executive Summary closes with this statement: "If the U.S. manufacturing base continues to shrink at its present rate and the critical mass is lost, the manufacturing innovation process will shift to other global centers. Once that happens, a decline in U.S. living standards is all but assured."

While less comforting, this is my view as well. In the final analysis, I do not believe it is possible to continue healthy economic growth without a significant manufacturing sector. We cannot transition to a manufacturing-free, "post-industrial" information economy without enormous problems.

Ten years ago, manufacturing was 22% of GDP. In 2005, manufacturing was 12% of GDP. If this percentage continues to decline, and we depend on just the service economy for our future, we will end up a nation of credentialed lawyers and consultants, baristas, temporary workers, and retail "associates." There is nothing wrong with these jobs as part of a balanced economy. But if this is all that's left, well that's something else entirely – a "hollowed-out" economy without the capability to make its own future.

The Answer: We Need a Strong Industrial Base.

It is my contention that transitioning to a "post-industrial" economy that will somehow sustain us without affecting living standards is a dangerous myth. We are already faced with declining living standards – and it could get worse.

While not every job or every manufacturing company can be "saved," I do not think there is any alternative than to work to prevent manufacturing from slipping below the critical mass size. We have to stop the decline of manufacturing. We will lose jobs and plants to globalization but we must not allow manufacturing to shrink below that "critical mass" size.

I do not know what it will take to get the policy makers and politicians more interested in this problem, and I don't think protectionist measures are the long-term answer. But I do know some things individual manufacturing companies can do to survive, and, in some cases, prosper.

And that's what this book is about. Not saving giant companies or offering big policy solutions to big government. It is not a position report making a case for Congress to pass protectionist legislation. It is a human-size book for manufacturers. I don't know if we can maintain the critical mass, but I am optimistic that thousands of small and midsize manufacturers can survive and grow in the new economy by transforming their companies to the new realities of globalization.

Saving American Manufacturing is about Competing

This is not going to happen merely by improving internal processes. Small and midsize manufacturers need to go on the attack and seek out the new opportunities being created by globalization. To compete means finding new customers and markets, inventing new products, changing sales channels, and offering new services.

We can do this by transforming SMMs from process-driven, operations-driven companies to what we call "Prospector" organizations that are designed to find new markets and opportunities.

This book is a blow-by-blow, "nuts and bolts" description of all of the changes necessary to make the transformation. It shows you what you must do to become a 21st Century manufacturer – one that can compete in a global economy. It is focused on saving as high a percentage as possible of those small and midsize manufacturers who want to be saved.

We won't save them all – but we can maintain a critical mass of vital, productive manufacturing companies playing an essential role in a healthier, more balanced economy.

Our economy is like a giant skyscraper with manufacturing as its foundation. Manufacturing is like the basement of that skyscraper with all of the service industries housed in the floors above. The lower floors of the service sector are crowded with the many desks of the data processors and other low-paying service jobs. The top floors are the spacious and opulent offices of the credentialed elite who have the best views. And, as we discussed, this group is currently doing quite well and, in many ways, benefiting from globalization. But if the foundation erodes, the whole building is in jeopardy regardless of the floor or office you occupy.

I have tried to make the case for placing more emphasis (politically and practically) on saving or reducing the decline of America's manufacturing base and providing job opportunities for the middle class.

Manufacturing and the middle class are inextricably linked. I am convinced that if we can make revitalization of the manufacturing base one of our shared national goals, we can have a healthier and more balanced economy.

Notes:

1. "Technology and the American Economic Tradition," Office of Technology Assessment, 1987.
2. Bureau of Labor Statistics, U.S. Department of Labor, 2002.

Chapter 1
Introduction: Success through Transformation

It is time to think differently about how we can stop the decline of American manufacturers and consider new ways to grow in this globalized world. If we are to have a chance at growth, all manufacturers need to examine the obstacles to growth with unflinching reality.

This book makes the case that contrary to the doom and gloom scenarios, manufacturers can compete in the new economy and against foreign competitors – but not as they competed in the past.

The premises on which this book is based are:

1. **We Must Grow** – As the American economy has recovered from the 9/11 recession many manufacturing companies have stopped declining and are treading water. Stopping the decline of manufacturing industries and companies is not enough. We must find ways to grow.

2. **Process Solutions** – Process solutions like Lean Manufacturing have kept manufacturing in the global game. These process solutions have led to cost and waste reduction and more plant capacity for more sales. But they do not automatically lead to sales growth and there are definite limitations on how much cost and waste can be reduced.

3. **All Customers Are Not Good Customers** – Many customers, in their own efforts to survive globalization, are demanding too much from their suppliers – particularly in forcing suppliers to discount prices. When the supplier cannot keep up with the demand for price discounts by reducing costs, the result is lower and lower margins. These kinds of customers can put the supplier into financial jeopardy. More often than not, these types of customers are not worth keeping over the long haul.

4. **Finding New Customers and Markets** – Pruning bad customers will always mean looking for new customers to replace them. For most manufacturers developing a Growth Plan will be based on finding new customers and new markets.

5. **A New Organization** – Most manufacturing organizations are Defender organizations that are designed for internal efficiencies. A Prospector organization is designed to explore markets, develop new products, and find new opportunities. Growth requires finding new customers and markets, which requires an organization change. We must change our companies and go on the attack.
6. **Mindset Change** – Perhaps the most fundamental and difficult change will be converting manufacturing cultures from an operations driven mindset to becoming market driven.

WHO ARE THESE MANUFACTURERS WE NEED TO SAVE?

According to the 2002 Census of Manufacturers, there are 344,000 manufacturing establishments. Of these establishments, 98% have fewer than 500 employees.[1] I call this group **Small and Midsize Manufacturerers (SMMs)**. These companies and the managers who run them are the focus audience for this book. They are also the manufacturers who will have to adapt to the changes brought on by globalization. To understand who these small and midsize manufacturers (SMMs) really are, one needs to consider three important factors.

1. Four Types of Manufacturers

First is the fact that manufacturing companies in the U.S. are not a homogeneous group. From more than 30 years of working with manufacturing companies of all sizes, I suggest that there are at least four distinctly different groups. Figure 1-1 shows there are logarithmic differences in the four types in terms of resources, knowledge, experience, staff, and the where-with-all to deal with change

2. Resource Limitations

The second important point is that all small and midsize manufacturers are restricted by resource limitations. "FACTS" is an acronym that best characterizes the reality of the small manufacturing environment. It stands for:

F – <u>Fear</u> of making a wrong decision

Figure 1-1: The Collins Classification of Manufacturers

	Type 1 Micro	Type 2 Family Owned	Type 3 Professional Managed	Type 4 Giant Public
Employees	1-19	20-99	100-499	500 plus[2]
Assets	Few	Growing	Collateral	Huge
Cashflow	Awful	Erratic	Positive	Enormous
Focus	Any Sales	Sales	Profit	Bottom Line
Plan	None	Verbal	Budgets, Forecasts	Strategic
Org. Type	Sole Prop.	Family Corp.	Private Corp.	Public Corp.
Systems	Beginning	Manual	IT	Sophisticated
Costing	Poor	General	Detailed	Detailed
Customers	Some	MVC	Market Niches	Large Markets
Sales	Internal	Inside Sales, Some Channels	Sales Force, Sales Channels	Many Channels

A – limited <u>Access</u> to capital
C – <u>Cashflow</u> problems
T – <u>Time</u> constraints
S – small or no <u>Staff</u>

A Type 1 manufacturer might be just a few people managing a small shop with very little operating capital and a day-to-day worry of generating enough cash flow to keep the doors open. A typical Type 2 manufacturer is a family-owned business with around 50 employees, known customers, and decent cashflow. Type 2s, however, are generally very good technically but lack the knowledge and staff to do industrial marketing. Type 3 manufacturers are midsize companies from 100-500 employees that are usually managed by a professional staff and well-developed systems (such as cost accounting). These 3 types of manufacturers are so different in their knowledge and resources, that one solution does not fit all three. Hence suggested solutions and strategies need to be tailored to the type of SMM.

3. SMMs Are Not Small Versions of Large Manufacturers

Third, and perhaps most important, is the understanding that small manufacturers are not small versions of large manufacturers. One of the most popular approaches to helping SMMs is the assumption that the same theoretical concepts or solutions pioneered by giant manufacturers will also work for SMMs. If the solution does not consider "FACTS" and the "type" of company, it can harm rather than help SMMs. In a medical analogy, one must be careful that the dose of medicine does not kill the patient or make the symptoms worse. In my experience, the strategies and solutions designed for Caterpillar Tractor won't work for ABC Fabrication. The Hippocratic Oath must be observed in helping save America's SMMs – Do no harm!

On the other hand, there are the Type 4 publicly held manufacturers who have the power to control entire industries and supply chains. They are probably going to do whatever they see as most profitable for their shareholders, and there is probably nothing that their suppliers or anyone else can do about it.

I am hopeful that Type 4s will take a longer view and work at developing true alliances with their suppliers and maintaining the critical mass of U.S. manufacturing for the good of the entire economy. But, I think everyone concerned about saving American manufacturing should not assume Type 4 companies are going to change unless there are financial advantages to change.

How to Read this Book

This book is not about how to reduce costs or improve efficiencies. It assumes that most SMMs are already doing or have done process solutions. This book is about how to grow and find new opportunities in the changing marketplace.

Growth is an external phenomenon that is driven by customers and markets. The book is designed to help the owners of SMMs visualize the process of transforming their companies based on customer and market needs and then working backwards – developing the strategies to support the new customers and markets.

If growth is the primary goal, then it is only common sense that the organization must change to explore these external opportunities for growth. This type of organization is called a Prospector organization, which has the ability to:

- Monitor customers and prospects
- Identify the good and bad customers
- Find new customers and markets
- Develop new products for new market niches
- Offer new services to offset the loss of some customer sales
- Create new sales channels to reach these customers
- Continuously change their organization to compete.

Success through Transformation in Five Stages

The premise of the book is based on the assumption that how we competed in the past is not at all the model for survival in the future. To compete successfully against foreign competitors and in changing markets with customers who can buy globally will require a holistic approach to transforming the company to the new realities of the marketplace. It is presented in five stages:

I.   Customer/Market Diversity
II. Organizational Transformation
III. Cost Reduction, Cost Accounting, and Pricing
IV. Workforce Education and Training
V.   Growth Planning

I. Customer /Market Diversity
Monitoring Customers and Finding New Customers and Markets.

Customers are in charge of the forces that are changing manufacturing everywhere. Customers force price reductions, drop suppliers, find offshore vendors, demand customization, and expect high quality as a standard at no extra cost. Markets and customers change rapidly and make it difficult to maintain a competitive advantage, unless you monitor them.

The number one problem that must be solved to help manufacturers survive and grow is learning to do a much better job of diversifying into new customers and new markets. By this I mean both developing the information systems to monitor customers and markets as well as developing the methods to find new customers and markets.

Up until globalization began to change everything, most manufacturers did not have to be market- or customer-driven, and they did not have to invest a lot of time and money in prospecting for new customers. Instead they devoted most of their efforts to making internal processes more efficient. This solved some of the problems but it did not make a company market/customer driven, and it did not assist manufacturers in finding new ways to grow.

All this requires gathering external information on customers, competitors, and markets. It means continuously monitoring what is going on outside of the plant and capturing new information on purchasing patterns and specific needs of customers in a way that can be used for management decisions.

In his book, *Confronting Reality*, Larry Bossidy (former President of Allied Signal) says, "The only way you are going to have differentiation is by knowing the people you're hoping to sell to better and sooner than everybody else. You get that knowledge by observing, learning, and thinking about the end user and viewing your own business from the end user's perspective."[3]

This means visiting your prospects and end users, calling them on the phone, and getting to know them, which for many manufacturers is very scary and a whole new way to do business. Gathering external information is an art not a science.

I would like to convince you that gathering the necessary external information is not as difficult as it may seem. Some of the most progressive

SMMs in the U.S. that are finding and capitalizing on new opportunities in the new economy have already figured out how to do this. They have made the commitment to be customer/market driven and know how to gather the external data to find prospects for new customers. Many of these manufacturers, featured in stories throughout this book, reveal their methodologies and the tools they used.

Profiling Customers

Profiling means developing the capabilities to identify bad customers, and develop profiles of the best customers. In fact, because of the pressures of globalization, many customers will not be good customers. In their efforts to survive, some customers will demand too much from their suppliers. They can inadvertently put you out of business. So continuously finding new customers and even firing some customers is necessary for survival. This is perhaps the most important point in the book and it has many ramifications.

Finding new customers and markets means taking an aggressive approach to dealing with external issues. It will require new methods for prospecting in external environments and new sales channels to sell them. This will, in most cases, automatically lead to changes in products and services.

The goal of this external approach is finding new customers and markets. It is the necessary front-end strategy that will drive manufacturers to become more market driven and less internally focused. Market focus is the first step in the process to be more competitive. It can be defined as focusing on the right customers and the right markets, and gaining or developing a competitive advantage.

II. Organizational transformation

In their book *Fit, Failure, and the Hall of Fame*, Raymond Miles and Charles Snow make the case that a company's organization and strategy must be tied to what is going on in their marketplace. "The process of achieving fit begins, conceptually at least, by aligning the company to its marketplace – by finding a way to respond to or help shape current and future customer needs."

They go on to say, "Some firms achieve success by being the first, either by anticipating where the market is going or by shaping the market's direction through their own research and development efforts. We call these firms Prospectors because they continually search for new products, services, technologies, and markets."

"Other successful firms move much less quickly. Instead they study new developments carefully, wait until technology and product designs have stabilized, and then apply their competence in developing process efficiencies that will allow them to offer a standard product or service of high quality at a low price. We call these firms Defenders."[4]

This is a huge insight, which is very applicable to manufacturers who are generally some variation of a Defender organization. To use a Defender organization and strategy requires a healthy, stable, and predictable environment. But in the new global economy, customers are driving changes that make most markets unstable, unpredictable, and sometimes unhealthy.

One of the premises of this book is that small and midsize manufacturers will have to change their organizations and strategies to fit the new demands of their customers and markets. This is the second most important problem and a huge change for SMMs. New customers, and even current customers, are relentlessly demanding faster response, customized products, new services, and lower costs. To meet their needs will require faster response, quicker decision making, and a more agile and flexible organization.

The pyramid or functional organization used for so long to efficiently manufacture products will (by its very design) not work. There are too many levels of management, it is too bureaucratic, and the decision making is too slow to compete in the new economy.

To succeed in the marketplace will require some variation of the decentralized Prospector organization, which is designed to monitor customers, find new markets, and continuously offer new products and services.

III. Cost Reduction, Cost Accounting, and Pricing

Another big challenge is reducing costs. In most industries customers relentlessly drive price reductions and compare U.S. supplier prices with foreign suppliers. So, cost reduction has become a necessity to survive and compete in the new economy. In many highly competitive markets today, it is no longer possible to pass on price increases, and manufacturers are forced to maintain their margins by cost reduction.

Cost reduction is even more important when your company is prospecting for new customers. To capture an order from a customer that is already being served well by another supplier will either require a superior product or service or a lower price.

Another problem is that U.S. supplier prices are constantly being compared to foreign supplier prices. In many cases keeping a customer will require matching foreign supplier prices. And in some cases staying in the manufacturing business may require matching the foreign supplier's prices or outsourcing part of the work. For any or all of these reasons, cost reduction is a challenge that must be met. Fortunately, most manufacturers are involved in some type of continuous improvement program to reduce waste and lower costs using Lean Manufacturing techniques.

Reducing costs on a continuous basis is the most pressing issue and it requires a new approaches to cost accounting. There is also a need to improve the accuracy of price and cost systems. The rule-of-thumb costing systems used in the "good old days" probably won't work in the future, particularly if you are being compared by your customers to foreign supplier prices. Most SMMs need to take a new look at how to develop their prices and to learn how to use contribution margins as a basis for pricing.

IV. Workforce Education and Training

The fourth stage of the transformation process is absolutely critical to the success of American manufacturing. It is about improving the education and training systems for the new manufacturing workers needed in the 21st century. This is a three-dimensional problem.

The first issue is quality, in terms of the type of worker that is needed. Manufacturing needs highly skilled and educated employees. Over the last 15 to 20 years, manufacturing has shifted towards jobs requiring higher skills. The shortage of skilled workers is most serious for jobs such as machinists, technicians, electricians, engineers, and people who can maintain and operate automated lines.

The second issue is creating new education and training programs for these kinds of jobs. Apprentice and craftsman type job training has been abandoned in many industries. Programs to educate and train these types of skilled workers will largely have to be created from scratch.

The third issue is quantity, in terms of how many people are needed. A report by the National Association of Manufacturers, "Keeping America Competitive," states that the babyboomer generation of manufacturing employees will be retired within the next 15 years. The report predicts that 10 million new workers will be needed to replace these retirees by the year 2020.

An entire chapter is devoted to the problem of workforce education and training, because if we don't find ways to recruit, train, and educate the manufacturing employees of the future, all other efforts to become competitive will be academic. We must be able to empower the skilled workers in manufacturing to compete. To succeed will require the commitment of both small and large manufacturers as well as the government and educational institutions. Failure to meet these challenges will result in the continued decline of manufacturing.

IV. Growth Planning
Developing a Comprehensive Growth Plan Based on Finding New Customers and Markets

If your company is going to accomplish the first two stages of survival you will also need a process that ties everything together. What most manufacturers want is a breakthrough growth-planning process designed specifically for their products and resources. Growth Planning will help you adapt to the changing customers and markets and find opportunities. It is a plan for SMMs...

- Who have lost some of their MVC (most valuable customer) accounts
- Who need to diversify into new customers and markets and to get rid of unprofitable customers
- Who are in stagnant or declining industries with too many competitors
- Who are not growing
- Who are no longer making the profits they deserve.

If the company has already been forced into a financial crisis because of margin erosion, the plan will more than likely be a Turnaround Plan designed to help the company survive. Before a company can develop a growth plan it must get its finanical house in order and fix cash flow and other financial problems.

SMMs have all been exposed to the typical business and strategic plans with flowery mission statements and ponderous visions, all carefully described in a long narrative report. Most SMMs don't communicate with narrative reports and they see strategic plans as an academic exercise that takes a lot of time and money and leads to vague or poor results. In addition, manufacturers do not believe that these reports can be implemented or really lead to action steps. They are not interested in a plan that tells them what is wrong. They need a plan that tells then how to make the changes necessary to attain breakthrough growth results.

What I offer is a simple plan that summarizes everything to be accomplished in one year in less than 15 pages. This is a plan that is built from the bottom up by the key people in your organization. A plan that addresses the key people's problems with solutions and defines how they will be measured and who will do each task and carry out each agreed on strategy. Short goal statements defined by dollars, not vague mission statements, drive this plan. It is a realistic plan that adapts your company to the new economy. A plan designed and executed by the very people who are going to have to do the work,

This is a plan designed specifically for the needs of SMMs, which has already been proven in many turnaround situations. It is called a QUAD plan and is described in Chapter 9.

Companion Handbook

Saving American Manufacturing is supported by a companion handbook, *Growth Planning Handbook for Small and Midsize Manufacturers*. The methods suggested in this handbook are based on years of industrial research, experimentation and the development of many information tools, and the street smarts that comes from doing it. The Handbook is designed to support the transformation approach described in *Saving American Manufacturing*.

It begins with the Six Essential Questions that must be answered to develop a transformation or turnaround plan for growth. The solutions to these six questions are answered in detail with examples, charts, and how to do it procedures. The handbook also describes how to do competitive intelligence and market analysis in three different levels that fit Type 1, 2, and 3 manufacturing companies. In other words the solutions are designed to fit the resources and understanding of these three types of manufacturing companies.

There are also sections in the handbook that will show:

1. Six methods to determine sales potential.
2. How to do sales prospecting by phone and trace leads to sales.
3. How to identify the best sales channels, evaluate rep performance and provide the factory support needed to make sales channels work.

It concludes with a comprehensive growth plan that can be used to either get back on a growth track or as a turnaround plan for a manufacturing company that has lost its way in the marketplace. This last section of the Handbook describes two different types of Growth Plans – for type 2 and 3 manufacturers. These plans are detailed enough to explain the entire planning process, and both use example companies based on real-life plans.

This Handbook is written for the thousands of small and midsize manufacturers who offer industrial products and services. Many tables, charts, and "how to do it" methods developed over many years are described in detail.

My commitment was to write a handbook that could be immediately used in your business. In this regard I have tried to stick to the following principals:

- Tell them how not what – You will find that this is not a textbook that tells you the general principals. It is a how to do it book.
- Use small business language – The methods are explained in common language. MBA business terms are avoided.
- Always use examples of small and midsize manufacturers – All examples are Type 1,2, or 3 manufacturers (both product manufacturers and job shops).
- Tailor solutions that can fit their budgets – Most methods and tools are described in three different ways to fit Type 1,2, or 3 manufacturers.
- Emphasize one step at a time – Most methods are step-by-step instructions.
- Simple visuals – All sections use checklists, exercises, tables and spreadsheets.
- Never offer solutions used by the giant manufacturers – Small manufacturers are not small versions of large manufacturers. What worked for Boeing probably won't work for Joe's Welding shop.

Conclusion

It seems self-evident that finding the answers on how manufacturers can differentiate themselves to compete and survive in the future must begin with the people who are driving all of the changes – the customers. Yet so far, only lip service has been given to focusing on customers and being market driven and nobody has spent much time explaining how to do it.

America's flagship manufacturer, General Electric, is now beginning to voice the need to be more customer driven. General Electric is the company that championed Six Sigma and it seems that manufacturing in all industries followed their lead. GE's newest program is (ACFC) or "At the Customer, For the Customer." The program is based on getting good information about their customers' needs, problems, and intentions. The president, Jeff Immelt says that "At the Customer" can mean that you are literally present with him. "For the Customer" means that you learn their industry, business model, competitiveness, and segmentation and you help them succeed in multiple ways."[5]

This idea may seem obvious but I see it as major change in manufacturing. GE is making a case that just doing Six Sigma is not going to be enough. To compete in the future will require very good external information from customers.

Saving American Manufacturing is the missing business book written for the thousands of small and midsize companies that manufacture industrial and technology products. The chapters represent key areas that must change to make manufacturers more competitive. It begins with the most important change – learning how to find new customers and markets, which includes techniques to monitor customers and identify good and bad customers.

Notes:

1. Statistics for all manufacturing establishments, U.S. Census Bureau, 2002 Economic Census.
2. These employee numbers are also confirmed by the U.S. Small Business Administration. Their titles are MicroEnterprise, Small Enterprise, and Medium Enterprise.
3. Larry Bossidy and Ram Charan. *Confronting Reality.* Crown Business: 10/19/2004.
4. Raymond E. Miles and Charles C. Snow. *Fit, Failure, and the Hall of Fame.* The Free Press. New York: 1994
5. See Note 3.

Chapter 2

Finding New Customers and Markets

To survive in the new economy, industrial manufacturers of every size will have to find new markets and customers as a defensive strategy. This is your first transformation, and the reasons for it are clear.

Manufacturers at all levels are faced with the challenges of globalization. These include, but are not limited to, changes forced on them by changing customers and changing markets. These changes start with the giant customers at the top of the supply chain and then they are pushed down the chain to the smallest suppliers. Now those changes are everywhere.

You are probably dealing with a number of the following problems:

1. Customers are closing plants and moving offshore.
2. Customers are moving product lines offshore.
3. Customers are sourcing goods and services from foreign suppliers.
4. Customers are driving cost reduction so relentlessly that many SMMs cannot continue to do business with them.
5. Some customers are in markets and industries that are dying.
6. Some customers are too important to lose. These customers are MVCs or Most Valuable Customers. These are the small group of customers (often just 2-3 customers) that account for 80% of either sales volume or profits. When one of these customers abandons a supplier it is a disaster because they are such a big part of sales volume and hard to replace.

For any or all of these reasons, developing a system to find new customers and markets on an ongoing basis will become a high priority.

The core of this chapter is a step-by-step methodology for identifying your best customers and markets on an ongoing basis. Real security for manufacturers is to develop a diverse group of customers and a portfolio of market niches that will help your company "ride-out" the cyclical nature of many industries and the fickle nature of many customers.

As old industries dwindle, new industries emerge, and large customers evolve to adapt to globalization, your company will be part of this change.

And change can be good news as many new industries, hundreds of new market niches, and thousands of new applications will emerge. (I am fond of saying there are always opportunities in chaos.)

New and Growing Industries

Certainly there are going to be many industries that continue to decline and perhaps some, like semi-conductors, apparel, and shipbuilding, will never come back. But there are other industries that are emerging and evolving that will provide new opportunities for manufacturers in the future. This is where many of your new customers will come from.

Advanced Manufacturing Industries

As some traditional industries die, they will be replaced by new and emerging high growth industries. Among those industries are many technology industries – manufacturing in areas like biomedical devices, nano-technology, nano-manufacturing, informatics, biotechnology, pervasive computing, analytical instrumentation, and optic electronics.

Some of these industries can become very high growth industries and the technology will eventually be used by SMMs for new products.

But first let's look at traditional manufacturing.

Traditional Industries

Many huge traditional industries are not going to go away. They are U.S. industries that have a long history of growth. Although growth may not be spectacular in these industries, most will continue to grow and continue to change to be more competitive. Table 2-1 offers a sample of these industries and their recent growth.

Industries like chemicals include hundreds if not thousands of market segments and they are supplied by manufacturers of all sizes.

Though large, most of these industries have considerable volatility. Because of the changes going on within each of these industries and the ongoing growth, there will continue to be literally thousands of opportunities for new products and services, particularly in process and production line automation.

Figure 2-1: Growth of Traditional Industries

Industry	Growth-from 2003 to 2004
Paper	7.8%
Chemicals	9.8%
Plastics/ Rubber	9.0%
Primary Metals	24.8%
Metalworking machinery	20.6%
Industrial machinery	13.7%
Material handling machinery	11.1%
Construction machinery	35.7%
Industrial instruments	13.2%
Dairy Products	17.1%
Meat, poultry, seafood	9.0%
Heavy duty trucks	14.5%
Petroleum and coal	38.3%
Defense aircraft/parts	11.2%
Wood products	20.3%

Source: Value of Manufacturers' Shipments for Industry Groups, U.S. Census Bureau, and Economic Census 2002.

A good example is packaging and the packaging industry. Every time a large consumer product manufacturer changes the packaging of their products, it can cause a chain reaction of opportunities down through the OEM suppliers that supply machines for their production lines.

For example, saving money by eliminating the traditional corrugated or cardboard cartons and replacing them with some kind of shrink-wrapped package or plastic bag may cause every machine in the production line to be redesigned or changed in some way. In every major industry there are thousands of packaging changes that result in thousands of opportunities for new applications of machines and new machine designs.

Your transformation will also mean selling and marketing outside of your market region and perhaps enlisting the assistance of new sales channels. Most assuredly, it will mean devoting considerably more time to sales activities than you have in the past.

Most manufacturing books acknowledge that customers are the ones who pay the bills, send your kids to college, and are the ones we absolutely have to satisfy. Some even admit that the process centered approach should "start by determining what customers really want from us and then we will work backward from there." They even go on to say that all of the processes should be "customer centric." But it seldom happens. Why?

The reality is that most manufacturers still look at the customer from the inside out, not the other way around. That inside out perspective makes it hard to be "customer centric." This happens because most manufacturers are Defender type organizations that are designed to be very good at internal operations and processes but not necessarily good at dealing with external information. Most manufacturers have never had to aggressively prospect in the marketplace or monitor customers and markets.

Selling involves developing new skills. It's just one of the aspects of this transformation.

It means calling people you don't know, prospecting on the phone, becoming a good interviewer, and exploring totally new applications and market niches. This is not a matter of simply hiring a few extra sales people or spending more money on promotion. The key point in this chapter is that transforming yourself from an order taker to an order maker is about creating a new type of organization – a Prospector organization.

Anytime there is rapid growth or massive change in industries, thousands of new market niches, and hundreds of thousands of new applications will emerge. Since U.S. manufacturers are geographically closest to these industries they can seize the initiative for finding the best solutions to these new applications. It's all about staying close to customers and their problems. This is a common behavior for consumer marketers, but it is relatively uncommon for industrial marketers.

As your company transforms itself, you will discover more unique aspects to modern industrial marketing.

Industrial Products Are Not Consumer Products

Industrial companies sell to other manufacturers – not to consumers. That's the first reason industrial products are not like consumer products.

Consumer products are usually very standard and *have predictable margins*. This is a critical point because with low-priced and predictable margin consumer products, one can make the case that any customer is a good customer.

Industrial products and services can be very different from the consumer model. The Product Range Chart shown in Chapter 4 illustrates this.

At the top of the range there are standard products with predictable margins much like consumer products. For these kinds of standard products, it can be fairly easy to identify customers and markets. In this case, "basic marketing" techniques can be employed.

But as you move down the product range, industrial products become more complicated, and margins become more unpredictable. These industrial products and services are sold to very specific customers, in very special market niches.

So finding new customers to grow is not just about finding *more* customers and markets; it is finding the *right* customers and markets.

So the emphasis is not just on sales volume. It is critical to identify the best customers in markets where you have a chance of getting a reasonable price and margin. All customers are not created equal.

So Where Do You Begin?

The first place to start digging is in your own data. Manufacturers usually have a "gold mine" of information that can be used to find new customers and markets. First evaluate your internal information on quotations, lost orders, and costs to determine what has happened historically.

Second, you'll need to gather external information on customers, competitors, and markets to know where to go in the marketplace. Again, much of this information is already available but it may be scattered around the company.

As you begin looking for new customers and markets, here are Six Essential Questions that should be answered.

The Six Essential Questions

1. Can you identify the best customers – now and in the future?
2. Do you know which market niches (customer groups) to focus on now and in the future?
3. Do you know what kinds of products and services the best customers want?
4. Can you compare your products to the competitor's products in terms of price, delivery, key features – model by model?
5. Do you know the specific reasons you lost orders to competitors for every known lost order in the last year?
6. Do you know if you are making adequate margins on each product line, model, or job?

If you can't answer some or all of these questions, don't worry, you are not alone. You are in the large majority of manufacturing managers who have never had to do this.

For the small manufacturer, getting the answers to these six questions may appear to be a daunting task. But it is not as difficult as it may appear.

The following is a practical step–by–step process that explains how to gather this necessary information with methods that can be used by any manufacturing company (no matter how small) with a little determination and creativity.

It's well worth the effort. Because getting the answers to these six essential questions is key to survival and the initial basis for gathering the necessary information you will need to increase sales.

Let's take them one by one:

Essential Question 1: Profiling Customers
Can you identify the best customers to sell now and in the future

Profiling your customers is the first step in the Six Essentials because really knowing your customers is absolutely vital to everything else you do. Selecting new customers and markets will drive decisions and changes to products, services, organization, and manufacturing. It is important to know how to profile the best customers, the right customer, a profitable customer, and ones with future sales potential. You will need this knowledge to grow your business profitability.

The simplest way to achieve this is to carefully profile the ideal type of customer; then find more like them.

Usually, you can do this by examining the best of your current and past customers. This is a process designed specifically for manufacturers of complex industrial products and services.

Here is how to objectively profile your customer:

Begin by printing a list of all accounts sold in the last 12 months (can vary from 1–3 years) by sales volume – from the largest volume to the smallest volume account.

It is also very helpful to include the average profit margin percent of each account before overhead. (This is known as the contribution margin or sales minus direct materials and direct labor.) Getting an estimate on the average margin for a customer account requires aggregating cost information from work orders and jobs. This may appear to be a difficult task - do it anyway. The information will pay off over and over again (as explained in later chapters). If you can't provide margin information, then begin with a list by sales.

Next, assign NAICS codes to each customer account (See Figure 2-1). The government has devised a method of classifying all products with a code. It is called the North American Industrial Classification System (NAICS). You can find this information on the Internet by going to www. census.gov/naics. The NAICS system replaced the old SIC system and uses a 5- or 6-digit code (depending on the market) to designate specific sub-industry markets. If you have old SIC numbers, the website has conversion tables that allow you to find the new NAICS codes that replaced the old codes. You can also look up codes by product.

For instance, if you want to find the product code for a ship mounted marine crane, you would do the following:

- Go to the website for North American Industry Classification System at www.census.gov/naics
- On the left side of the page click on Product Classification/manufacturing
- Then choose Manufacturing Machinery 333
- Then choose construction machinery 333120
- Under this classification you will find "pedestal or shipboard mounted marine cranes or NAICS # 3331201188.(the larger the number the more detailed the description)

Figure 2-1: Sample Customer List and NAICS Code

Example: Assemble customer list & Assign NAICS Codes

NAICS Code*	Customer	Sales	Profit Margin %
33441	DEKA	800,000	24
33441	OECO	575,000	40
32614	Puget	570,000	41
33392	CLARK	290,000	38
33152	PCC	235,000	10
33429	FLIR	149,000	61
33111	BOISE	20,000	-4
33411	Tekko	110,000	25
33829	Warner	85,000	24
33321	Allied	80,000	-4
33211	Aptec	60,000	30
33399	MARKO	44,000	30
	ALL OTHERS (126)	850,000	19

*North American Industry Classification System Codes

Evaluate Good (+) and Bad (-) Customers

Now that you've developed the list, you have the beginning of the information you need. One of the first things to look at is profitability. In Figure 2-1, you can see that two of the small customers are losing the company money and one account (PCC) is only a 10% margin. All three of these accounts are marked negative (-) in Figure 2-2. Currently, they are considered "bad customers."

The next step is to dig deeper and determine strong and weak customers. To begin, we will simply mark each customer account + or -.

Profitability is one factor, but not the only factor to consider. To make a judgment on good (+) or bad (-) customers, one should consider the following questions.

Evaluating Your Customers

	Yes	No
1. Are they profitable? (Sales - C.O.G. Sold = gross profit)	___	___
2. Does the customer have potential for significant future revenues?	___	___
3. Do they truly value what you do well?	___	___
4. Are they a springboard to other like customers (referrals)	___	___
5. Can you serve them better than competitors?	___	___
6. Is this customer financially healthy?	___	___
7. Do they pay their bills on time?	___	___
8. Do indirect expenses reduce your gross profitability, such as: Returns/allowances, warranty, paperwork, field service, special engineering, credit terms, complexity of quotes, high number of sales calls, senior managers time, inventory demands, price discounts, special delivery, overtime?	___	___

Based on these questions, rate your customers. I've found that going from three pluses to three minuses will give you the ratings you need. Here's how it looks for our customers in Figure 2-2.

Figure 2-2: Rating Your Customers

Evaluate Good (+) and Bad (-) customers

NAICS	Customer	Sales	Rating
33441	DEKA	800,000	+++
33441	OECO	575,000	+++
32614	Puget	570,000	++
33392	CLARK	290,000	++
33152	PCC	235,000	-
33429	FLIR	149,000	++
33111	BOISE	120,000	---
33411	Tekko	110,000	+
33829	Warner	85,000	+
33321	Allied	80,000	---
33211	Aptec	60,000	++
33399	MARKO	44,000	+
31132	KC	34000	+
31181	Banatam	32000	-
31194	Mazoline	30000	++
31142	De Fort	29000	-
31141	Frozen Fresh	28000	---
31151	Bell's	25000	+++
	ALL OTHERS (126)		

Best Customer Profiles

Now go through the list of your good/"plus" customers and you can easily determine the ideal customer profiles with the best future sales potential. The NAICS codes for these Best Customer Profiles will help you "find more like them."

What about the customers marked (-)?

This profiling method also forces you to consider what you will do with bad (-) customers. You and your company are entitled to a fair margin. And good customers – even tough ones – will recognize that you, too, are entitled to make a profit. All manufacturers should be working at ways to further reduce costs through new manufacturing methods – this is another way for you to improve margins. But those who will not let you make a reasonable margin, for whatever reason, are probably not customers you will want long term.

You may need to prune some customers because they will not allow you to make a decent margin. If this happens you will immediately be in the position of having to find customers to replace them. Again, we have an example of how better information can start to assist you in making better decisions

A good example is a Tier 2 supplier in the auto industry. The big car companies have been hammering on their suppliers for years for lower prices and at the same time forcing them to adopt expensive programs such as ISO 14000. In recent years, the price discounts have been mandated as part of their contracts. Many of the suppliers who have tried to "hang on" to the auto business and have accepted these terms have found themselves in financial trouble. They have been rewarded for their trouble by an announcement in October 2005 that Ford intends to eliminate 50% of its suppliers.

This may seem like an extreme example, but it makes the point that in the new global economy SMMs must defend themselves. They must recognize bad customers and take action to replace them before these kinds of customers put them into financial trouble.

For the moment let's focus on profiling and finding new customers, and work at defining what constitutes an ideal customer – and let's think hard about how to get more of them.

The point is this. It is better to go on the hunt for a customer that will see the value of your price than to continue accepting losses or to hope for some manufacturing miracle that will change your margins short-term.

We've already made progress, now we're going to get smarter about our markets.

Essential Question 2: Focus

Do you know which market niches (customer groups) to focus on now and in the future?

Group Customers into Market Segments

Each customer account was assigned an NAICS code, (shown back in Figure 2-1). The next thing we are going to do is to group these customers into market niches. If your customers are in a spreadsheet, you can sort the NAICS Codes from the smallest to the largest number.

The market segment groups can then easily be identified and grouped together as shown in Figure 2-3.

For clarification, an industry is usually a 3-digit code such as 322 in the paper industry. Tissue/towel is a general market segment with a 6-digit number. A very specific market niche can be a 6-12 digit NAICS code number.

We know what some of our potential markets might be. Now let's see how big they are.

Determine Market Size by Prospects

This next step requires that you access a database such as Dunn and Bradstreet's I-MARKET and find out how many prospects are in each market segment. This will give you a preliminary idea of the market size you will be "prospecting." For instance, the market niche designated as tissue towel (NAICS 322122 in Figure 2-3) has 221 prospect companies in the U.S.

Prioritize Market Segments by Sales Potential

Once you list all market segments, the next step is to prioritize them in terms of sales potential, profitability, and known purchase order opportunities. In our example, Figure 2-3, the markets are ranked from 1-13 by priority. This is a qualitative (not quantitative) process. It is about deciding which market segments are the most important in terms of your priority.

Figure 2-3: Market Segment Priortizing

Priority	Market Niche	NAICS	# of US Prospects
YEAR 1			
1.	Tissue/Towel	322122	221
2.	Bottled Water	312112	132
3.	Dairy (cheese, ice cream)	311520,311513	1833
4.	Meat Products	311612	1,344
5.	Canned Foods	311423	638
YEAR 2			
6.	Frozen Foods	311410	474
7.	Cereals,	311234	556
8.	Pasta	311823	161
9.	Soap, Cleaner, Bleach	325611	621
YEAR 3			
10	Candy, Confections, Nuts	311320,311330	315
11.	Pharmaceutical prep.	325412	878
12.	Publishing	322291	494
13.	Fats and Oils	311225	4853

The last step is to decide how many market segments you can go after in each year. This will help you make decisions on which markets to budget for, promote or develop a specific sales plan for each year.

Prioritizing market segments is custom work based on your understanding of customer and market opportunities based on quotations, lost orders, and historic sales. Here is where your specific knowledge and information on Best Customer Profiles will be valuable.

At the same time, you need to appreciate some of the new perspectives you have uncovered through your NAICS Code analysis. With that in mind, look over the previous example (Figure 2-3), and then get ready to do your own customer/market identification program.

ACCOUNT LIST SEGMENTATION

By developing profiles of your best customers and markets using NA-ICS codes you can now find more prospect companies like the profiles. All of the market segment NAICS codes listed above were found on the D and B online database. Each code revealed the number of potential prospects for the entire U.S. You can also look up these prospects by state and county and purchase a list of the prospect companies for any specific geographic area.

I call the entire process from best customers to best markets with the number of prospects in each market Account List Segmentation.

Develop a Marketing or Sales Plan to begin making sales calls

Congratulations. You now have the information you need to develop a marketing or sales development plan. This plan will usually include:

- Lead generation program
- Prospect qualification system
- Telemarketing to explore new markets
- Target account list for each territory
- Sales call schedule (discussed later in this chapter).

The Growth Planning Handbook

This entire process is explained in a more detailed 10-step process in the *Growth Planning Handbook*. All of the specific tools that support the process and all of the spreadsheets and charts are included. You can obtain a copy online at savingamericanmanufacturing.com.

Essential Question 3: Monitoring Customer Needs

Do you know what kinds of products and services they want or need?

For some small manufacturers, this is the most difficult of the steps they must take to become customer centered. For others, it is almost joyful and liberating, as you develop new and meaningful connections with your customers.

It can be a bit difficult at first. For most of us, listening to customers and monitoring their needs is not a natural ability – it must be systematically developed. But it is one of the most immediately productive ways for you to increase your business intelligence.

In his book *Confronting Reality*, Larry Bossidy offers a good answer to the question of monitoring customers. He says, "Of all of the external information you can gather, knowledge of the customer is the most specific and valuable in assessing your business model and strategies." I think everyone would generally agree with this statement. But Larry, unfortunately, doesn't tell us how we are supposed to do it – just that it is vitally important.

Developing a systematic way of monitoring customers is where you will find many ideas for new products and services. I've found that monitoring customers is almost always the key to success in increasing sales and finding market opportunities regardless of whether it is something you're naturally good at, or it feels like pulling teeth. It must be done if you are to compete in a changing economy. As we said, it's not always easy, because customers are external to the situation and not easy to monitor.

Whether easy or hard, it must become a regular part of your operations, just like maintaining your equipment. You may have to begin by hiring a third party to help you get started or perhaps another employee with these skills. But, you can no longer afford to operate in an information vacuum. Your future depends on it.

When there is no formal procedure to track customer comments, the chances of not meeting customer needs increases, which leads to customer defections.

How to Listen to Your Customers: Nine Simple Methods

Here are some basic techniques that will work with a small staff and a tight budget. It might sound trite, but the very first thing you need to do to find out what your customers want and need is to *ask them*.

I don't mean chit chatting on the phone when they call you. I mean developing systematic ways to gather information on an ongoing basis.

There are many complex and expensive ways to gather customer information but let's start with Nine Simple Methods you can use to begin monitoring customers.

Note: Methods #3 and #4, Lost Order Analysis and Quotation Analysis, are explained in great detail with extensive "how to" instructions in the Industrial Marketing Handbook.

1. **Use Lunches** — Budget 10% of your time to have lunch with key customers and other industry gurus. This is low cost research. For a start, this means at least one lunch a week.

2. **Phone Customers** — Randomly select some names and call them up. Try to have every employee occasionally phone customers. Don't make this complicated, just ask them what they think of your products and services. Then ask if they have any suggestions. In most cases, you will discover one or two employees who are better than average at doing this. They will become your part-time customer research staff. Have everyone send his or her customer notes and information to a "Customer Intelligence" file.

3. **Lost Order Analysis** — This is discussed in Essential Question #5, to follow, and at greater length in the Handbook.

4. **Quotation Analysis** — It is easy to design a database that provides a running analysis of quotations and orders. This analysis usually includes the number of orders lost and won, the dollar amount of quotations, a quotation "hit" rate, and the quote to order ratio. This gives your sales manager a very quick look at the sales history of any given account and is excellent internal information that could be used for a variety of analysis.

5. **Make Sales Calls** — Monitoring customers will inevitably lead to sales calls – usually at the customer's plant. Many job shops and small manufacturers have never had to do this – or they may have relied on sales reps to do it.

    It is important that owners and Presidents occasionally make sales calls on their own to find out why customers buy or don't buy. Placing yourself on their premises, where you have no control, strips away assumptions and is a fast way of gaining empathy for their problems and their needs. If you feel you don't have the time or are uncomfortable making these calls, appoint someone who can.

6. **Dissatisfied Customers** — Have all managers go into the field and make customer calls. Make sure they call on customers who favor the competition or are not fully satisfied. They will quickly find out about customers' wants and needs. In fact, these calls are magical because they are experiential. The closer you get to the customer's pain the more you understand. And we often learn more from those we haven't pleased. They help us understand how and where we have to improve.

7. **Training Sales People** — Sales people get to see competitive products, competitor bids and pricing, they listen to customer complaints about your company and they are told about product weaknesses from buyers. However, they don't know exactly what you need to know from customers. Enlist their support by introducing the information gaps you need to fill at the next sales meeting, and tell them specifically what information you need. And if you don't know what you need to know, that's all the more reason to learn.

8. **Customer Intelligence File** — In some cases, this can be surprisingly useful. Remember, the changes that you're facing are hitting your competitors as well. Begin a file to collect information on competitors, lost orders, customer changes, etc. Have everyone who receives a valuable call about any of these three subjects write you a quick memo or e-mail. Appoint someone in the office to be the collector of all of these memos.

9. **Independent Rep or Distributor Council** — If you use reps or distributors, pick out the most productive and experienced reps or distributors to form an information council. Get them together as soon as you can, and then once a year listen carefully to their feedback from customers.

10. **Display the Information** — Since you have now spent time and money collecting all of this good information you must put it to

use. All key managers and supervisors should know what customers want and don't want. Post everything on the walls of the conference room once a quarter for anybody to examine.

Essential Question 4: Competitive Advantage

Can you compare your products to the competitor's products in terms of price, delivery, and key features – model by model?

The first reason competitive intelligence information is important is that it shows you whether you have a competitive advantage.

Many job shops and product manufacturers find themselves trapped in competitive situations where they have little competitive advantage and dwindling profits. They need to gather critical competitive information to find out if their company can differentiate its products and services from the competition well enough to maintain margins and, hopefully, grow the business.

Initial Intelligence

When the objective is to find new customers and new markets it is important to find out:

- How many competitors there are for each product line or service
- How your products or services compare to their products in terms of customer buying perceptions
- How your prices compare to their prices from customer buying perceptions.

If you can't answer these basic questions, then you will have to wait to find out at the point of sale whether you have competitive advantage or not. It goes without saying that it is very expensive to find out you don't have a salable product or service at the point of sale.

Competitive Matrix

A good first step to finding out whether you have competitive advantage product by product is to design a simple matrix. On one side of a page list all of your direct competitors. On the top of that page list some key factors like company size, models, selling price, discounts, type of distri-

Figure 2-4: Sample Competitor Matrix

Manufacturer Model	GMH Model 400AB	OLSON Model ANT22	ACME Model 4459
Base Price	$112,000.00	$???	$???
Specifcations			
Speed	10 per hr	???	13 per hr
Load ht. capacity	61"	???	52"
Max. opening	52" x 26" x 18"	54" x 24" x 25"	???
Input	Side	???	Rear
Motors	Reliance	Baldor	SEW
Gear boxes	Cone / Electra	Tinsmith	???
Upper plate	Steel	Aluminum	Titanium
Max. load weight	9000 lbs.	???	???
Upper guides	STD	STD	Optional
Lower guides	STD		
PLC	OPCON	???	Micro
Drive belts	Optional	STD	???
Lift mechanism	Hydraulic	Pneumatic	Electric
Rollers dimension	3.5"	4"	5"
Keyboard	Monotonic	ABB	???
Discharge	Shuttle	Chain	Chain
Interface	STD	Optional	STD
Cylinders	Atlas	Parker	Lao Xingr

bution, delivery time, and other factors you need to know to be competitive. Now fill in the matrix and see where you are missing information. See Figure 2-4 for an example. Here we use a comparison of three material handling machines that carry pallet loads.

This exercise is a quick way to find the information gaps shown as (???) that need to be filled in before you can truly find out how your product compares to the competition from a customer's point of view. Once you get enough good comparative information and a sell price, you will have the same information the customer looks at in a buying situation. Getting an "apples to apples" price comparison is absolutely necessary if you're going to find out whether your products or services are competitive in the marketplace.

A more complete range of methods for gathering competitor intelligence is provided in the companion Industrial Marketing Handbook. *These methods begin with fairly simple techniques using only internal data and progress to more complex techniques requiring field research.*

Essential Question 5: Lost Orders

Do you know the specific reasons you lost orders to competitors? Do you have that information for every known lost order in the last year?

One of the best indicators of whether a marketing or sales program is working is the ratio of orders to lost orders. Knowing why customers buy or don't buy is vital to industrial marketing, and I have included it as one of the Six Essentials. The reasoning is simple – it is difficult to know what to do to prevent future lost orders or lost customers if you don't know why you are losing current customers and orders.

Keeping track of lost order information is critical to perpetuate long term growth and is a fundamental part of the foundation you must build of continuous improvement, customer satisfaction, and quality programs.

My own surveys and interviews during the '90s showed that more than 75% of small manufacturers do not track lost orders and 95% do not know all of the reasons customers dropped them as a supplier.

The bottom line is you can't really develop a plan to increase sales growth or even survive in the new economy without knowing why you lose orders and customers.

How to Build a Lost Order Analysis

Begin by developing a list of all orders that were lost in the last year (see Figure 2-5). Get everyone together who was connected to the quotes and sales effort. Now review every lost order to find the best reason.

If no one has been keeping records, try to review as many of the accounts as people can remember and go through the list quickly to determine the basic reasons. You will probably find that, as in the example in Figure 2-5, many of the lost order reasons are not known (???). Some will be very obvious and other reasons may be simply guesses.

Figure 2-5: Sample Lost Order Analysis

Here is a partial Lost Order Analysis – There are 150 orders, total.

Start by developing a code for Lost Orders: P – price; SP – couldn't meet specs; LT – lead time; SR – sales rep; SCP – superior competitor product; ??? – unknown.

Note the real important accounts – the ones you cannot afford to lose with an X.

NAICS Code	Customer	Model	Sales	Reason	
33441	DEKA	100	800,000	???	
33441	OECO	10	575,000	P	
33152	Maggot	400b	570,000	SP	X
33392	CLARK	f400	290,000	P	X
33152	DFC	f500	235,000	???	X
33429	RIR	1000	149,000	P	
33111	BOISE	100A	120,000	SCP	X
33411	TEKKO	100A	100,000	???	X
33829	Warner	100b	85,000	SR	
33321	Allied	100c	80,000	???	X
33411	TETCO	25B	60,000	LT	
33152	Marko	25C	44,000	P	X

List goes on with 138 other lost orders

NAICS Code	Customer	Model	Sales	Reason	
31133	MK	400A	34,000	???	X
33431	DEKA	400b	32,000	P	X
31194	MAZOLINE	400c	30,000	???	X
31142	DEMNT	1000	29,000	???	X
32455	Capricorn	10bdf	28,000	LT	
32134	LECH	10	25,000	???	X

Next comes what may seem difficult. But it's critical. You, or someone else at your company – such as the appropriate sales person – will have to call each of these customers and find out the real reason for their decisions. If you don't have a person or the time to get the answers, hire an outside service to get it done. This is important

In some ways, finding out about lost orders is as important as getting orders. You've begun to develop a simple system to follow-up on every quotation to a final resolution. Get involved and oversee the lost order analysis process.

Four Types of Lost Order Information

There are 4 types of information you can gather on lost orders that will help you in making strategy decisions

- **Customer Information** — If you can find out the real or complete reason the customer decided to buy a competitor's product, you will have an insight as to what strategy you must change in the future to get the customer back or get the next order.
- **Sales Rep Information** — By comparing bookings to lost orders it is easy to see which rep groups are having trouble selling your product lines.
- **Model Information** — Grouping lost orders by model reveals which models might not have competitive advantage and should be considered for redesign or a pruning decision.
- **Competitive Information** — Most importantly, it is necessary to find out exactly which competitors you are losing to. If you have 25 competitors but you lose orders to only 3 of them 70% of the time, you will know where to focus your strategies.

For more information, charts showing examples of each of these methods of assembling lost order data are shown in the *Industrial Marketing Handbook*.

Essential Question 6: Product Costs and Margins

Do you know if you are making adequate margins on each product line, model, or job?

To have a chance of competing in the new economy, you will need to find out if you are making adequate margins on each product line, model, job, or service. Many small manufacturers have good sales records but rarely keep summaries of profitability. Maintaining detailed records on profit by customer account, product line, and even product model is necessary to make customer selection decisions, to change selling and pricing strategies, and to identify "product dogs" that should be dropped.

But there's one more reason. The most important reason costs and margins are important is that it is dangerous to find new customers or go after large accounts or to bid on large projects when you do not have good cost information. Most Type 3 manufacturers have good cost information but most Type 1 and 2 manufacturers don't. Examples of the kind of data needed are described in Chapter 7 in a section describing the fundamentals of designing a basic costing system.

Once you've identified new customers and markets as described earlier the next challenge is contacting them. The good news is you probably now have some of the best customer and marketing information you've ever had.

Sales Prospecting by Phone

Once you have identified new customers and markets, the next problem is contacting them. More specifically, once you have a list of prospects in various markets all over the United States how do you find the qualified buyers?

The cost of in-person sales calls ranges from $100.00 to $300.00 per call so it is expensive to make cold calls. The answer to this problem seems obvious — **use the phone to qualify prospects**.

I don't mean just calling prospects. Phone prospecting requires a systematic method and discipline. There are essentially 4 steps:

1. Define "qualified." In general, a qualified lead or prospect will be someone who has a need for the product; has a budget for the product, or is planning to request funding; and either has the authority to buy or is a member of a team that will make the purchase.

2. Conduct an interview. Don't just wing it; develop a list of questions to ask in order to qualify each prospect. The questions should
   - Explain the purpose
   - Probe the prospect about applications, short- and long-term needs
   - Determine if the prospect is a qualified buyer and has purchasing authority
   - Determine if there is a budget and the time line for the purchase
3. Send information – mail an inquiry package within 24-48 hours of the call.
4. Follow up.

Why most sales people don't do it.

Almost all industrial sales reps agree with lead and prospect qualification and would welcome focusing their time on 50 qualified prospects with projects rather than 1200 general inquiries. Today's industrial salesman is required by their factory or principals to do quotations, customer follow-up, training, service, and a wide range of administrative tasks. Most do not have the time or patience to spend hours on the phone qualifying hundreds of leads.

There are 3 solutions:

1. Convince the sales reps that it is their job – you might be able to force them if they are employees and their jobs are threatened.
2. Another answer is for the factory to hire their own telemarketing person to qualify all leads before sending them to the reps.
3. Perhaps the most practical solution to this problem is hiring a sales prospecting service. These are independent telemarketing services that have operators that are trained to handle industrial prospects, and can do a lot of the prospecting and qualifying at a relatively low cost.

Other Methods for Finding New Customers and Markets

The techniques for identifying the best customers and finding new markets (Account List Segmentation) discussed in this chapter are very basic, but provide you with the fundamental information that is necessary to begin the process of finding new customers and markets.

Now we are going to look at other practical methods used by successful SMMs. They range from simple shotgun methods to complex methods of market analysis. These examples will show you that a good deal of niche marketing is common sense. It's a matter of profiling customers and beginning with a list of general prospects, and then continuously narrowing the list down to a specific group of buyers.

Here are eight real-life methods used by SMMs that will help you decide which methods will work best in your company.

1. Use "Shotgun Marketing" to Find New Customers

Example: Small, high-tech manufacturer of microcontrollers with no outside sales force

Shotgun marketing is the use of a wide variety of marketing techniques to sell to any type of prospect. There are no specific customer profiles or target markets. Shotgun marketing is selling to anyone who says they can buy.

When you are just beginning to market a product or are starting a company and don't know the markets or the customers, Shotgun marketing is a good way to start.

Many small manufacturers began as shotgunners and many have also had strong sales growth with shotgun techniques. Shotgun Marketing is most successful for manufacturers who build standard products and have consistent costs and margins. But at some point in time the company needs to focus on the right customers and markets to succeed over the long haul.

Here's a story, though the names have been changed.

I'll call this company Shot Tek. This is a real company, but I'm disguising it a bit. This firm, a manufacturer of microcontrollers, got off the ground with a shotgun mail-order program – one that reached everyone from hobbyists working in their basements to engineers for Fortune 500 companies who were designing plant production systems.

The company drummed up more than 250 new customers a year by running ads in high tech magazines and by mailing a catalog showing all of their products. Many OEMs used the micro-controllers as primary controls of their own products, and they began buying in large volumes.

From those beginnings, the company grew at 20% per year and eventually reached $1.2 million sales. They reached $1.2 million in sales volume because they inadvertently stumbled onto a half dozen OEM-type customers who began using large quantities of Shot Tek's micro-controllers in their equipment.

With this volume also came some problems in quality and customer service.

In hindsight, Shot Tek should have refocused their company on the OEM market and organized themselves to develop a quality control system and the new customer support systems and technical manuals the OEMs needed.

They were victims of their own success with shotgun marketing. All they had wanted was a simple way of selling their products through a mail order system, but they inadvertently got into trouble when they sold to technical OEMs rather than hobbyists. Their shotgun had brought in a few big birds that needed more special care and feeding.

The shotgun marketing techniques that had led to their early growth eventually created big customer problems. In trying to serve so many customers, Shot-Tek didn't really satisfy anyone. So the downside was that the company couldn't retain customers long enough to establish a good sales backlog. This forced them onto the exhausting treadmill of continually seeking out more new customers. Eventually the lack of repeat business and ongoing service problems caught up with Shot-Tek. The company lost most of its best OEM customers and had to lay off employees.

The moral to the story is that shotgun marketing works and is a good way to get sales started but at some point the company has to decide where they will focus in the market. Or, to put it another way, when you go hunting with a shotgun, pay attention to what you hit.

Shotgun marketing techniques do work. The only limitation is the money you can afford to spend. Here are some tips:

- Attend as many trade shows that represent your products as you can afford
- Run advertisements in as many trade journals as you can
- Pay all reps a commission based on just the gross sales amount so that they will be inspired to find any kind of sales in their territories
- Require that all reps make cold calls every day
- Quote any prospect who contacts the factory to increase the chance of more orders
- Use price discounting as a primary sales technique. Discounting can get hard-to-sell customers interested in a hurry.

If you have the money to use all of these methods and don't have to worry about product costs and margins then I will virtually guarantee that you will increase sales.

Long-term, there may be issues, but, as Peter Drucker observed, "Volume solves a host of problems."

2. Using telemarketing to prospect for new customers

Example: Independent rep agency selling packaging equipment

Okay, time for another story.

This one is about a small rep agency that was given the chance to prospect for sales in the Greater Chicago area. The only problem was that this market was 6 hours away from headquarters. The company simply could not afford to drive over to Chicago and make cold calls. They needed to find a more cost-effective way to explore the market and do sales prospecting. The following describes the primary factors.

- Rep agency: a 4 person firm selling mostly in Ohio, New York, and Pennsylvania.
- Sales call cost: Approximately $300 per call
- Product represented: A system used to detect the fill quantity of cans in a production line

- System prices: Orders ranged from $14,000 to $55,000
- Markets Identified: NAICS Codes 312120, 311421, 311422, 311920, 311941, 311111, 312111, 311999
- 763 PROSPECT COMPANIES.

The prospect list was developed from the factory profiles of existing customers purchasing detection systems, and from the ten most likely NAICS market niches.

Since none of the four agency salesmen currently on staff had the time to do the phone work, an outside telemarketing service was hired and two scripts were created using a two-step process.

Step 1:
In the first step, all 763 prospects were contacted and qualified in terms of their production process, buyers, types of products processed, and capability of buying the detection equipment. It was discovered through a very short phone interview that 517 plants did not qualify and could not use the detection system.

The telemarketing firm found that there were 246 companies that were really qualified to buy the detection system. All of these prospects were sent a packet of literature.

Step 2:
In the second step, each of 246 qualified prospects was re-called.

Results: The process was slow and deliberate. It eventually resulted in 38 quoted projects with a sales potential of $840,000. Not every sale was made, but these quotes led to $500,000 in sales.

The total cost of the telemarketing-prospecting program was $5,358.00 including salary benefits, phone, fax, literature, and supplies.

This came out to $141.00 per prospect ($5,358/38 = $141.00). Compare that to the cost of attempting to contact the 246 qualified prospects face to face. It would have been nearly $75,000 ($300 X 246 = $73,800).

This example is very instructive for SMMs who are looking for a low cost way of finding new customers in geographically distant markets.

It typifies an industrial selling situation, where industrial buyers can be somewhat difficult to identify and qualify.

3. Focusing on market niches and new customers using account list segmentation

Example: A family-owned, Type 2 machine shop.

This story is about how a family owned machine shop used account list segmentation to focus on the right customers, the right market niches, and the right prospects to grow their business. The steps they used generally follow the description for identifying customers and markets earlier in this chapter. Their process was done in seven steps:

Step 1: Identify Guidelines — The process begins with the company deciding on or estimating the increase in sales for the next 12 months. The second guideline was to set a minimum for profit margins by customer – established at 20%.

Step 2: Account List Segmentation — This step begins by printing a list of all accounts sold in the last 12 months (can vary from 1-3 years) by sales volume – from the largest volume to the smallest volume account. In a second column the list includes the corresponding profit margin percent of each account before overhead. Once the list is constructed, determine the number and percent of accounts that make up 80% of the volume. In this company's case, 12 accounts (8.5% of 140 customer accounts) were 84% of total sales. These are their Most Valuable Customers (MVCs).

Step 3: Good (+) and Bad (-) Customers — All customer accounts were marked as Good (+) or Bad (-) by the owners of the company. Good (+) customers are the accounts the company wants to retain. Bad (-) Customers fell below the guideline. Three MVC customers and many of the smaller accounts fell below the minimum standard of 20% gross profit. It was decided that prices would be increased for the MVC accounts that were losing money, and other small accounts that had gross profits below the target minimum would be pruned from the business. On the other hand, several MVC accounts contributed large sales volumes and gross profits above 30% in the electrical and metals market niches.

Step 4: Find More Like Them — By developing profiles of these companies using NAICS codes and employee size, the company decided to look for similar prospects in these niches by purchasing prospect lists in a specific geographic sales area.

Step 5: Group Customers — This step groups customers into market niches. Each customer account was assigned a NAICS code, and then grouped into defined market niches. The market niches are then prioritized in terms of sales potential, profitability, and known purchase order opportunities.

Step 6: Competitor Analysis — It was also decided it would be prudent to examine all known direct competitors in these markets. The company commissioned an outside consultant to do a competitive intelligence project on 32 known competitors. The information was compiled in a matrix to compare machine tool capabilities, tool sizes, quality systems and labor rates. This helped the company assess its competitive advantage and to know the strengths and weaknesses of each competitor during the bid process. The competitor intelligence methods are described in the Handbook in Section I-4-H.

Step 7: Marketing Plan — The last step was to use all of this information to develop a marketing plan that included:
- A one-year proforma sales and budget projection
- Selection of the target accounts for face to face sales calls
- Decisions on marketing strategy such as trade shows, direct mail, catalogs, and telemarketing
- In some instances they changed estimating procedures and pricing for certain accounts and jobs
- They also decided to approach several competitors with lower labor rates to become suppliers in an alliance rather than expand their shop.

Results: Company sales volume grew from $3.6 to $5.2 million.

4. Finding new customer and market opportunities by focusing on the components of a larger product or system

Typically, Type 3 market leaders are somewhat complacent about market trends and technological innovations. Here's why:

1. They often don't perceive threats as imminent.
2. They often disregard tiny competitors as not being in the same class.
3. They tend to focus all of their attention on current products and, particularly, the total system.
4. They seldom spend a lot of time or money monitoring their own customer wants and needs.
5. The larger the company grows, the more attention they pay to "big ticket" products and systems and conversely less attention is paid to parts, service, and components of systems.

As a result, they leave themselves open to attack from innovative newcomers. There is a message here for small manufacturers – *There are always opportunities to find new customers and markets by focusing on the weaknesses of relatively complacent larger competitors.*

One approach that is much easier than developing new products and new market niches is simply to look for a component that is a small part of a larger product or system, and then offer a better product with superior services.

Here are two examples.

Example I: AJAX FOUNDRY, INC.

In 1973, a consultant to the paper industry brought Ajax Foundry a casting called a refiner plate. This was used as a wear part in a larger machine called a refiner. The consultant had received the plate from a local paper mill that was interested in finding another supplier of the wear part because the original equipment manufacturer was high priced and they were unresponsive to repeated complaints. This is a classic case of a large OEM focusing on the overall product but not paying attention to the small components or support services.

Ajax forged an alliance with the dissatisfied local paper mill and produced a refiner plate that could replace the existing part and sell for about 25% less.

Results: The OEM never responded to Ajax's competitive challenge and eventually lost all of the refiner plate business. Ajax has grown from a small local foundry to $20 million, and a dominant supplier serving these market segments worldwide. The primary reason for Ajax Foundry's success was that they chose not to compete on the entire product, which would have been extremely expensive, but to focus on an area of weakness, where they could gain a competitive advantage.

Example II: GRIPFAST, INC.

In 1975, a large OEM introduced projectile weaving machines in the textile industry. Projectile weaving machines were designed to weave a piece of cloth 144" wide, which made large scale production of polypropylene possible (it didn't exist 30 years ago).

These machines used special grippers to grip the polypropylene fabric. The original grippers designed by the OEMs had a short life because of wear problems. This reduced the overall efficiency of the machine.

A worker in one of the textile plants saw that the company was buying a large number of gripper parts and, in 1975, formed Gripfast, Inc., to offer a solution to parts problems. With very little capital, assets, or machinery, Gripfast went into the business of making wear parts for textile machines.

They designed a new gripper with longer life than the OEM's gripper and guaranteed the part to last at least one year. They offered personalized services, guaranteed deliveries, and just-in-time service to lower the customer's inventory. They reduced the industry lead time on this part from 16 weeks to 48 hours and, as you might imagine, their business grew very quickly.

Results: The OEM company never reacted to Gripfast's competitive challenge. Today, two of every three grippers sold in the U.S. are Gripfast products.

These two examples demonstrate that monitoring competitor weaknesses can be a low cost way of finding new market ideas. They also demonstrate that it is possible to eventually dominate the market niche and enjoy phenomenal growth.

5. Hiring your first outside sales manager

Example: A small, high-tech plastic injection molding shop.

The Plastics Group (TPG) is a high tech injection molding shop specializing in the development and manufacture of critical plastic products and components. The staff consists of a team of manufacturing professionals ranging from well-trained operators and assembly people, through expert molding and laboratory technicians to seasoned engineers having a wealth of experience with plastics and their applications.

The company's molding capacity includes 20-ton to 300-ton presses. The quality system is modeled after ISO 9001. All tooling design and construction is supervised by TPG's tooling engineers, as is the in-house repair service. TPG services encompass a complete range of secondary operations including custom packaging, assembly, post machining, ultrasonic welding, decorating, and painting.

The company also has a sister company, Plastics Engineering Labs (PEL), that specializes in product design and development services. PEL has developed numerous products from scratch, as well as FIRST-ARTICLE army inspection. This engineering expertise is a core competency of TPG.

The company was founded in 1992, but in 1995 TPG began having financial problems. Sales and margins were erratic and one large customer dominated the company. They did not have a focus in the marketplace or a way to find the right customers and markets that fit their core competencies.

In late 1995, TPG asked the local manufacturing extension partnership center for assistance. A field engineer from a regional office of Georgia Tech was brought in to examine the manufacturing problems and offered to do a layout for a contemplated move to a new building. Another specialist was brought in from Georgia Tech to identify cost reduction opportunities and to analyze the company's financial statements relative to industry benchmarks. After analyzing the financial statements and looking at customer information, the Georgia Tech specialists suggested to the general manager, Sam Brockway, that he "had a serious sales problem." Sam said that he thought that most of his problems were production problems, but the specialist made him realize that his major concern should be marketing and that he should seriously investigate customer profitability.

In early 1996, company management was invited to attend several seminars hosted by Georgia Tech. One of these seminars was a closed circuit TV broadcast that I presented on niche marketing. Sam, his son, operations manager Buzz Brockway, and the newly hired sales manager Dave Flood attended the broadcast. After the broadcast, they purchased my first book, *The Manufacturer's Guide to Business Marketing*, and they began studying the fundamentals of industrial marketing.

The shotgun checklist in the book showed that the company was using shotgun marketing to find new customers, and the section on "MVC Analysis" presented a methodology that helped Sam Brockway examine some of his customers. The company did not have a formal cost accounting system but they could recover labor and materials information from work-orders to show contribution margins. Sam and Buzz manually costed out all of the jobs to determine which customer accounts were profitable.

TPG's Six-Page Marketing Plan

TPG management decided to take a totally different approach to the market. They decided to hire their first outside sales manager and develop a brief marketing plan to find the customers that best fit the company and its core competencies. The marketing plan was very succinct (6 pages) and included the following:

1. One page on the company profile. In 2 paragraphs they explained the company's core competencies and services. In one paragraph they described the marketing niche. It says "our best clients will be companies that are currently buying injection molding, who all have new products or improvements coming on-line on a regular basis."

2. One page showing the sales goals and a four-year MVC and sales projection. This is a simple matrix showing the number of MVC customers and their total sales by year, and the total number of

accounts and their total sales by year. The forecast covered a 4-year period and there is a note on the bottom of the page that says their goal is that no one account will have more than 10% of the total sales dollars.

3. One page showing the "Criteria for Most Valuable Customer." This is a key page in the plan because it defines the MVC customer in terms of sales potential dollars and relates the profiles to TPG's core services and capabilities. Sam Brockway decided that it costs as much to do business with a $10,000 account as a $100,000 account, so why not focus on larger customers and send the small accounts to his competitors. His criteria describes the billing they expected from the new customer, the sales potential for the future, a willingness to see the value of TPGs services, the customer's growth and financial stability, and the most important factor – the customer's willingness to deal with TPG as a partner rather than a parts maker.

4. One page describing the marketing strategy for finding new business and customers. This page is entitled the "Marketing Plan" and describes sales prospecting from a master list to personal calls.

5. One page describing the sales force and potential channels of distribution. The plan describes using independent reps to sell their services in 5 states with territories defined in terms of sales potential dollars.

6. One page describing the systems that would be needed to achieve the sales goals. This page makes the case for gathering information in a database on competitors, customers, and prospects and doing a customer survey.

Once the MVC criteria were established the sales manager developed a list of several hundred potential customers in Georgia alone. He called all prospects on the phone and most were sent mailers. After an account was qualified, a visit was arranged for personal contact and a verification of needs, usage, and potential. With this qualification processed they eliminated the large list of prospects down to 12 companies with the best potential. All of these companies had personal visits from TPG management and the company gradually began to get sales contracts from them.

Results: The company moved from a small financial loss on $1,100,000 in sales in 1996 to a solid profit in 1997. Their marketing plan and new focus on specific market niches began to pay off in 1997 with new customers and solid growth. By early 1998 the company had grown from 16 employees to 42 employees and was fast approaching their $3 million 1998 sales goal with a corresponding increase in profits.

The TPG case study is not only an inspiring financial turnaround story; it also illustrates some of the key points of industrial marketing.

1. First of all, the story shows that it is very hard to make money or to satisfy customers using shotgun marketing or selling anything to any customer.
2. Second, it shows that it is very difficult to really focus in the marketplace until the company develops a profile of the customers that are really needed for long-term growth.
3. Third, it shows that customer selection or selling to customers that best fit and value your competencies and services is the real key to long-term profitability and growth.

6. Finding new markets using independent sales reps, integrators, and specialized distributors when customers and markets are unknown

Example: Manufacturer of robots.

Willamette LLC is a manufacturer of material handling robots. They started in 1990. A key assumption was that the market was growing so fast and their products were so good that sales would simply happen. They were correct in their first two assumptions.

The market was growing fast and these Japanese-built robots were excellent. But sales did not simply happen.

The company did not focus on the right markets, the right customers, the right applications, or the competition. They did not have a real business plan beyond a one-year budget and they employed shotgun-selling methods in an attempt to make the sales forecast.

Like many start-up companies, Willamette LLC began by selling products wherever they could find buyers. This shotgun approach to the market eventually led to erratic sales, significant losses, confusion, unhappy owners, and a negative net worth. All of this characterized the first three years of their existence. They found themselves in a bad situation where most stockholders were simply tired of the losses and wanted to shut the company down.

The company needed to find a way to focus on the right customers and on the market segments.

If you've got a niche, scratch it.

Identifying small market niches (groups of customers) is a process of slowly narrowing a wide range of potential prospects with unknown needs down to a small group of qualified buyers with specific needs.

If you have a factory sales force and fairly identifiable customers, the salesman can do the qualifying process.

However, if you are using independent sales channels and the markets and projects are not easily identifiable an inquiry generation system is one of the most cost-effective ways of finding the right customers and projects for your company. Good qualified leads are also the quickest way to get independent channels working for you.

With that in mind, here is a good example of how to explore and exploit a market niche.

Using Sales Prospecting and Niche Marketing Techniques

Here is a four-phase niche-marketing plan:

Phase 1: Assign NAICS Codes. Assign them to all orders and quotations.

Phase 2: Examine Quotations and Leads. By examining quotations and leads, the sales group discovered there were opportunities in the dairy industry. Under the new NAICS system this was a four-digit NAICS code – 3115 – that showed 2,300 plants in the U.S.

Phase 3: Narrow Your Focus. In the next phase, the Dairy industry was further narrowed down to plants that produced various cheese products. This is a six-digit NAICS code – 311513 – that had 1300 locations.

Phase 4: Find Your Best Fit. By using quotations, sales calls, and lead analysis it was possible to narrow the market even farther to a specific cheese by-product, "dry cheese whey." This is an 8-digit NAICS code – 31151316 – that had only 150 plants. Once this specific application was known, it was possible to focus the marketing techniques and make sales calls on the plants.

The primary advantages of using this approach to identify specific market niches are:

- The manufacturer can customize products and services for that specific application
- The manufacturer often gains an advantage by offering a system that is superior to that offered by competitors
- By aggressively marketing to the other identified prospects of the niche you may have enough advantage to command a good price and maintain margins, and dominate the market niche – until the competition can respond
- Qualified leads will inspire independent sales channels to make calls and spend their money on sales efforts.

Results: In this case, the sales forecast was achieved in just one year. This is a terrific result that went from unhappy customers, poor sales, and serious losses to a significant profit in just one year.

Many factors and systems contributed to this turnaround, but the primary reason for success was focusing on the right market niches – though that was just the beginning. From that they evolved to changing the channels of distribution, monitoring a wider range of competition, and developing a competitive advantage with products for specific applications – ones where they could get their price and maintain margins.

The company then went on to develop many more market niches in the seed, chemical, and cement industries. Within three years, they were growing at 15% per year, while the company achieved their sales and profit goals. Within five years, the company had tripled its size.

Inquiry generation is one of the most cost efficient ways of diversifying your company into new and different types of niches. It will, to some extent, avoid the plague of economic downturns. For when some of the markets are declining, others are growing. It also shows how the transformation process can work to revitalize a company. Transformation can be "catchy." Once it starts in one place, the habits of changing for the better can permeate a company.

7. Identifying an emerging market niche from quotation analysis

Example: Manufacturer of palletizer machines.

In the 1970s a new application emerged in the paper industry that demanded new high-speed methods and equipment to handle the cartons of copy paper without damage. This special request was one of 500 different requests for quotes received during 1975.

The company I worked for, Columbia Machine, modified a standard machine design and added a new "turntable" device that would gently turn the Xerox cases in either direction without touching the sides of the cases. This simple line extension gave us a unique competitive advantage, and we received an order for nine machines from a large paper company.

In 1975, I had the opportunity to work with an engineer at Nekoosa Paper Company, one of our customers, to refine this "turntable" machine so that it would connect to a new German high-speed sheeter manufactured by E.C.H. Will of Hamburg, Germany. A sheeter is a huge production machine that converts large rolls of paper into sheets of photocopy paper. Will's new sheeter could run three times faster than equivalent American machines.

I visited the Nekoosa plant site and found that they had purchased the second new German sheeter installed in the U.S. Everyone in the paper industry was waiting to see how the new German machines would impact the marketplace. Even though the machines were more expensive than their American counterparts, they were supposed to increase productivity enough to pay for the investment in a few years. I knew that if this proved to be true, there would be opportunities for the new sheeters in many American paper companies with converting operations. By carefully following one new application and designing a unique approach to case handling, we had discovered a completely new market opportunity.

We built several of our modified palletizers for Nekoosa, and they worked very well. At this point, I decided to do a little research and define this emerging market niche more clearly. I started by analyzing the profile of our customer, Nekoosa. Here's what I found:

1. It was a large multi-plant paper company with converting lines.
2. The company had several of the original, low speed Lenox (American manufactured) sheeters.
3. Nekoosa was interested in the new German sheeter because it provided higher speeds, less down time, more precision, and higher quality copy paper, and it boosted the overall level of production.

In researching further, I found that the copy paper segment of the paper industry was growing 10% to 15% a year and that many large paper companies had special converting lines and contracts to make copy paper. From several paper industry associations we obtained lists of all paper and pulp mills in the U.S. The total was less than 200 companies. In this case, it was a simple matter to find other mills with the same profile as Nekoosa.

E.C.H. Will, the German Company, had already done a good job of examining the U.S. market and had targeted many paper mills as candidates for new lines in the U.S. I had a good contact at Will, so I knew which mills were being targeted. We also found, by visiting the mills, that every manager and specifier in them was a member of TAPPI, the major paper industry trade association. These members gave us enough in-depth knowledge of the customer's needs to refine our machine even further and build overwhelming competitive advantage.

From the beginning, we were determined to dominate this market niche and stay ahead of our competitors. We devoted part of our advertising budget to buying targeted ads in a paper industry trade journal.

As a result of our efforts, we won a number of new long-term customers, and the modified palletizer had the highest gross margin of any of the machines in the product line.

Results: This niche strategy worked well for both E.C.H. Will and Columbia Machine.

Between 1975 and 1984, 100 of the Will sheeters were installed in the U.S., and Columbia Machine received 99 of the palletizer orders for these new lines.

8. Using a direct sales force when customers are known

Example – Manufacturer of sawmills with direct sales force.

This last example shows what can happen when you are using a factory direct sales force with customers and prospects that are well defined.

In this case, the product is sawmill machinery.

Forest industry trade directories list about 3,000 sawmills in the U.S. The market for automated sawmill machines can be further sub-divided into a segment of 300 to 400 large sawmills – the ones that are most likely to buy complete plants or automated machinery.

Since virtually all sawmill locations are known, it makes sense that the best method to find new prospects for sawmill equipment is to have direct sales reps stay in contact with each plant.

The company also did some brand (image) advertising in the trade journals and attended two trade shows per year. But lead generation was not the primary method – or even the most cost-effective method – for finding new projects.

This company had annual sales of more than $100 million. They could afford to hire a factory direct sales force. They used five salesmen in the Southeastern U.S. and five on the West Coast.

All sales people were assigned to geographic territories with a specific number of accounts to cover every year. This sales force coverage and the prospecting was so good that the company regularly was able to bid on more than 95% of all projects occurring in the United States.

Finding the projects was not a problem. Their challenge was closing enough of them to make their forecast. The lesson from this case? When all prospects and projects are readily identifiable and you can afford a factory sales force, lead generation is not the best technique to find new projects.

Conclusion

Finding new industrial markets and new customers seldom begins with sophisticated computer models and statistical techniques. In most cases, it's a matter of experimentation, and trial and error with many customers and markets. A good portion of it is frequently intuitive.

Another portion is just plain hard work. Digging up the facts about your own particular market and profiling the customers who will be right for you.

Successful SMMs start out with a large list of potential prospects that might be interested in buying. They gradually narrow their focus (reduce the number of prospects), by systematically eliminating prospects that don't fit their customer and market profiles. If they are persistent in their sales prospecting and lead qualification, the focus eventually defines the right customers and markets.

It's all about identifying the right customers for your company and the right markets – specific customer groups with specific needs

Key Points

The general premise of this book is that the key to competing and growing in the 21st century is to get out of declining industries and markets and get rid of customers that will drive you into bankruptcy. This, by definition, requires finding new customers and markets. This chapter provides a step-by-step methodology for identifying good and bad customers and identifying new markets on an ongoing basis.

Suggested Action

Print out a list of all of your customers and try to group them into market niches by size, product, NAICS code, or any parameters suggested in this chapter. Can you profile customers in each niche well enough to develop a mailing list and find more like them?

Transition and Transformation

You now know how to profile your customers, analyze competitors, and define market segments. You also know many other unconventional techniques used by SMMs to find market segments. Finding customers and markets is the first step.

Once you have sold these new customers you will usually find they want different kinds of products and services. This sets the stage for a process that will increase your chances of developing the right products that will sell. That will be the focus of Chapter 3.

Chapter 3
Developing New Products: Transformation through Innovation

In addition to finding new customers and markets the other key factor is product development. New customers. New markets. New products.

Continued investment in new product development is one of the most critical factors in competing with the rest of the world. This is true for both small and large manufacturing companies.

A report from the National Association of Manufacturers summarizes this importance:

> "Manufacturing's innovation process is the key to past, present, and future prosperity and higher living standards. The intricate process starts with an idea for a new product or process, prompting investments in research and development. R&D successes lead to investments in capital equipment and workers, and to 'spillovers' that benefit manufacturing and other sectors.
> "This process not only generates new products and processes, but also leads to well-paying jobs, increased productivity, and competitive pricing. Yet while this process produces wealth and higher living standards, most of it is hidden from view and poorly understood."[1]

There seems to be an endless number of articles written about why all manufacturers must become more innovative. They suggest that this thing called innovation is a function of creativity, and that creative ideas will lead to successful new products. The implication is that an increase in creative ideas will lead to an increase in new product success.

And there's something to it. Anyone who has traveled extensively and worked with Small and Midsize Manufacturers (SMMs) will quickly see that there is no shortage of creative ideas. SMMs are clever and we can always count on them to produce endless ideas for new products.

The challenge isn't coming up with new ideas; it is in the successful commercialization of the idea. This problem is actually many problems. They lie in each step of the implementation process. Simply put, getting it done right at each stage will increase the probability of achieving commercial success with your innovation. In companies of every size, ideation of concepts is usually good, but implementation is generally poor.

The Difference between R&D and New Product Development

Many books and articles talk about new products and R&D as if they were the same things. But let me make what I think is an important distinction in understanding new products as developed by SMMs.

True research and development is the primary research that is done in federal labs or in giant companies such as Bell Labs or the IBM Watson Center. These research labs are the ones that invent new technologies such as self-cleaning glass or microprocessors with circuits down to one nanometer wide. You can make a case that creativity plays a big role in this type of primary research.

SMMs seldom do primary research with scientists and large labs. However, they will often use the results of this primary research to design their new products. This process is called "spillover" by the government. This does not diminish the importance of their new product contribution because they have to be very creative to see the new product possibilities and very clever to design the new product or related application.

The real problem in companies of every size is that a very low percentage of new product concepts are successful.

A study by Booz Allen Hamilton shows that only one in seven new product concepts becomes a commercial success.[2] Another recent study of both large and small manufacturers shows that one third of new products fail at market launch.

To repeat my point, the real problem is not innovation, or creativity, but commercial success.

The objective of this chapter is to help you increase the probability of success of your new product concepts. It is also about how to reduce the risk of losing a lot of money on new product ideas that are not unique or saleable. And it's about how to address the types of problems common to various stages of the process.

This chapter will present an iterative process (successfully tested by the author) to evaluate new product concepts from the idea stage to successful commercialization. This process evaluates risk and costs at every stage and only allows big money to be spent on new products with significant commercial potential that can be executed with your SMM's financial resources.

Why New Products Fail

Let's begin with a discussion of why new products fail and the critical success factors that SMMs should consider to enhance the probability of their success. This is very important. If we can reduce the number of failures and increase the percentage of successful products we can get a better return on the money we commit to new product development

A study by Robert Cooper of the New Products Institute in Toronto, Canada, entitled "Why New Industrial Products Failed," analyzed 150 industrial product firms, large and small, and discovered that most (though not all) of the reasons for new product failures had to do with marketing rather than technical problems.[3]

Specifically, SMM companies made three basic mistakes:

- They underestimated the number and strength of competitors
- They overestimated the number of potential users
- They overestimated the price customers would pay for the product.

Other studies have come to similar conclusions. They show the primary cause of new product failures to be market-related rather than technical.

Most of the reasons have to do with failing to do the upfront work required to ensure that the idea is competitive, has potential customers, and is unique enough to have an advantage over similar products in the market.

American manufacturers can increase their competitiveness by simply improving their new product success ratio. Or, to look at it another way, by decreasing the failure rate. And here's some good news – 70% of the information you need to increase your chances is from the market and is not technical in nature.

Once again, external customer and market information is the critical ingredient. As we go through the process, you'll see how to get at that information. (The handbook worksheets can help you further.)

More good news. American manufacturers have an advantage here. It is very difficult and expensive for foreign manufacturers to gather the necessary market data to design new products when they are on the other side of an ocean.

Robert Cooper's study listed seven different causes of new product failures. They are listed below, ranked by the percentage of companies citing the reason. (Sometimes more than one reason was cited.)

45% – Inadequate market analysis
28% – Product technical problems or defects
25% – Lack of an effective marketing effort
19% – Higher costs than anticipated
17% – Strength of the competitors
13% – Poor timing of the introduction
12% – Technical or production problems

As you can see, understanding the marketing problems and effective execution of a marketing program are critical.

Certainly the product has to be technically competent, but in my experience SMMs are pretty good at making things.

It is developing an understanding of the marketing of the things they make that is the real challenge. That's where expertise is often lacking.

Building a Better Mousetrap Isn't Good Enough Today

Emerson once wrote that if you build a better mousetrap the world would beat a path to your door. Emerson's contribution to literature is unquestionable but it is very questionable how he would develop a better mousetrap in today's business markets. Even if he did, would he know how to bring it to market? And would the market even care if catching mice was already being handled by current technology.

New product development is a high stakes game that can catapult a company into riches or plunge it into bankruptcy in a short period of time. Studies by the Conference Board and other research organizations show that approximately one third of all new products introduced to the marketplace are failures. When you include all of the new product concepts that never made it to the commercialization stage, the success rate is even lower. We estimate that it's only one out of every seven new product ideas.

More Mousetrap Fallacies

Most of the small and midsize manufacturers I know still want to believe that you can invent a better mousetrap and riches will follow. They are enamored by the Apple computer stories – tales of garage inventors who made it big.

The myth of inventing new mousetraps is a particular problem for SMMs and entrepreneurial inventors who are technically oriented. The mouse-trap approach appeals to their technical, creative, and entrepreneurial needs, it may be the reason they started their business in the first place. Inventing new mousetraps is truly the fun part of manufacturing.

But instead of looking at it from the perspective of the mouse or the mousetrap inventor, let's look at it from the all-important perspective of the thing you need to make it work – the cheese – or, in this case, the money you'll need.

Look at It from the Investor's View

Wayne Embree of Cascadia Pacific Management in Portland, Oregon, looks at many new product and technology ideas and reviews a lot of business plans. When asked what these inventors and entrepreneurs can do to increase their chances of commercializing their product idea, Wayne has a clear and simple answer. "They should spend a lot of time developing a case as to how their product idea is going to have a compel-ling competitive advantage."

Once again, this translates into marketing – gathering information on competitors, channels of distribution, and customers so that you can achieve that "compelling competitive advantage." That's the kind of information you need if you are going to convince anybody to invest time and money in your new product idea. Wayne's take on the mousetrap fallacy is "An ounce of marketing beats a pound of technology."

The Four Mousetrap Questions

Perhaps these problems can be put into perspective with some modern day corollaries to Emerson's original catchphrase. You need to ask these four questions about your "mousetrap."

1. What Are Customer Needs? Just because you can invent a better mousetrap doesn't necessarily mean anyone needs a mousetrap. You need to spend some time finding out if there is a need. You absolutely must define the customer problem that will be solved.

2. How Tough Is the Competition? As the old saying goes, "People don't need three-quarter inch drills, they need three-quarter inch holes." How are these needs being met right now? Who is meeting them? In fact, you may need to really roll up your sleeves on this topic.

You need to do a competitive analysis. Many SMMs find out the hard way that there are already many similar mousetraps that offer the same benefits. You need to identify the other competitive and substitute products to make sure yours is unique. This means examining all known competitor products thoroughly enough to compare them to your product in a matrix. Finally, remember that "nothing" can also be a big competitor. How vital is your product and the competitor's product. Is it critical or is it something customers can do without?

3. What Is Your Value Proposition (Cost/Price)? Can you deliver your new product for a cost you can afford at a price they'll pay? Even if it is a clever or even unique mousetrap users may not want to buy it if the cost exceeds the benefit. (Nobody wants a $10,000 mousetrap that catches an occasional mouse). My friend Bruce calls it "catching mice with a cheese truck." You need to get a feel for what users will pay or if they see enough value in the improvement you offer to justify the price.

4. What Does a Market Analysis Tell You? How many mice are out there? How cost-effective is it to reach the people you need to reach? And when you do, can they afford your product? A market analysis will help you answer these questions. There may not be enough customers or they may be too hard to reach. Hope is not a strategy. You need to find out if there is a demand for the product (testimonials are excellent evidence) and if there are enough "reachable" buyers in the market.

Cooper also points out another reason for new product failure – industrial firms in general suffer from an inward orientation. Cooper found that industrial firms (large and small) will spend enormous amounts on R & D and prototype developments but only tiny amounts on market research or defining customer wants and needs.

The message for industrial firms of every size is obvious – a greater market orientation is needed in new product development. A better job must be done connecting mousetrap ideas with mousetrap user needs.

The next part of this chapter will explain the different kinds of new products and examples of the SMMs who developed them. It will show different techniques and approaches used by other companies just like you. We'll show you six prototypical examples – though, of course, there are many variations and combinations.

Finally, we'll focus on a seven-step approach to new product development. It describes the development process in stages and shows all of the information necessary to make the probability of success higher at each stage. This common sense approach helps to dissuade SMMs from "betting the farm" when they don't have the necessary information.

Types of New Products

Developing new products differs greatly in terms of risk, investment, marketing, and promotion. The Classification of Manufacturers (shown on page 3) clearly shows that there are different types of manufacturers with very different resources and capabilities.

Some smaller manufacturers are simply not in a position to develop leading edge products because of the investment required and risks involved. But that does not mean they can't develop new products. It just means they need to focus on the types of new products that are within their capability and budget.

It's the same with larger companies. For a big company like McDonald's, new products involve cooking up something new and serving it. At that stage, it's an easy entry proposition with relatively low cost.

On the other hand, a company like Kimberly-Clark may have to build a whole factory – or at least dedicate a part of a factory to the manufacture of a new consumer item. This is a very different matter. SMMs fall in the middle. Sometimes it's as simple as "adding cheese" or offering a "supersize," but usually there's a lot more to it.

Now let's look at those six types of new products.

1. Inventor products
2. Line extensions
3. Customer ideas
4. Reverse engineering
5. Replacement and substitution
6. Leading edge products

1. Inventor Products

This is a small but important category of new products.

There are many failures in this category, yet these products are so numerous that they deserve special mention.

Inventor products are ideas thought up by an individual, not a company. The individual inventor is always short on money and long on enthusiasm. They are usually motivated by visions of hitting the jackpot with a creative idea. They usually ignore The Four Mousetrap Questions and totally endorse Emerson's "build a better mousetrap" statement. This group is important because it is large in numbers and has a spectacular failure rate.

A good example of an inventor product is a special vise I will call the Vise Tek. The Vise Tek offers adjustments in two directions for wood or metal. It has the precision of a machine tool and has superior craftsmanship.

The problem with inventor products like this is that they are always new to the inventor but are seldom really unique in the marketplace. In the case of Vise Tek, there were actually hundreds of other similar products that may not be exactly like the Vise Tek, but that perform the same functions and for much less money.

The inventor likes to believe that there are no competitors and no products quite like the inventor's product. They always believe that their products are unique and sales will materialize just based on faith. Sometimes inventor products do become a success story in *INC* magazine where they are portrayed as a Horatio Alger story of the little guy beating the odds. But, as we said, "Hope is not a strategy." The problem is that inventors have very little capital and usually run out of money before they figure out the channels of distribution, promotion, pricing, etc.

Many inventors have genuinely good ideas, but they need help early in the process to evaluate competitive products.

2. Line Extensions or Product Modifications

Included in this category are redesigns of existing products to reduce manufacturing costs, products that are given new features, and new models that are introduced to expand the product line. The commitment and risks involved in developing these products are relatively low. This is "adding cheese." The strategy will usually be to sell the new products to the same customers and markets.

In this situation, the sales department may need some training on the new product and the appropriate sales promotion tools, but, in general, should be able to use the same sales approaches and channels.

A line extension is a product that is a derivative or modification of an existing product. For instance, a machine that is redesigned to produce more output or speed. For example, a Model 20 machine that operates at twenty cases per minute is redesigned to operate at thirty cases per minute. The new product is called the Model 30. It functions just like the smaller model except that it has more speed, a higher price, and is designed specifically for a group of customers in the food industry with lines in a specific speed range.

3. Customer Ideas

Another innovative and often overlooked opportunity for SMMs who want to find or add product lines is to use customer ideas to develop a new product. Erik Von Hipple, a new product guru from MIT, notes that "lead users – often the trend setters in an industry – are often better sources of new product ideas than the manufacturers themselves."

- von Hipple estimates that in the high technology field as many as 80% of the new product ideas originate with users.
- One study shows that 77% of 111 new scientific instruments came from scientists and researchers – not manufacturers.
- Another of von Hipple's studies shows that 67% of printed circuit board innovations came from end users.
- In pultrusion (a fiber-reinforced plastic for aircraft) von Hipple says 90% of the innovation in that field comes from end users.

A customer may find that they need a new product in their process but they don't want to design it. Or, they may have a specific idea and even design the product but they don't want to (or can't) manufacture it.

Perhaps another supplier's product is not meeting the customer's needs and they want to find a new supplier to design and manufacturer a variation of the product. An example of the latter is Delta Equipment, Inc., a company that manufactures the equipment used in dental offices.

In 1983, there were several large OEMs who dominated the U.S. dental chair market. These OEMs didn't pay attention to their component parts business and dentists began looking for new suppliers.

Dentists wanted to replace the existing components of their dental chair systems except they wanted higher quality components, lower prices, and faster deliveries.

Delta was launched in 1983 at a Chicago trade show where the founder rented a part of an eight-foot table in another company's booth and displayed a syringe, a drill, and a vacuum valve. He met dentists, competitors, and distributors at the show, sold $3,500 worth of product, and got a good feel for the market.

After the show, he decided to focus on selling direct to dentists with a combination of mail order and direct sales. As sales progressed, the dentists gave him ideas for new products and services.

Based on these customer ideas, he used a contract designer to develop higher quality and better looking parts.

Because of his low overhead and the fact that he didn't use wholesalers, he could offer the dentists high quality products at a lower price. In this case, he didn't really need to do a lot of market research because his information was, in an important way, already based on market research – it was coming from his market.

In many ways, market research is an antenna where we try to tune in to what our customers are thinking. When customers come to us and tell us what they're thinking, it's like gold ore delivered to your door.

But, of course, even gold ore has to be refined. Delta uncovered other important opportunities to improve and differentiate their offerings.

To take advantage of the poor parts and service offered by the OEMs, they offered a guaranteed two-day delivery to all customers and a personal phone call on each order to provide that extra-personalized touch.

It probably won't surprise you that their business quickly blossomed. By continuing to monitor the competition's product deficiencies, Delta continuously added more new products that were tailored to the specific needs of dentists on his mailing list.

After a few years of selling direct, Delta decided to market their products through distributors to expand the number of dentists he could reach and service around the country. They used many of the same marketing methods to gain a foothold in Europe.

As a result, Delta's home-based, mail-order business has grown into a $100 million company that markets its products in 54 countries.

4. Reverse Engineering

One approach that is a fairly easy way to develop new products is to copy a competitor product and then improve it by offering some unique features or superior service. This is called reverse engineering. The big advantage of reverse engineered products is that the basic concept, customers, and markets are known.

If you can reverse engineer a competitor's product and lower the cost significantly, you may be able to offer the exact same product without unique features or services. The Asian countries do this everyday to get into U.S. markets. Here is how it usually works:

A large U.S. customer (usually a retailer) begins marketing a U.S. manufactured product. If the product sells well and sales grow, the retailer will ask for a price reduction with a promise to sell even higher volumes. If the manufacturer can't lower the sell price to the customer, the retailer sends the product to a country like China to be reverse-engineered and offered as a "knock-off" product. This may sound unfair but it is a fact of globalization (particularly with high-volume consumer products).

To avoid being knocked off by foreign manufacturers, American manufacturers must:

- Develop very unique products that are hard to copy
- Develop patentable products
- Or develop a continuous stream of new products to stay ahead of the copiers.

On the other hand, there are opportunities for U.S. manufacturers to reverse engineer unique designs coming from foreign countries like Europe. For instance, European countries have been very progressive in inventing new products and technologies for packaging machinery. They are often 5 to 10 years ahead of American manufacturers in inventing clever new methods of packaging and filling, and are very aggressive in marketing to the wide variety of American industries that buy this type of equipment.

By simply walking one of the large European packaging shows, American manufacturers can find many unique ideas and designs that can be reverse engineered and offered in the U.S. at lower cost.

Many small American manufacturers also reverse engineer their U.S. competitor products as extensions of their product lines. This works best if they have superior manufacturing processes that will help them develop a similar product but with higher quality, more benefits, or lower prices.

To pursue reverse engineering as a strategy to develop new products, a manufacturer should make sure they do a good patent search and search out all known competitors. Once all competitors are known it is best to evaluate the competitor products in a matrix with a price to make sure they can offer a competitive product. The methods to do this are described in the *Growth Planning Handbook* in Section 2.

However, building a good competitor product, which has competitive advantage, is only half the battle. SMMs who attempt this may be entering a new market with new customers, which may require a new type of sales channel and a lead generation program to gain market share.

5. Replacement and Substitute Products

Some products may be new to the manufacturer but similar to other products in the market. These are what I refer to as replacement or substitute products.

For instance, an electronic component manufacturer might develop a data acquisition device for monitoring production machines. There may be hundreds of similar products on the market that will do essentially the same thing.

In this scenario, the salesman must learn about all competitors and must face the task of selling to many new prospects, often in new market niches. The sales person needs the following:

- Product training in the user benefits
- Profiles of the target customers
- A list of the target prospects
- An advertising program to find new prospects, and
- Identification of the market niches in terms of NAICS codes and mailing lists.

An example of a substitute product is a machine called a load transfer machine, which transfers loads from pallet to pallet. The design of this machine was very new to the manufacturer but not new in the marketplace. There were already a number of competitors with similar machines and specific markets and customers who purchased them.

Before the company could finish their design they had to carefully research all competitive designs, competitive prices, and existing customers and markets to establish the sales potential of the new product.

The danger of substitute products is that they will be seen as "me-too" products by the customer. They won't be unique and won't offer enough of a meaningful advantage to motivate current users of competitive products to switch. So the challenge is to make sure there is a competitive advantage before launching the product into the market.

In the case of the load transfer machine the design did have several competitive advantages. These advantages matched up well with a number of market niches. With that information in hand, the right customers and markets were chosen to get the product off the ground.

6. Leading Edge Products

Leading edge products are those that are new to the manufacturer and unique in the marketplace (maybe even new to the planet). An example of a leading edge product was the initial development of a high-tech product called computer aided engineering (CAE).

In 1981, Gerry Langeler and his partners left the electronics giant Techtronix to start a new company. Their plan was to develop a new software product for the emerging computer aided engineering market. They had little funding and worked out of their homes. They named their company Mentor Graphics.

They believed a market existed for their new idea. But they had to go out into the marketplace to test out their ideas and find evidence for the market. Like many leading edge new products, this product idea would take years of experimentation and millions of dollars of investment to perfect. Leading edge products like this one are very risky because:

- Markets are totally unknown and have to be developed

- Potential customers are only vaguely known
- Applications have to be developed from experimentation
- Sell prices and costs are unknown
- Demand is only a vague estimate of potential
- A great deal of capital has to be raised to even build and test a prototype.

After spending weeks developing the specifications for the new product, the partners had progressed to a point where they were convinced that their invention could revolutionize the CAE market. Unlike the founders of many high-technology start-ups, Langeler and his partners knew they had to get a reaction from the marketplace before they asked people to invest the large sums of money that would be needed to launch the product. They chose 20 companies in the United States that they considered potential customers in this emerging market niche. They discussed their product idea with these companies.

The target companies not only told Langeler and his partners about their needs and problems but also helped in the process of changing the specifications to meet their future needs. After a whirlwind customer trip, lasting four weeks, the partners returned home with a completely revised software product and several potential customers.

There was still a lot of work to be done, but the founders of Mentor Graphics had defined both customer needs and the proposed product well enough to estimate costs, selling prices, sales potential, and market segments.

In a presentation I attended in 1990, Gerry Langeler, president and COO of Mentor Graphics, spoke about the lessons he had learned during the process of starting up the company. I believe these lessons apply to every manufacturer who wants to develop leading edge products.

1. Let the market determine the specifications for your product. Use potential customers as collaborators in the design process.
2. You have more competition than you think. None of Mentor Graphic's most important competitors were even identified in the initial business plan.

3. Talk to potential customers during the design phase. For the founders of Mentor Graphics, seeing potential customers face-to-face was an essential step in refining the new product idea and establishing market potential.

Results: Leading edge products are risky and have a high failure rate. But when they are successful, the returns are truly spectacular, and can lead to the creation of whole new markets. In this case, Mentor Graphics achieved phenomenal success. In its first year of business, this customer-driven company achieved revenues of $1.7 million. Within eight years, they had grown to $400 million in sales.

Three Other Approaches to Developing New Products

Above are the six key new product categories for SMMs, but three other approaches are worth mentioning.

They are:

7. Spillovers
8. Customization
9. Capital equipment

7. Spillovers – Using Developed Technologies

For small and midsize manufacturers in the U.S. there are endless opportunities to develop new products and serve specific needs simply by using technology developed by larger companies.

Manufacturing R&D expenditures in 2002 were estimated to be $127 billion or 57% of the total private R&D expenditures in the U.S. Small manufacturers represented about 18% of this total.

Big changes caused by advanced research at the top of the supply chain can cause a chain reaction of opportunities that cascades down the supply chain.

For instance, R&D that develops new cars or airplanes will require new machine tools, production line equipment, and materials from suppliers. This "cascading" effect of research will provide thousands of opportunities for new and modified machines, machine tools, electronics, and chemicals, to name just a few categories.

Smaller manufacturers can be very innovative and competitive by constantly adapting these new technologies to existing products. This process is known as "spillover." It occurs when a new product uses new technologies (developed by another company) to create a "product modification" or "line extension."

By using new technologies to solve new customer application problems, manufacturers can stay ahead of foreign competitors in specific market niches. This is a cost effective and very efficient way to develop a continuous stream of new products with new prices and good margins.

A good example is Container Inspection Inc., which manufactures equipment to detect quality problems with cans, bottles, jars, and other containers. The company originally used an acoustic technology to detect product "duds."

After ten years of product development, Container Inspection now has a modular product line that can detect a range of problems: leaking products, fill levels, missing labels, missing containers, damaged containers, low vacuum products, and swelled cans. All this at speeds up to 2,000 containers per minute.

The driver in the marketplace that creates these new product opportunities is that consumer manufacturers are constantly changing their packaging, containers, and lids. They're making these changes to save money or to appeal to the consumer – often, both.

This change creates many opportunities for new product development.

Container Inspection uses a four-step process in their product development process.

1. **Market Research** – They monitor package and container design changes by working with container manufacturer associations and individual manufacturing members.
2. **Field Calls** – They find new customer applications by using their existing sales channels to call on end users and by quoting new applications.

3. **New Technologies** – They monitor new technologies by constantly monitoring competitive designs and the technology used in other packaging machinery.
4. **Standard Modules** – They have developed a modular approach to all of their designs so that various modules can be used independently or combined with other modules to form a standard system. This manufacturing process allows Container Inspection to build standard modules yet solve special applications.

Since beginning with their original standard acoustic technology product, Container Inspection has used X-ray, load cell, DSP, proximity, and laser technologies combined with the latest computer controls and software. The combination of the new technologies and product modules has resulted in many new products, which can be used on literally hundreds of different packaging applications. With these new products, the company has grown 20% per year, including solid growth through all three of the recent recession years.

8. Customization

In industry after industry, customers are demanding and getting more and more customized products.

Customization is becoming a big part of innovation and the new product process because:

- It can lead to new models and product lines
- It is a way to retain your Most Valuable Customers
- It is difficult for foreign competitors to emulate.

There is a growing requirement for products that are "one offs," customized to a specific application, or built from unique specifications.

Foreign suppliers are generally taking away products from U.S. suppliers that are standard, commodity-type products, which are high volume and low cube (low shipping volume in a container).

For obvious reasons, one area where they don't (and can't) compete well is in customized products.

Custom products used to be considered low priority to most manufacturers of standard products because they could make more money on high volume standard products.

But now, customization is a weapon that favors U.S. manufacturers.

If done right, customization can provide a manufacturer with ongoing competitive advantages and profitability.

The problem with customization is that it is often done indiscriminately. Manufacturers customize their products and services without targeting customer needs, evaluating competitors, considering the re-use of engineering, or examining long-term sales potential. They don't answer the big question of "Is the sales and profit potential worth the costs incurred?"

Every customization decision or order is an investment decision. If made wrong, customization can squander limited resources (like engineering hours) and lead to poor margins.

However smart customization will lead to strong growth and profitability, even in mature industries.

For some SMMs in the supply chain, becoming good at customization may be a matter of survival. For others, customization is the key to growth when competition is fierce.

A study by Booz Allen Hamilton found that "The way a company responds to demands for customization can make a difference between performance that leads a sector and performance that lags that of industry peers.

"Indeed, companies that more effectively balance the value that customization brings to their customers with complexity of costs it can impose generate organic sales growth and profit margins significantly higher than their industry average."

A good example of how customization can provide competitive advantage and growth is Jacquart Fabrics in Ironwood, MI. Since the 1980s, 483,000 jobs have been lost in the apparel industry. Most of these jobs were eliminated because apparel goods are now manufactured in Vietnam, China, Pakistan, India, and other Asian countries.

It might appear at a time like this that we are in a "last man standing" scenario and no U.S. manufacturers will be able to compete in the new century.

But this is not true. A few U.S. companies are surviving and even growing in this industry. That's right, there are small American manufacturers that are not only surviving but thriving in this declining industry.

As the U.S. apparel industry continues to shrink, Jacquart Fabric Products has been growing at a rate of 18% per year. How do they do it?

Jacquart is a "cut and sew" operation that manufacturers customized products – from doggy beds to special outdoor hats. Their manufacturing operation has seven business units that include pet beds, cat accessories, winter clothing, stadium seats, canvas covers for boats and truck trailers, upholstery, and retail sales.

Jacquart has been successful because they offer customized products to targeted market niches. Most importantly, Jacquart is a master of customization.

What Jacquart Fabrics has accomplished is instructive and their methods should be considered by manufacturers trying to survive in many other mature industries that are threatened by foreign competitors.

The real key to Jacquart's success is their ability to customize products and deliver them literally overnight. For instance, the company offers 500 different SKUs of doggy beds in hundreds of different colors and materials. From the time of order they can deliver the custom bed anywhere in the continental U.S. in 3 days.

9. Capital Equipment

There's one more critical aspect that must be mentioned. Capital equipment – which is at the very heart of the innovation process.

As mentioned earlier, R&D successes lead to capital equipment investments. This is an interrelated process between small and large manufacturers. The large manufacturers are generally the giant consumer product companies that have the large R&D budgets and staffs needed to continuously invent new food, chemical, computer, drugs and other consumer products.

These new products then drive changes in the production equipment used to produce these products. Production line equipment is generally manufactured by SMMs. In a manner of speaking then, SMMs are joined at the hip with their large customers in the innovation process.

The design, redesign, and upgrade of production line and other capital equipment is also important because innovation can lead to greater speed, capacity, operation, and flexibility of the equipment. This usually translates into lower unit costs, quicker delivery, higher quality, and higher productivity for customers.

That last factor, productivity, is extremely important in keeping U.S. manufacturers competitive.

Even as jobs and output declined from 1991 to 2003, productivity increased 6.2%. Half of this productivity gain was due to capital equipment investments.

So the large manufacturers need innovative suppliers who can help them reduce costs and increase productivity.

As a result of this innovation process, SMMs who manufacture capital equipment will have many opportunities to develop new products. And they must make the most of these opportunities.

The U.S. cannot afford to lose the manufacturing and innovative design of capital equipment to foreign manufacturers. Capital equipment is the "heart" of American manufacturing. And here's some good news. U.S. suppliers do have an advantage over foreign manufacturers because of proximity to their customers and all of the support services necessary to keep these machines running for years.

However, U.S. suppliers must be able to keep up with the changing needs of their large customers and continue to offer them innovative designs, the latest technologies (spillovers), and world-class service.

Customization, collaboration, alliances, and technology can all be combined to maintain U.S. supplier OEM dominance in capital equipment.

And this is one more important weapon in the battle to maintain that vital base of American manufacturing jobs.

We now have a good overview of the types of new products that can succeed. How can you make this happen in your company? That will be the focus of the next section of this chapter.

A 7-STEP APPROACH TO NEW PRODUCT DEVELOPMENT

This will introduce you to a 7-step process for managing new product projects from idea to launch in the small to medium sized industrial firm (Figure 3-1).

Figure 3-1: The 7-STEP Process

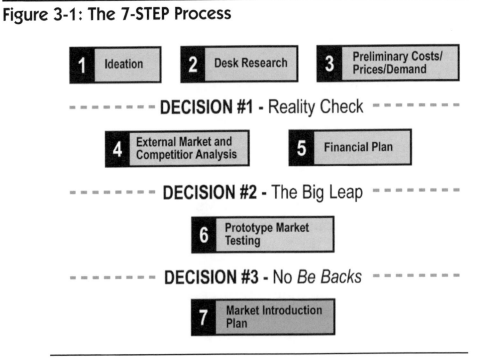

The process begins with an idea and progresses through a series of well defined steps. These steps, or activities, are explained in the order shown in Figure 3-1. The 7-step process is designed for a complex capital equipment product in a Type 3 manufacturer. However, in the case of some more simple industrial products, where the market and customers are known, some steps can be combined, or the process can be done in fewer steps.

There are also three different decision points interspersed between the steps. Each step contains a set of prescribed and concurrent activities, incorporating industry best practices. It is important to remember that activities during a step are executed in parallel, not in sequence. This ensures that they are carried out quickly and effectively.

Getting Started

Because the process is based on collective decision making, before beginning, a team needs to be appointed. The team members will usually be department managers who control resources or functions within the companies. They are a cross-functional group that usually represents marketing, sales, R&D, engineering, production and finance.

The team members can choose to go ahead, kill, hold, or recycle the project. At the end of a team meeting, a decision must be reached. If the decision is to go, this ensures that there will be resource commitments and support from management for the project. Team members use a pre-set list of criteria and rules – they can't play favorites.

A Key Concern: Cost vs. Risk

Figure 3-2 shows all seven steps of the process and the three decision points as they relate to cost. This is an important chart because most manufacturers do not have a way of viewing the costs of development, only a total approved budget figure.

This particular chart is based on a real new-product project managed by the author, and the original approved cost was $600,000. The graph makes the point that cost is fairly low until a prototype is designed and built. The third decision is obviously the riskiest one, because once the prototype gets into the market and a decision is made to launch the product, costs increase logarithmically. The graph suggest two conclusions:

1. If the product is not saleable after product launch these costs will continue climbing and it will be extremely costly to modify in the marketplace to get some sales.
2. If the idea does not appear unique or saleable, it's best to terminate the project on decision point 1 or 2 when costs are still fairly low.

Figure 3-2: The Costs of New Product Development

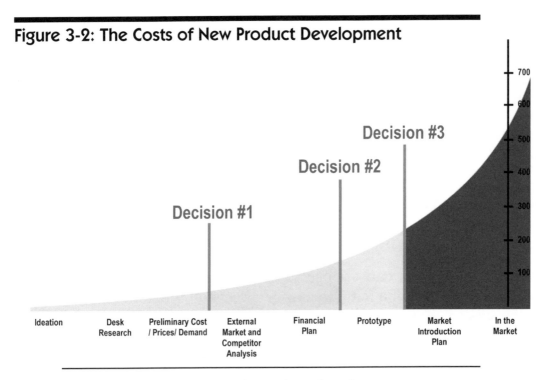

Here is the 7-Step Process explained in detail.

STEP #1 Ideation:

After coming up with the idea, or ideas, the key question is "Is the idea unique?"

This is the number one success factor, coming up with a unique idea that can be differentiated from competitive products with unique benefits and superior value. Unique doesn't just mean different – a purple mousetrap does not qualify. The benefits must be meaningful to the market, and the price/value must be attractive.

This step begins with the submission of a written suggestion for each product idea or ideas. You should get ideas anywhere that you can – from internal or external sources. At this stage, there can never be enough ideas, but to submit an idea to "The Hopper" they must be written and explained.

This process is very much like a hopper – the top is wide open for many ideas and narrow at the bottom where the final ideas come out. Using our process, only the good ones make it through the hopper no matter how many you start with. This is illustrated in Figure 3-3.

Then, if you have more good ideas than money, just do the ones with the best potential. Also, during this first step; don't ask for a lot of backup for an idea, just the basic thought should be enough.

FIGURE 3-3: The Idea Hopper

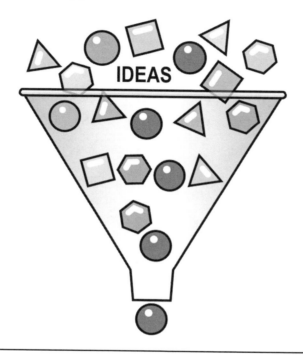

Step #2 Desk Research:

During this stage we'll need to do a quick and inexpensive analysis of the product ideas we've selected. This stage features a quick and inexpensive way of doing a preliminary investigation of the product idea. It is based on using secondary information from sources such as

- Internet
- Trade journals
- Competitive literature

- Library
- In-house reports and surveys
- Key customers
- Published reports
- Government agencies
- Trade associations
- Company's own sales and service people.

The objectives of Step #2 are to:

- Define the market into specific market niches
- Identify all direct and indirect competitors
- Define preliminary product features and benefits
- Do a preliminary patent check
- Make a preliminary evaluation of "make vs. buy"
- Make a preliminary evaluation of sales potential.

Sales Potential Example:

For instance, the product could be a gas valve for new residences. One could find out the number of housing starts in a market region to start, then estimate the number of valves sold by competitors and an estimate of the percentage of total market that could be supplied by the new product based on positive assumptions of the valve advantages. At this stage, this would be all that is needed to estimate a preliminary market size and market share, which would give you the necessary sales potential information to begin.

Step #3 Preliminary Costs, Sell Prices, Demand

Right at the beginning you should estimate the selling price and cost. It is easiest to do this if you know several competitor prices.

A major problem is that too many products get built without estimating a preliminary cost or a market sell price. Then after all the work has been done, the product bombs in the market place simply because there were other competitor products that were less expensive.

Perhaps you can get a premium price with a truly superior product. But don't be too optimistic at this stage – better to be a cold-eyed realist.

This step is a preliminary financial assessment that generally estimates the product costs, price, margins, and potential sales revenue. You don't want to spend too much time on this step. Just get the facts required as best you can in the allotted time. There will be plenty of additional time for investigation in subsequent stages.

> **Decision # 1** – Reality Check – This first decision is based on qualitative judgements and preliminary data. The reality check decision is a simple review of the ideas and is based on each team member rating the new product idea with the following six questions:

1. Does the product idea fit with the company's strategy?
2. Is the product idea unique or does it appear to have a competitive advantage?
3. Does there appear to be an attractive market?
4. Is it technically feasible?
5. Are the perceived financial rewards worth the risk and costs of development?

This first decision only requires a simple majority of voting team members to move the idea forward. You're not spending a lot of money yet, so it's better to move an idea to the next step to gather more information than to kill it too quickly.

Step #4 – EXTERNAL MARKET AND COMPETITOR ANALYSIS

The objective of this stage is to build a strong business case for taking the product to the development stage. This is perhaps the most difficult stage for any small or midsize manufacturer of industrial products because it requires gathering external information.

The detailed investigation should include:

- Defining the user wants and needs – this includes using personal interviews with potential users
- Defining market segments, market growth, and market size
- Defining the final product specifications
- Doing a thorough job of analyzing competitor products and the competitors themselves

- Testing the idea on end users with drawings, slide programs, models, or even prototypes
- Doing a competitor matrix of all competitor products complete with sell prices
- Doing a legal patent assessment
- Proving there is demand for the product.

The methods required to do a good job are:

- Desk research
- Interviewing techniques
- Phone research
- Basic competitor intelligence methods
- Competitor matrix
- Field research – interviewing customers, prospects, distributors, manufacturing reps, and others about sales potential; visiting customers in the field.

This is the critical stage. You must develop detailed and reliable market information. If it's wrong here you're in trouble. If you can't do this step yourself then it is a good idea to invest money in a third party service. You will need one that can prove they know how to research industrial markets and products. This is especially true if you are looking at a market you do not currently serve. (Note – Three levels of competitor intelligence and three levels of market analysis are explained in Sections II and III of the *Growth Planning Handbook.*)

Step #5 - FINANCIAL PLAN

In this step, you must gather enough competitive information, market information, and customer information to do the following:

- Finalize the sell prices
- Determine the total cost of the unit and gross margin
- Define what part of the product will be purchased or farmed out
- Develop an accurate sales forecast.

With this information, Step 5 is completed by developing a proforma sales forecast and budget for the first five years. The forecast/budget should also include marketing costs and a preliminary determination on how many years it will take to achieve "payback" on your investment in the new product.

DECISION #2 – The Big Leap – Steps #4 and #5 are summarized in a summary report for all team members. The team then discusses the project in detail to be sure everyone is on the same page after reading the summary report. This second decision is a more rigorous screening procedure than Decision #1. It includes questions about competitive advantage, a fit with other product lines, market attractiveness, technical feasibility, and financial rewards. Each team member rates each of the questions shown in Figure 3-4 either yes or no.

FIGURE 3-4 : New Product Evaluation – Decision #2

1. Does the product have a competitive advantage?	YES	NO
2. Are there unique benefits to the customer?	YES	NO
3. Is the market niche adequately defined?	YES	NO
4. Do you know the size of the market?	YES	NO
5. Do you have evidence that the market niche is growing?	YES	NO
6. Will the new product idea fit user needs?	YES	NO
7. Have you defined the final product specifications?	YES	NO
8. Have you thoroughly analyzed competitor products?	YES	NO
9. Are you sure the new product will be competitive?	YES	NO
10. Have you tested the idea on end users?	YES	NO
11. Have you completed a competitor matrix with sell prices?	YES	NO
12. Have you made sure there will be no patent infringements?	YES	NO
13. Have you proven there is demand for the product?	YES	NO
14. Have you finalized the sell price?	YES	NO
15. Have you determined the total cost of the unit?	YES	NO
16. Is the estimated gross margin adequate?	YES	NO
17. Is the five year sales forecast and budget complete?	YES	NO
18. Have you estimated the payback in terms of years?	YES	NO
19. Is the payback (return) acceptable?	YES	NO

Each team member should circle a "yes" or "no" answer. If you have as many "no" answers as "yes" answers, you probably need to go back and get more information. If you have answered most of the questions, the team members should vote either to go to the next step or to kill the project.

Again a majority of team members have to vote "go" to allow the project to move ahead to the next step – prototype development. This decision is usually where significant time and money are committed. Only the best new product ideas continue. Other candidates may be killed or just put on hold, particularly if resources are limited.

Step #6 - PROTOTYPE DEVELOPMENT AND MARKET TESTING

Once the decision is made to go to the development stage, the new product project becomes visible and costs will increase dramatically.

The primary activities in the development stage are:

- Development of the prototype
- Finalizing the product specifications
- Resolving all legal and patent issues
- Defining the production process
- Defining all manufacturing requirements
- Developing a preliminary market launch plan.

A prototype of the new product is built to see if it works, to test the technical capabilities, to confirm the projected costs, and to finalize how the company will manufacture the product.

This is the technical test to see if a product can be made at a reasonable cost and performs such that it satisfies the market needs that were identified in Step #4.

For the market-testing stage of Step #6, the objectives are to:

- Test the prototypes at the factory
- Test the prototypes with customers in field situations
- Demonstrate the production and manufacturing process
- Finalize the market launch plan.

This is the acid test to see if any customers will buy the product.

It's no longer a question of whether the product is interesting or whether they like the idea in the abstract, but if they will buy it in the real world at a realistic price. If there are no customers willing to "admit" that they would buy it when it's commercially available, the project will most likely be killed at the next decision point.

If the company cannot get a good enough reaction from potential customers on whether they will buy the new product, they may decide to make more new products and do more testing until they can make a decision on demand.

> **Decision #3** – No Turning Back – The decision at this stage marks the beginning of the commercialization process. The final decision is based on all of the factors shown in the New Product Evaluation Chart. This chart is designed specifically for small and midsize manufacturers of industrial products. It takes less than fifteen minutes to complete and produces a numerical score on the pluses and minuses of undertaking a new product development project.

Final Evaluation: Instructions

> Quickly read each of the questions and the corresponding answers shown in each box. Mark an X in one of the columns on the right side of the page, indicating whether the answer is +2, +1, -1, or -2. Once all questions are answered, determine the total of all minus values and all plus values at the bottom of the columns.

> If a majority of team members have more minuses than pluses, this indicates that you are developing a new product with too many unknowns and the risks will be very high. Before continuing with development you should re-examine each of the minus answers to see if there is a practical way to find the information and improve the score. Or kill the project.

> If a majority of the team members have mostly plus answers you have done a good job of answering all of the new product development questions and are ready to go to the next step.

If the final evaluation shows very mixed results and the team cannot make a decision, the next step is to focus on all of the risks versus the company's ability to survive the financial loss if the product fails.

If a product failure could cause serious financial problems or threaten the future of the company, you should reconsider whether it is really practical to develop the product. You might also ask the opinion of an outside expert or simply spend more time analyzing the commercial and market questions until you prove to yourself whether the product has a strong chance of success.

Step #7 - MARKET INTRODUCTION PLAN

This step opens the door to full-scale production and market launch.

It involves implementation of the market launch, fine tuning manufacturing, developing the quality program and monitoring all plans.

This step is the execution of all previous plans. This is not the time to be inventive. It's time for following through with the project as described in all the past steps. We use timelines and detailed schedules for all activities necessary for a successful launch.

A market launch plan usually includes an advertising campaign, trade shows, literature, CDs, and direct mailings to the defined prospects. In addition each manufacturing rep is given a list of target accounts to call on that were determined by the market research.

Advantages and Disadvantages of the 7-Step Process

The major advantage of using this 7-Step Process for developing new products is that it provides the structure and discipline needed to gather all of the information necessary to make a new product commercially successful. The process also includes tools that help the company ask the right questions, and to make objective decisions.

Probably the most important advantages of the 7-Step Process are:

- It forces the company and team members to make decisions based on facts rather then preconceived notions or emotional attachments to the ideas

- It eliminates bad or mediocre ideas early in the process before a great deal of money is spent on them
- It also has these additional advantages:
  - It uses a team and collective decision making so there is no bias from one inventor or promoter
  - There is an agreed upon voting method at each decision point
  - It makes the team continuously focus on both costs and risks throughout the process
  - It gives the company three chances to either modify or stop the project if the new product does not meet the basic requirements
  - Most importantly, it lowers the risk of getting a bad product into the field where it will lose more money for the investors
  - And, by a process of continuously asking the right questions and changing the design, it increases the chance of market success.

The Major Disadvantage

The major disadvantage of the process is that it runs counter to the methods generally used by small and midsize manufacturers to develop new products. In some cases, they have had just enough success developing new products with the old methods that it lends credence to them. In other words, small manufacturers will say "We never had to use a structured process before. Why do we have to now?" The answer, of course, is that most small and mid-size manufacturers cannot afford to have two failures for every one successful new product that makes it to the prototype and introduction stage.

The 7-Step Process is not a guarantee. But it is a proven process that will certainly improve the probability of success. It was designed for Type 3 companies with departments and staffs of competent people. (See page 3 for Classification of Manufacturers.)

However, the fundamental questions raised in each step remain the same. And when it's all said and done, even the smallest manufacturer will have to find a way to answer basic questions on competitors, customer demand, prices, costs, and whether the idea is unique.

Figure 3-5: Resource Factors in New Product Development

	TYPE 1 SURVIVAL MODE	TYPE 2 FAMILY OWNED	TYPE 3 PROFESSIONAL MANAGED
Cashflow	Awful	Erratic	Positive
Costing	No/Poor	General	Detailed
Capital	Little Capital	Limited Financing	Debt or Equity Financing
Sales	Owner Sells	Inside Sales, Some Channels	Direct Sales Force, Sales Channels

Figure 3-5 shows some of the key resource factors that define the three types of manufacturers. Both Type 1 and 2 manufacturers have definite limitations in terms of cashflow, product costing, sales channels, and access to capital. To control risk and costs, it makes sense to match the resources of the company with the type of new product.

Perhaps the best approach for Type 1 and 2 manufacturers is to carefully examine the six types of new products explained in the beginning of this chapter and to select the type of new product that has the lowest risks and investment.

For instance, line extensions, customer ideas, and reverse engineering new product projects tend to be good for Type 1 or 2 manufacturers because the customer is known, investment is minimal, and the risk is low. This type of new product is likely to succeed even if the company gathers minimum information in the 7-Step Process. And, if the product doesn't succeed, the company will probably survive the loss.

Leading edge and substitute products are considerably riskier because the customer and markets are not known and the investment required is often quite large. Type 3 manufacturers usually handle these types of new products because the development requires considerable market analysis, staff, testing, and capital. There are, of course, many exceptions where very small manufacturers decide to invent a new product without knowing the customers, markets, competitors, or the costs of the project. In this case smaller manufactures have three choices:

1. Finance the cost of hiring an outside professional firm that can do industrial market and competitive analysis.
2. Do the entire 7-Step Process themselves.
3. Pick a new product where customers and markets are known.

Other progressive manufacturers have used similar processes.

Here are two case studies showing two different approaches – both were successful.

The first case study actually describes my first new product project, which utilized some very basic (and unsophisticated) methods. This may be closer to your experience the first time out.

The second case study uses more comprehensive techniques. This will probably be closer to your experience once you get the hang of it.

CASE STUDY #1 – SeaLift Inc, Roseburg, Oregon

In 1970, I was given my first complete new product project. The task was to investigate the potential market for a ship-mounted, hydraulic marine crane.

The parent company had plenty of financial, engineering, and manufacturing expertise; but the concept of industrial marketing was both new and somewhat misunderstood.

I'd graduated from college in 1964 and the only class that was available was on consumer marketing. At the time there was no class you could take on industrial marketing and no one in the company to mentor me. But I had found a book written by Aubrey Wilson in England entitled *Industrial Marketing Research*. Starting there, I began to teach myself how to do market analysis in the industrial environment.

Ideation – Here's where we started. There were already some converted truck mounted loaders on various types of vessels, but they did not work well on rolling ships and they were not resistant to salt water. Based on our initial ideation, these two problems – common to most marine applications – were identified as the two key challenges.

I had an idea for a new design that would work in a corrosive salt-water atmosphere on various vessels.

Since most vessels used a traditional lift boom with ropes or cables as a hoist, this new idea was to replace some of the old style booms with hydraulic knuckle-boom cranes (sort of like a backhoe). At the time, this was essentially replacing an accepted and cheap design with a relatively new technology.

A good example of the advantages of the hydraulic crane over the traditional live boom is on a salmon tender. A pair of cranes can unload each side of the vessel at the same time with a crew of two instead of a three-man crew. Not only that, but each crane can unload fish twice as fast as the live boom. In terms of operating costs, each tender costs the cannery approximately a nickel per can of salmon. By eliminating one man on the crew and increasing the volume of fish loaded per hour with the crane installations, the tender can unload more times per season which lowers the price per can of salmon (or increases the margin).

Price Cost Demand – I reported to a product committee. They assessed the cost of my new design and dictated the gross margin. The sell price for the medium capacity Model 81M was set at $5,500, this was justifiable in less than one year on a salmon tender.

Desk Research – I used the 1967 "Census of Commercial Fisheries" and another government document "Fisheries of the U.S. 1969" to document the types, numbers, gear, and functions of all vessels.

My original desk research included charts showing:

Appendix A: Total number of commercial fishing vessels by region
Appendix B: Types of fishing with corresponding vessel
Appendix C: Vessels by type of gear, and lengths
Appendix D: List of all fishing ports by number of vessels
Appendix E: Influential fishing companies and managing owners
Appendix F: List of all types of non-fishing utility vessels

Competition – Most vessels at that time still used hoists and there were only four competitors offering hydraulic cranes. All of the cranes were truck mount hydraulic cranes, which were adapted to be used on a vessel. I saw Hiab (Swedish) cranes on shallow draft barges, straight boom National Cranes on offshore supply vessels, and Pettibone cranes on research vessels. But, none of the competitors had designed a true marine crane that would withstand salt air corrosion. I did a competitive matrix that compared all of these models in terms of specifications and price with my design specs.

I had an idea to develop three models of true marine cranes that would be unique and have a competitive advantage over all of the competitor designs.

External Market Information – I spent time visiting ports in San Diego, Long Beach, Portland, Seattle, and Alaska and found that there had already been many attempts to replace old style hoists with hydraulic type cranes.

There were applications on tuna seiners, salmon tenders, Coast Guard vessels, crab boats, oyster dredges, elevating barges, offshore supply vessels, tugboats and research vessels.

I worked with the government to help determine the exact number of vessels of each class in use. And I researched all shipyards to determine the types of new vessels planned for construction.

During the market analysis of the marine crane idea, I spent time on Long Island Sound fishing with oyster fishermen, and visited Woods Hole, Massachusetts, and talked to scientists on their research vessels. I went on sea trials on new tuna seiners in the Pacific, sailed around Puget Sound on workboats, and I visited salmon canneries in Alaska.

It was this fieldwork that really gave me the intuitive insights into both making an accurate forecast and convincing Sealift management that this design had a true competitive advantage.

The total market included fish companies, chartered vessels, new vessels, salmon tenders, crab vessels, tuna seiners, floating canneries, canning plants, oyster dredgers, tugboats, and government vessels – in total, a potential of approximately 9,000 vessels. This provided a rough fix on the market – and management was pleased to be dealing with this comprehensive overview of the market. It was very clarifying.

Financial Plan and Sales Forecast – Even with all that information, I could not figure out how to estimate a conversion factor to forecast sales so I focused only on new vessels under construction and the tuna fleet.

A sales call in San Diego put me in touch with the most influential owners of the U.S. tuna fleet. I spent the time to get interviews with the six most influential owners, who owned 50% of the fleet, and who were building all of the new modern seiners.

During that visit, I talked one of the owners into buying the first four cranes with options on ten more to demonstrate the inherent demand. From this success, I estimated we could sell at least twenty cranes per year and made a conservative forecast for five years.

Prototype Testing – The first two prototypes were installed on a brand new tuna seiner, the "Bold Contender." I was on this new vessel during trials in the Pacific off San Diego to gather technical information and to evaluate what did and did not work.

The Bold Contender was going to fish off West Africa, but a boom cylinder collapsed on the way to the Panama Canal. I flew to Panama with our service man, Bob Mott, and he repaired the prototype SeaLift crane in the harbor.

I continued to follow every problem of the new cranes on the Bold Contender and other tuna seiners during the first year. We continued to change our design to be the best hydraulic crane available for salt air corrosion.

Results – Solid success. We continued to sell SeaLift cranes to the tuna fleet and many other marine markets. By 1972, the marine line was so successful that the company sold the engineering and all inventories to a marine company in Wisconsin for a substantial profit.

I learned the value of comprehensive market research and the importance of gaining as broad a perspective as possible. For example, in

Oregon, we have a salmon perspective, but the tuna fleet was where SeaLift needed to go fishing.

Case Study #2 – Michael C. LaRocco, American Made LLC, Ambridge, PA

Developing successful new products can be viewed in terms of three different skill sets:

1. First, being able to envision a good idea as a solution to a specific customer problem.
2. Second, finding a solution by using a new or developing technology.
3. Third, knowing how to gather enough market, customer, and competitor information to make sure the product will have a meaningful competitive advantage and will sell in the marketplace.

Michael C LaRocco, president of American Made in Ambridge, PA, is one of those rare manufacturers who does all three very well. He does them so well, in fact, that his company may be the fastest growing manufacturer in the Pittsburgh area.

Mike began his entrepreneurial career as a student at Penn State. While trying to get a Masters Degree in Market Research, Mike developed an idea to replace the traditional grease bearing surface of a truck's fifth wheel with a "non-grease" plastic bearing surface.

He got this idea while in graduate school based on a chance conversation with someone interested in the "greaseless" bearing problem. He became very excited about the idea, did secondary research and determined the following:

- How many trailers were produced every year
- How many were in use in the U.S.
- Whether there were any direct competitors with a similar idea.

He also did some fieldwork and called on a few local trucking company end users to determine the costs of greasing fifth wheels annually.

His preliminary market research showed a high probability of customer demand. So his next step was to investigate various types of plastic bearing surfaces that would do the job and be cost competitive.

In 1983, he started his first company, American Made, Inc., in Ambridge. He then did the marketing plan to launch the new product.

He described the product as a "Final Lube, Solid Grease Plate." Because of the easy-to-understand benefit of savings per year to the trucking companies, sales for the product took off immediately and he was on his way.

Mike knew that he could not reach all areas of the country by selling direct, so he began appointing dealers. Right from the start, Mike had an extraordinary ability to visualize new product solutions and think like a market researcher, a salesman, an engineer, and a manufacturer on any given business trip or sales call.

This multi-tasking mind set was very important to his success. I also believe it contains a good lesson for other manufacturers.

The idea is to view every field trip or sales call as an opportunity to find out about customer needs/problems that could lead to new products and applications.

The two fundamental skills are listening and interviewing.

During his early investigations of the trucking industry, Mike discovered the problem of dump truck beds. Back then, most dump truck liners were either steel or aluminum and would scuff easily, corrode, or have products stick or freeze to the bed.

Mike immediately saw the need to develop some kind of dump truck bed liner that would reduce or eliminate these problems.

Mike did some preliminary desk research. He discovered that the average dump truck company was small, rural and dumped 5-6 times per day. He also determined a preliminary market size. He found the total number of dump trucks built per year, the number in operation in the U.S., and the number replaced annually.

In his competitive search he found that there were no manufacturers offering a liner kit but that there were a few people in the Midwest who were attaching plastic liners to truck beds with 500-1000 fasteners as "one-off" experiments.

He then did a little more field work to find out what people would pay for a liner kit. He found that the initial kit would have to sell for $3,000 and be easily mounted with few fasteners and in just a few hours. This research information proved that there was a very high probability that there would be sales potential if a liner could be developed that would wear well.

Mike got some additional help from the Federal Government in 1987 when a law was passed that limited bridge loading. This forced manufacturers to design lighter weight aluminum dump bodies with longer trailers than the original dump bodies. With these longer dump trailers, the load had to dump easily or the long trailer would have to be raised to a high and unstable position. In addition, the new aluminum trailers did not wear as well as the old steel bodies. These two factors combined to propel the liner idea into the forefront in this market.

His next step was to investigate the advances in polymer science to develop a rigid polymer lining that was lightweight, abrasion resistant and stick resistant.

The development of these new products also required a good technical understanding of polymers in order to both design a product with the new wear characteristics and to develop a new manufacturing process to make it. Mike learned about polymers by simply studying available information and doing "trial and error" experiments.

Through experimentation he found the product he needed by using polyethylene plastic.

He called this second new product the "Re-Pro Heavy Duty Liner." In the process, he had developed a rigid polymer lining that could be used for aggregate, rock, sand, fly ash, coal, and limestone. He went on to develop "Black Fire – Hot Asphalt liners" by modifying his polymer lining with special heat stabilizers to hold mixes up to 375 degrees.

The Re-Pro products were launched in 1985 and were commercially successful by 1989. Again, Mike knew that he could not sell every liner himself so he began looking for dealers that could sell, service, and repair his liners. By 1989, he had appointed 200 dealers to sell them.

By this time, Mike LaRocco had become very experienced in various segments of the trucking industry. By working with his truck dealers, he learned of yet another new problem/opportunity in trailer vans.

This time, the problem was that typical van wall panels did not hold up to the scuffing and abrasion of fork trucks. His preliminary market research showed that both end users and truck trailer OEMs wanted a wall panel that would wear much longer than existing panels.

For this project, Mike began by doing research on various types of new plastic and glass materials.

A small article in a trade journal led him to a trade show to meet a company that had just developed a brand new high strength fiber material.

Mike and his design team experimented with the new fiber product and figured out how to build a very hard (but very light) panel that was stronger than steel.

He called this new composite product Bulitex because it would stop a 45-caliber bullet fired from 20 feet.

It sounded tough and, once the product was successfully tested on some trucking company vans, he began to design the special process and machines to build the van panels.

The manufacturing process takes a multi-layered woven fiber material and processes it through heating, compression, and cooling stages, to create a final rigid panel. The Bulitex panel turned out to be (pound for pound) the most impact resistant material available. It was water-resistant, withstood extreme temperatures, and eliminated cracking, splintering, and snagging.

They were an immediate hit with all eight of the major OEMs who manufacture dry van trailers. This product saved the OEMs both in material and in the downtime it took to replace trailer wall panels. Mike went on to discover additional applications for the material in translucent roofs and for walls and ceilings of refrigerated trailers and railcars. Bulitex has even been used for molded auto bumpers, containers and for military applications.

At a time when only one of seven new product ideas reaches successful commercialization, Mike LaRocco's companies are three for three. Part of the reason for this success is knowing how to gather the "non-technical" market information. Remember, this is 70% of the reason for most product failures.

Mike says that, at a minimum, manufacturers who want to develop new products should gather the following information

1. **Ideas** – If you come up with a good idea, try it out on people who are not familiar with the industry and see if they understand the value. Then test the idea on average buyers in the industry – not lead users who are always looking for new ideas and may not be indicative of the market.

2. **Competitors** – Get on the Internet as soon as possible to see how many competitors make a similar product. Get their literature, prices, and any other information they may have published. Then qualitatively review their products very carefully to make sure your idea has competitive advantage.

3. **Patent** – If you think you have an original product with unique advantages, file for a provisional patent. This will cost you $1,500 and it will protect you for one year while you are trying to get your product off the ground or do more investigation.

4. **Customer Needs** – Get on the phone and call customers in the industry to test the validity of the idea and to get an initial idea of sales potential. If the reaction looks promising, take a model, a drawing, or a prototype out to some of the most interested or influential end user customers. This requires going into the field and having good interviewing skills. Don't just think – listen.

5. **Markets** – The next step is to break the potential customers down into market niches that can be identified with an NAICS code. Many manufacturers make the mistake of thinking they are selling to large general industries like the trucking industry. In Mike

LaRocco's case he was developing his Re-Pro Heavy Duty Liners for a very specific segment of the dump truck market, which is only 7% of the truck industry. If you do this step correctly you should end up with a list of all of the potential buyers you are going to try to sell in the first year.

6. **Sales Potential** – This is probably the hardest step. But you're a lot more ready now than when you started. After doing steps 4 and 5, you should have enough information in the form of testimonials, interest, and an initial "snapshot" of the number of potential buyers in the niche you're aiming at to convince yourself and perhaps other investors that the product has sales potential. The big leap of faith is to determine how many products can be sold in the first year. In the case of the dump truck market, Mike's challenge was to estimate how many of the existing dump trucks could be converted to liners with field installed kits. And, how many OEMs of new dump trucks could be sold in the first year.

7. **Financial and Cost Analysis** – Mike LaRocco says that this step "is as important as the idea itself." As soon as a cost of the product can be estimated along with a margin and a price point you should begin doing a financial analysis – either in your head or on paper. In step 5 you should have found out what most customers will pay for the product and have some idea of the sales potential. You must have a clear idea of how many units you must sell a year to break even and how many years it will take to recover your investment. If you haven't gathered enough information to do this calculation, you should either go back and get enough information to be convinced or abandon the new product idea.

Mike says that "some people just have the 'knack' to know what customers want and what will sell." You can enhance your own chances greatly if you are willing to make sales calls and do field interviews of end users. And remember, don't just talk – listen. Mike's listening to customers was a key source of information for each of his successful business ideas.

Mike has always made sales calls and explored markets for new product opportunities. He says, "competing in the new economy is a matter of continuously looking for new product opportunities and new markets. The secret is to continuously change, be flexible and quick."

American Made has had double-digit growth from the beginning. LaRocco's marketing and new product methods are very progressive and a good model for other manufacturers trying to compete in the new economy.

The New Product Challenge

Growth based on new and improved products will be critical for every SMM that wants to survive and grow in our new economy.

This chapter began with a description of six types of new products – each with varying degrees of risk and investment.

Having a clear idea of the differences between risk and investment is important. Having read this chapter, you're already on the right track. Because now you understand that there are big differences in the types of new products you might choose to pursue. You should make a choice based on what you and your company can afford and how much you and your partners can risk.

Almost all SMMs can develop some kind of new product; the real question is should they "bet the farm" when they commit to development. In most cases, the answer to that question is "No!"

You can see from just these two case studies that there are many approaches to developing new products – from simple to complex.

SeaLift and American Made used two very different approaches, but they had a few important things in common. Both approaches answered the most vital questions on prices, costs, competition, competitive advantage, customers, and markets.

In the end, all of the new products were successful and sales projections were attained. These cases demonstrate that there are different methods for gathering the information, but that the vital information you will need to gather is almost always the same.

As these and many other case studies demonstrate, many progressive

SMMs are beginning to successfully adopt new methods of doing new product development. Some are enjoying spectacular success.

Because of their size, flexibility and creativity, SMMs will continue to play a key role in new product development. Innovation and the design of new products have always been an American advantage. If we can meet these challenges with resourcefulness and hard work, we can ensure that this country will continue to have a strong and vital manufacturing base.

The good news is that the accelerated change caused by globalization will continue to require constant innovation and more new products. The opportunities are there.

Key Points

The most popular method for developing new products in America is what I like to call the "inventor/gambler" method. This method focuses all time and efforts on developing a product that is so unique and clever it will sell itself.

The inventor/gambler method has worked and is the most popular method for manufacturers by far. So what is the problem? The problem is money. You have to gamble that the customers will buy it and there won't be comparable products already in existence. But the fact remains that only one out of three prototypes is successful, as measured by sales and return on investment. So, if you can afford the potential losses that come with a new-product gamble, go for it. Otherwise, you should be investing in the analysis of customer needs, markets, and competitors.

This chapter makes the point that you can increase your success rate by using a system. Here are five key points that are worth repeating:

1. The whole idea of developing new products is to sell them successfully as a final result.
2. You can increase the chance of selling the new product and making a sales forecast if you do a good job of evaluating your customers, competitors, and market.
3. You can increase the chance of coming up with a unique idea if,

at the start, you have many, many ideas to choose from.

4. It is possible to lower the risk of new product failure as the expenditures go up by using the 7-Step Process to continuously evaluate the new product from concept to market introduction.

5. Because risks and costs increase with each step of the process, it is important to have "set decision points" that will permit you to back off an idea that might not be commercially successful in the market.

Suggested Action

Fill out the New Product Evaluation Form (Figure 3-4) in terms of how you currently do new product development. This form is designed specifically for owners of manufacturing companies to help them through a "reality check" before they decide to spend the big money. Evaluate all of your "no" answers. What steps can you take to change your response to these questions? Each "yes" answer your able to give will likely improve your chance of success.

Notes:

1. Joel Popkin, *Securing America's Future: The Case for a Strong Manufacturing Base* (Washington, DC: Joel Popkin and Company, June 2003).

2. Adapted with permission from *New Product Management for the 1980s* (New York: Booz Allen Hamilton, 1982).

3. Robert G. Cooper, "Why New Industrial Products Fail," *Industrial Marketing Management* (April 1975): 315-326.

Chapter 4
Selecting the Best Industrial Distribution Channels

If you've ever tried to memorize the "Four P's" of marketing – product, price, place, and promotion – I'll bet you were brought up short the first time you saw the "P" of "Place."

Well, to make the Four P's acronym work – they made "Place" stand for distribution. This can range from being an actual place if you're a restaurant or a retailer, to the more complex concept of sales and distribution channels necessary for SMMs.

Today, getting this part of the equation right is more critical and more complex than ever. For a start, we have to do a better job – with limited resources to do that job. Our transformation has to extend out into our distribution.

One of the most obvious indications of the changes caused by globalization is that customers are driving cost reduction. They are demanding it from their vendors any way they can. Customers want more products and services at lower prices. And any way they can means exactly that.

If customers think they can eliminate middleman commissions from the price, they will.

This big change in buyer demands has also brought about changes in the tasks required to get a sale. One result of these efforts to get both more services and lower prices is a massive change in sales channels.

Manufacturers are trying to find the right combination of sales channels that can balance selling costs, selling tasks, and customer demands for more specialized products and services at lower costs.

This means the tasks required to get the sale have changed dramatically, and OEMs are struggling to develop or find the right distribution and sales channels to support these new customer demands.

Given the fact that almost everything else is changing, it seems clear that your sales channels are affected by the same revolution and they will also have to change to fit the new demands of the marketplace.

You have one more transformational challenge. Sales channels and strategies that worked in the past probably won't work in the future. The sales processes that worked for distributors, manufacturing reps, and integrators 10-15 years ago don't work as well today. Customers have largely driven these changes, and sales requirements continue to evolve and change with globalization. Technology is also driving change in distribution channels as products and services become more complex and more customized.

Many progressive manufacturers are in the process of changing their sales and distribution channels to fit this new mix of customers and their new needs. This requires a bit of experimentation. Not surprisingly, this new environment is driving many independent reps and distributors crazy.

In this chapter we'll begin with a coded list that describes all the types of industrial channels that can be selected by a manufacturer. Each channel is briefly defined in terms of the services provided. Various direct marketing methods are also described. Then, we'll go on to discuss the factors that must be considered in selecting industrial sales channels for your situation. These factors are very specific to industrial products and the sales tasks necessary in selling them.

Sales Channel Alternatives

Here are the simple codes for the eleven major types of sales channels:

MR – Manufacturers' Reps. Manufacturers' reps are also known as agents, brokers, and commissioned merchants, or simply as reps (a generic term). They are found in almost every industry and often substitute for direct salespeople. Reps generally sell a narrow line of non-competing products, do not take title to the goods, get paid on commission, and seldom stock inventory.

SMR – Specialized Manufacturing Rep. Specialized Reps are usually found selling very technical or complex capital products. They usually focus on selling 3-4 primary lines that complement each other. They are technically trained to do the same job as a factory sales person.

DD – Distributors/Dealers. This is a generic term for a variety of intermediaries who resell products. Distributors are also known as wholesalers, dealers, importers, brokers, franchises, and merchants. Depending on the products they resell, distributors can range from "supply houses" that carry inventory for local customers to specialized distributors who provide engineering, installation, and other technical services for a limited number of products. Distributors sell a wide range of products, carry inventories, and take title to the goods. They get paid on a discount (i.e. they buy goods at a discounted price), often provide service and installation, and can set their own prices and terms.

SDD – Specialized Distributor/Dealer. This is a variation of specialized, limited line distributors. They assemble or engineer different products into systems for the end user.

FS – Factory Salespeople. Factory salespeople, as the name implies, are full-time employees of the manufacturer. They are also known as direct sales people. Factory salespeople sell their company's products (and only those products) directly to end-users and sometimes to middlemen. They usually get paid a salary and commissions. Since factory salespeople are full time employees of the manufacturer, they can devote all of their time to selling specific products and accounts, and they can develop in depth technical knowledge of their products. The main disadvantage is the high fixed cost involved, since factory salespeople are not paid strictly on commission. It also takes a long time and considerable investments to build, train, and manage a factory sales force.

IN – Integrators. Integrators differ from industry to industry. Generally they are design engineering firms capable of designing, purchasing, installing, and servicing an entire system. They sell and represent product lines like reps. They buy and re-sell products like distributors. But, they engineer the system (unlike distributors) and provide installation and service.

MA – Major Accounts. A major account person is a highly trained factory sales manager who has the experience and a wide variety of technical abilities to handled the needs of very large companies with corporate engineering staffs and procurement officers. Sometimes they are also called national accounts managers if the customers provide large volumes and want to deal direct. The defining factors for using a major accounts manager or department is that the customers require direct contact with the manufacturer because they are so demanding in terms of information, communication, pricing, and discounts.

MC – Multiple Channels. This term refers to adopting combinations of sales channels to support a variety of different types of customers with different needs. For instance, if the orders vary from parts to small orders of less than $1000, to larger orders of $10,0000 to $100,000, to very large systems of $100,000 plus; the manufacturer may employ:

- C – Catalogs
- TM – Telemarketing/Telesales
- MR – Manufacturing reps
- FS – Factory sales people.

HY – Hybrids. This is another emerging channel that is designed as a creative way to cover the needs of customers and tasks at the lowest cost. Hybrids are creative combinations of factory sales, manufacturing reps, and distributors. Examples are factory sales people who are paid 100% commission like independent reps, stocking distributors who also function as reps, manufacturing reps who are paid by the factory to only represent the factory product lines, etc.

CDM – Catalog/Direct Mail. Although all industrial products have some kind of literature or catalog, selling by direct marketing techniques such as catalogs and direct mail is used mostly on standard products such as safety products, computer hardware, software, after-market parts, office supplies and equipment, and smaller material handling equipment. Catalogs and direct mail are also used as a separate sales channel to reach small and remote accounts.

TM – Telemarketing/Telesales. This is another direct marketing technique that has really come into its own in industrial markets. Although it is primarily used for sales prospecting, telemarketing or telesales can also be used as a supplementary sales channel for small accounts and remote customers.

ALL – Alliances and Agreements. Marketing agreement, private label agreement, licensing agreement, and OEM agreements.

Developing a methodology to show manufacturers how to change or select the right distribution channels is a serious challenge.

This is particularly true when the audience varies from small job shops who have never used outside sales channels to experienced midsize companies struggling with the change from traditional channels to complex multi-sales channels.

There are five primary factors manufacturers of industrial products should consider in channel selection.

Primary Factors to Consider in Selecting Channels

The five factors are:

- Affordability
- Product range
- Customer type
- Necessary technical information
- Necessary sales tasks.

Let's review them one by one.

1. **Affordability –** What Can You Afford? This is the most important selection factor in choosing sales channels and must be evaluated first. You may need factory-trained specialists to handle all of the customer requirements but may only be able to afford a variable cost solution because of the size of your company or your financial capability. This is the sales channel paradox. "What you may need you cannot afford." There are three simple ways to evaluate the affordability question.

   Can you afford a direct sales person? Industrial salesmen covering large territories with a car will often cost $100,000 including expenses. That means if you want to cover the entire U.S. you may have to hire 6–7 people for a minimum cost of $700,000. Many small manufacturers cannot afford to hire direct industrial sales people until the sales volume is large enough to justify the costs.

What is breakeven sales volume? If the salesman costs $100,000 per year and the company's overall sales expense to sales ratio is 10%: then $100,000 divided by .10 = $1,000,000. In other words, it will take a minimum of $1 million territory sales to break even. So, you must make sure the territory has considerably more sales potential than that breakeven figure.

What is the minimum order size? All sales people must cover their sales expenses with their commissions. If the cost of one sales call for a dealer rep is $100 per call (in a local area) and it takes four calls to get a sale, then it will cost a minimum of $400.00 in sales expenses to close an order. If you divide this cost by the company selling expense of 10% you will discover that the minimum order size should be $4,000 ($400/.10=$4,000). Order size is extremely important when selecting distributors and manufacturing reps. They may agree to represent your line but they will not dedicate much selling time if the order and their commissions are too small.

A specialized rep in a large territory selling capital equipment with long sales cycles is a very different story. Their sales costs are much higher and they have to split the commission with their employer. If a commission is not at least $5,000 and the order size at least $50,000, specialized reps are not very motivated to drive very far, or make many calls.

So the cost of a factory sales person, breakeven sales, and the minimum order size are all factors in selecting the right sales channel for your products and your company.

2. **Product Range** – Before getting into the details of choosing the right distribution channel, it is important to examine the wide range of industrial products and services. Many people believe that "marketing is marketing" and that the 4 Ps apply to all industrial products the same as they do to consumer products. The fact is, marketing strategies for price, sales, promotion, etc., vary a great deal with the type of industrial product. For example, the type of product or service often dictates the type of sales channel because of product complexity and

the technical information required in selling it. This is an extremely important issue to address when you are dealing with industrial products and services.

In general, a more specialized product requires a more specialized sales channel. For example:

- Dealer and manufacturers' rep sales people can sell fairly standard products such as bearings, electric motors, and lift trucks.
- Specialized reps, integrators, factory sales people or a combination of the three usually sell customized components and assemblies such as retainer plate castings or special engineered manipulators.
- A factory salesman usually sells special engineered and "one-off" systems and machines.
- And, very large systems that are specifically engineered, such as a high rise storage retrieval system, or a nuclear reactor, are sold by major accounts type factory specialists or a sales team from the factory.

Figure 4-1 illustrates this dynamic in the vast range of industrial products and services offered by SMMs and OEMs. The product range shows that as products become larger, more custom, more complex, and the sales cycle longer, the more specialized the sales channels have to be.

3. **Customer Type** – Figure 4-2 is an example of four very different customer types – each with very different needs and purchasing practices.

The large Type 4 multinational customers may require a major account approach to selling and supporting them. Many of these Type 4 customers no longer want to deal with manufacturers' reps or dealers given their drive to squeeze out costs.

The multiplant Type 3 customers will probably require a combination of specialized reps and factory sales.

The Type 2 customers can usually be handled by a well-trained specialized rep.

Figure 4-1: The Industrial Product Range

Standard Components	
Safety stairs	Direct/Dealers
Parallel processing computers	Direct/Dealers
Appliance hinges	Direct/Dealers
Design schematic software	Direct/Dealers
Pneumatic valves & fittings	Direct/Dealers
Compression rings	Direct/Dealers
Truck bed liners	Direct/Dealers
Gas valve (polyball)	Direct/Dealers
Bullitex wall panels	Direct/Dealers
Industrial fluid pumps	Direct/Dealers
Industrial gate valves	Manuf. Reps
Premixed resin products	Manuf. Reps
Dragline bucket wear parts	Direct/Dealers
Front end loader wear parts	Direct/Dealers
Manganese castings	Direct/Dealers
Lift truck attachments	Direct/Dealers
Lift trucks	Direct/Dealers
Mills for job shops	Direct/Dealers
Backhoes	Direct/Dealers

Specialized & Custom Components	
Custom designed crankshafts	Direct
Special gyroscopes	Direct
Microcontrollers	Direct
High Voltage air switches	Direct
Refiner plate castings	Direct
Specialized transducers	Direct/Specialist reps

Low	Customization	
Short	Sales Cycle	
Low	Price	
Small	Product Size	

Spec. & Custom Machines & Services

Load transfers	Direct/Dealers
Rebuilt packaging machinery	Direct Sales
Inspection systems	Specialist Reps
Palletizing machines	Specialist Reps
Concrete block machines	Direct Sales
Custom-built manipulators	Direct Sales
Industrial ovens	Direct
Forward-looking infrared	Direct
Ship-mounted hydraulic crane	Direct/Dealers
Industrial controls	Direct Sales
Foundry manipulators	Direct
Radar simulation systems	Direct
Home security cable systems	Direct
Plastic injection moldings	Direct Sales
Screw machine products	Direct Sales
Machining fasteners	Specialist Reps
Machining/fabrication	Direct Sales
Aerospace machining	Specialist Reps
Abrasive coatings	Direct Sales

One-off & Bid Spec. Assemblies

Nuclear reactors	Major Acct. Sales Team
Patrol vessel	Major Acct. Sales Team
High rise storage & retrieval systems	Major Acct. Sales Team
Complete concrete block plants	Major Acct. Sales Team

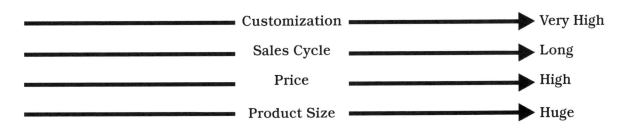

Customization	⟶	Very High
Sales Cycle	⟶	Long
Price	⟶	High
Product Size	⟶	Huge

Meanwhile, a Type 1 can be handled by most industrial reps.

Customer buying practices will dictate the tasks and costs in the selling process. If the sales channel cannot handle all or some of the selling tasks and costs, those functions will automatically be transferred to the manufacturer.

The point here is that customer types and sizes drive the specifications, requests for quotes, buying procedures, communication, and amount of paper work and technical information on each project.

In addition, some of these customers and their requirements may be more than a sales channel can be expected to do.

In this case, the manufacturer will have to find or develop a new sales approach to the customer or revise the commission schedule to fairly cover the tasks and costs.

4. **Necessary Technical Information** – The Industrial Product Range Chart in Figure 4-1 also illustrates that as you move towards selling more complex industrial products the technical information needed to make a sale becomes more complex.

   At some point, generic sales channels may not be able to gather and distribute all of the specialized information necessary to close a sale. Though the growth of online resources can, in many cases, provide the necessary technical information with some efficiency. The average independent rep and distributor is not willing or able to handle all of the technical information of complex products. It usually takes a specialist rep, integrator, or a factory sales person. It is important to carefully evaluate the quantity and type of technical information necessary to quote and close sales before deciding upon a sales channel or a commission schedule

5. **Necessary Sales Tasks** – One of the best places to begin when determining the type of sales channel you need is to define the sales tasks that need to be completed.

   This is a very critical area because customers continue to change their requirements, which changes the selling tasks every year. As

FIGURE 4-2   TYPES OF CUSTOMERS

	Example Customer	Annual Purchases	Average Order
TYPE 4			
Large multi-national	6 divisions		
Multi division	50k employees	$1,000,000	$400,000
Plants worldwide	120 plants		
Central purchasing			
Central engineering			
Specs and std. in books			
Large, RFQS			
Technical info – extreme			
Paper work – extreme			
Project mgt. – required			
Pre-sale info – extreme			
TYPE 3			
Large multi-divisional	3 divisions	$500,000	$150,000
Plants in North Am.	20K employees		
Plant purchasing	60 plants		
Plant engineering			
Specs & RFQS			
Technical info – moderate			
Paper work – moderate			
Pre-sale info – considerable			
TYPE 2			
Multi plant	1 company	$300,000	$150,000
Plant engineering	IK employees		
Technical info – light	5-10 plants		
Paper work – light			
Pre-sale info – rep calls			
TYPE 1			
Small plant	1 plant	$100,000	$100,000
Plant mgr.	75 employees		
Buyer			
Technical info – simple			
Paper work – simple			
Pre-sale info – simple form			

we noted at the beginning of the chapter, there are huge pressures to reduce costs in this area. Here is where the crunch often hits – in necessary sales tasks.

It is a fact that most customers now have leaner staffs. In some cases, this means they have transferred many tasks they used to do "in-house" to outside vendors and their sales channels.

Figure 4-3 is a typical list of sales tasks for specialist reps selling capital equipment. You might want to begin by using this typical list to develop your own list of sales tasks that need to be accomplished – regardless of whether your current sales channels are doing them all at this time.

Getting the sales process right is, in its own way, as important as getting your manufacturing right.

It is really worth your time to sit down and review all of the tasks that need to be accomplished to get a sale. Use a recent complex sale you received and break the whole process into the necessary tasks and who did them as shown in the example of Figure 4-3.

FIGURE 4-3: REP PERFORMANCE SCALE

Rep Name _____

1.	Ability to train customers	1 2 3 4 5 6 7 8 9
2.	Compatible product lines	1 2 3 4 5 6 7 8 9
3.	Ability to sell engineered products	1 2 3 4 5 6 7 8 9
4.	Follow-up on all leads	1 2 3 4 5 6 7 8 9
5.	Find new customers (prospecting)	1 2 3 4 5 6 7 8 9
6.	Use of telemarketing as support	1 2 3 4 5 6 7 8 9
7.	Ability to sell systems	1 2 3 4 5 6 7 8 9
8.	Have CAD proficiency to do layouts	1 2 3 4 5 6 7 8 9
9.	Use layouts as part of selling approach	1 2 3 4 5 6 7 8 9
10.	Ability to sell wide range of customers	1 2 3 4 5 6 7 8 9
11.	Ability to do complex presentations	1 2 3 4 5 6 7 8 9
12.	Pre-sale information gathering	1 2 3 4 5 6 7 8 9
13.	Use direct mail for market probes	1 2 3 4 5 6 7 8 9

14.	Response to product training	1 2 3 4 5 6 7 8 9
15.	Follow up on lost orders	1 2 3 4 5 6 7 8 9
16.	Ability to do proposals/quotations	1 2 3 4 5 6 7 8 9
17.	Sales & quotation reporting	1 2 3 4 5 6 7 8 9
18.	Assiduously pressing for the sale	1 2 3 4 5 6 7 8 9
19.	Overall communication with customer	1 2 3 4 5 6 7 8 9
20.	Achieving sales coverage & forecast	1 2 3 4 5 6 7 8 9

TOTAL SCORE_____

This simple performance scale is designed to give you a quick assessment of your rep or distributor firm. If the total score is below 100, you probably have problems that will eventually lead to termination. Look into them.

Note: A complete example with all of the details and steps on how to conduct a rep performance scale is provided in the Growth Planning Handbook.

The next step is to list the most important tasks that are needed to close the sale. Evaluate the most important tasks by circling the appropriate number in Figure 4-3.

As an example, ten of the most important tasks were selected as shown on a new scale in Figure 4-4.

Now use this list to rate each of your sales channels on a scale of 1–10. These scores will give you a quick look at the level of proficiency attained by each rep.

All ten of these tasks become more difficult to accomplish as the products become more complex and the customers larger.

The average dealer and manufacturing agent will usually score from 1–4 on technical products.

A specialized rep or integrator will score from 5–8 depending on their backgrounds and years of experience.

FIGURE 4-4: Sales Task Difficulty Scale

		Standard Products		Engineered Systems
1.	Pre-sale information gathering		1 2 3 4 5 6 7 8 9 10	
2.	Ability to do proposals/quotations		1 2 3 4 5 6 7 8 9 10	
3.	To provide customer CAD drawings		1 2 3 4 5 6 7 8 9 10	
4.	Ability to sell engineered products		1 2 3 4 5 6 7 8 9 10	
5.	Ability to sell a wide range of customers		1 2 3 4 5 6 7 8 9 10	
6.	Ability to sell systems		1 2 3 4 5 6 7 8 9 10	
7.	Ability to do complex presentations		1 2 3 4 5 6 7 8 9 10	
8.	Ability to train customers		1 2 3 4 5 6 7 8 9 10	
9.	Ability to do sales prospecting		1 2 3 4 5 6 7 8 9 10	
10.	Ability to communicate with customer		1 2 3 4 5 6 7 8 9 10	

To do many of these tasks in the 8–10 range usually requires a lot of factory participation.

The key point is that each task costs money.

If the sales channel cannot do the task, it will automatically be transferred to the factory or you will lose the order. If the sales channels cannot do some of the tasks (even with good training) then the manufacturer must look for a new sales channel or modify the amount of commission paid to the channel.

Now let's put them all together into what one of my friends calls a "BOE" or "Back of Envelope" checklist. It's an initial rough worksheet to help you get to the sales channel solution that, on judgment, makes the most sense for you, your company, your products, and your customers.

So, taking into account all we've just covered, let's work our way through the basic questions and write in a channel code as your best answer to each of them. We've put in a quick channel code guide at the bottom of the checklist – if you need a little more review, you might want to turn back to the earlier part of the chapter – where we covered this in more detail.

FIGURE 4-5: Five Key Questions

A Back of the Envelope Check List to Select Sales Channels

Channel Codes

MR	Manufacturer Rep	**FS**	Factory Sales
SMR	Specialized Manufacturers Rep	**IN**	Integrator
DD	Distributor/Dealer	**MA**	Major Account
SDD	Specialized Distributor /Dealer	**MC**	Multiple Channels
HY	Hybrid Channels	**CDM**	Catalog/Direct Mail
ALL	Alliances and Agreements	**TM**	Telemarketing/Telesales

Review each of the five primary factors and assign the sales channel code or codes (shown below) that best answer the question.

Write in a channel code

1. **What can you afford?** _____

   Consider the cost of a direct salesman. If you know you can't afford a direct salesman, you'll have to begin with some type of commission rep

2. **Type of product** _____

   Where are your products on the Product Range? If you have standard products you can use agents or distributors. But, if you have customized products, you will need a specialized or factory rep.

3. **Types of customer accounts** _____

   Are they small companies with buyers or giant companies with centralized purchasing and engineering? You may have to handle the large accounts direct and all the other customers with other sales channels

4. **Technical Information** _____

Is the technical information and paper work required to get an order easily handled by a rep or can it only be handled by the factory?

5. **What tasks to perform** _____

If you did the task exercise in Figures 4-3 and 4-4 you should know how many of the tasks can be handled by independent sales channels and what type of sales channel you need.

Eight Other Factors

Now, here are eight other factors to consider before deciding on the best channel solution. Again, write in the channel code that seems the best answer to each of the following factors – or at least the ones that you think are applicable. (Just write in "NA," not applicable, for the factors that aren't relevant – or cross them out.)

Competitor's channels_____   Frequency of calls_____
Geographic area to cover_____   Installation_____
Sales cycle_____   Local service/parts_____
Identifiable projects_____   Inventory_____

Which channel code was most frequently assigned? The next step is to eliminate channels you can't afford or are impractical. Then decide if you may require multiple sales channels.

Example: ABC Industries – Here's an example of how the checklist works. ABC Industries is a machine shop that builds special fasteners for engines, aerospace applications, and power generating systems.

The company wants to expand out of Ohio to all parts of the country. All orders are in small lots with considerable customization and specifications on each job. Bids are extensive, as is paper work. Orders range in size from $10,000 to $200,000. They have an inside sales manager and a good prospect database. The company has $5 million in sales. There are clusters of prospective customers in Southern California, Texas, New England, and throughout the Midwest.

Here are ABC's answers and the thinking behind them.

Figure 4-6

Back of Envelope Checklist to Select Sales Channels – ABC Industries

Review each of the five primary factors and assign the sales channel code or codes (See Figure 4-5) that best answer the question.

Write in a channel code

1. **What can you afford?**   **SMR**

   ABC wanted to expand to cover five major market areas in the U.S. and needed sales reps for each territory. A quick calculation showed that they could not afford factory sales reps and would have to use some type of independent rep.

2. **Type of product**   **SMR**

   ABC was a job shop and every order was built to spec. They wanted a factory rep, but decided that they would have to find or develop a specialized rep.

3. **Types of customer accounts**   **SMR**

   Most of the customer accounts were fairly large but they were not giant companies. On judgment, they could be covered by a sales rep and the factory had to get involved on a rare occasion.

4. **Technical Information**   **FS**

   The technical information and paper work required to get an order was not easily handled by a rep and all quotes had to be done at the factory

5. **What tasks to perform**   **SMR-FS**

   If you did the task exercise in Figures 4-3 and 4-4 you should know how many of the tasks can be handled by independent sales channels and what type of sales channel you need.

The last step is to consider the eight other factors before deciding on the best channels. Write in the best channel code that answers each of the following questions.

Competitor's channels_ none & FS _   Frequency of calls_ SMR _
Geographic area to cover_ SMR _   Installation_ N/A _

Sales cycle____SMR____   Local service/parts___N/A___
Identifiable projects___SMR___   Inventory___N/A___

The specialized manufacturing rep was most frequently assigned. The idea of having their own factory sales rep was eliminated for a very simple reason – they couldn't afford one. They would need multiple sales channels only in terms of having both the factory and the specialized manufacturing rep making calls on certain accounts.

The factory would also have to invest in lead generation and other appropriate marketing programs to find the prospects and leads for new projects.

Getting Ready to Interview:
How to Profile the Sales Channel

Once you've determined the type of sales channel to hire, the next step is to develop a profile of what you need. You should do this before you begin looking for candidates. You might also want to think of it as a job description.

To begin, you have to be very clear about what is needed for success. Whether someone is added through a formal hiring, or simply an internal shift in tasks or responsibilities, you still have to start with some clear benchmarks.

The following profile is based on one used for hiring a specialist rep for capital equipment. The profile is supposed to be unique enough to use in the hiring interview. Here are some guidelines for putting it together.

1. **List All Sales Tasks** – Manufacturers do not do a very good job of defining all of the sales tasks that are expected. Consequently, the relationship begins with a misunderstanding of what is expected for the commission paid. Figure 4-3 is a list of tasks for a specialist rep. Don't just copy it. It is designed to help you develop your own list – one that is right for your company.

2. **The Most Important Tasks** – Next, list the most important tasks needed to close sales. A list of these typical tasks is provided in

Figure 4-4. Again, use Figure 4-3 to create your own list. Then pick out the most important tasks by circling them on the list. The idea is to review all tasks with the candidate and then be able to show them the level of proficiency expected (and necessary) on the specific tasks.

3. **Define the Geographic Sales Territory** – Defining the geographic sales territory will only apply if the independent sales channel is going to get a contract based on geography. Many rep agreements today are defined by target accounts, or industries. However, geographic definition and protection can be extremely important to independent sales channels and should be defined up front. Independent reps tend to invest a lot more sales time when there is an exclusive contract that defines sales territories

4. **Define the Range of Order Prices in Dollars** – It is also important to define the range of orders from a minimum sale to a maximum sale (in terms of dollars) in the territory or in a similar territory.

   This will give the rep an immediate way of evaluating the sales potential and seeing whether or not the average commission will cover the sales expenses. This will also give both of you a more accurate picture of what you are offering. Be realistic. Over promising or being too optimistic is just one more formula for failure.

5. **Define the Sales Potential** – From historical records of orders received, lost order reports, quotes, leads, or from a composite market study, you need to define the sales potential of the territory in both dollars and units. This will help the rep determine the commission potential and enable the manufacturer to outline the realistic sales expectations or quota. Additional examples for defining sales potential are described in Section IV of the Growth Planning Handbook.

6. **Define the Commission Structure** – If the commission is paid based on achieving specific tasks, it is important to establish a clear understanding of the formula from the beginning.

   For example, some custom machinery manufacturers break down

the 10% commission into four segments.

- 2.5% – gathering pre-sale information
- 2.5% – for doing a layout in CAD and delivering the quote
- 2.5% – getting the purchase order
- 2.5% – the destination of the machine

7. **List the Markets and Customer Types** – A list of all market segment NAICS Codes as well as a list of known customers in the territory should be discussed. Evidence that the sales rep is already selling to these markets or, better yet, target prospects for the manufacturer is very good news. It is very important that you discuss the types of customers to be targeted.

If the customers and target prospects vary a great deal in size and complexity as shown in Figure 4-2, it is important to discuss the rep's ability to sell to the entire range of customer types. If they cannot sell the complete range, other sales channel alternatives or multiple channels should probably be considered.

8. **Product Line Synergy** – This is a complicated yet very important question. The question is about synergy between your product line and the other lines represented by the rep. If the same buyers who purchase your products purchase his other product lines, there will be two synergistic advantages.

- It will mean that the rep has a chance to sell his other lines when he makes a sales call the manufacturer or that your line will be considered when he is representing other products on the same sales call. The rep is twice as motivated.

- The manufacturer usually gets more sales from reps who have synergistic product lines because they call on a lot more qualified buyers. The rep is more efficient.

On the other hand, diverse groups of different (non-synergistic) products on the rep's line card will reduce the face-to-face (FTF) time in front of qualified buyers. The reason is simple: the rep must devote time to products that are sold in different markets and different customers from yours.

Establishing a clear profile of the type of specialized rep or distributor needed is critical.

Use these questions. They are based on years of experience in working with different kinds of industrial sales channels. They are specifically designed to be used in the rep recruitment and interview process. And they will improve your odds for a successful hire.

[Note: A complete interview sheet is included in the Growth Planning Handbook.]

Multiple Channels of Distribution

The changes in products, pricing, commissions, discounts, technology, customers, sales costs, and sales tasks are driving the revolution in sales channels. Manufacturers must now re-evaluate whether the sales channel can handle these new tasks or whether they must find a new or different combination of sales channels.

If you think you may not be getting the best or most cost effective sales coverage for your current customers, or that one type of sales channel cannot fit all customer needs, you may need to consider multiple channels.

This means reviewing the types of customers, their individual needs, their buying practices, the tasks the channels perform, the size of the order, and the sales costs.

Here's a quick way to do your own evaluation.

Step #1 – Print out a list of customer accounts by sales volume from largest to smallest. Then define the minimum cost of a sales call to get an order.

Step #2 – Now organize the customers into general categories based on obvious differences – their size and sales volume, or the number and complexity of the tasks you must do to service them.

Figure 4-7 is an example.

FIGURE 4-7

Evaluate The Customers And Sales Volume

	CUSTOMERS	SALES	UNITS	TYPE**
TOP 10 MVC*	Amberson	$6,100,000	19	4
CUSTOMERS	Colt Corp	$3,100,000	10	4
48% OF SALES	Kimfatton	$2,100,000	6	4
	Monarch	$1,200,000	9	4
	Banton Inc	$1,100,000	8	4
	Vogel	$900,000	5	3
	Golden	$810,000	8	3
	Johnson Inc	$750,000	8	3
	Cargille	$600,000	4	3
	MTS	$550,000	3	3
113 OTHER	BENNING Ind.	$500,000	5	3
CUSTOMERS	Denning Corp	$475,000	4	3
	Moore LTD.	$400,000	4	3
	Maygra Food	$89,000	1	1
	Amphilio	$79,000	1	2
	Los Lagos	$71,000	1	2
13 SMALL	Hi Lift	$29,000	1	1
CUSTOMER	Lotrali l	$31,000	1	3
ACCOUNTS	Food Ltd.	$35,000	1	2
IN TERMS OF	Quimby Sales	$38,000	1	3
ORDERS	Gold Star	$39,000	1	2
AND ANNUAL	Best Brands	$40,000	1	2
SALES	Shannon	$43,000	1	4
	Swan's	$48,000	1	3
	Flowright	$48,000	1	2
	MBC	$50,000	1	3
	Builtmor	$59,000	1	2
	Food Inc.	$59,000	1	3
	Conagra	$60,000	1	1

MVC means Most Valuable Customers, which are the customers with the largest sales volume as described in Chapter 2.

**The four types of manufacturers are described in Figure 1-1 of Chapter 1, under the Collins Classification of Manufacturers.*

Now, look at your list and answer the following questions:

1. Are some of the customers so large and do they require so much support and specialized services that a sales rep cannot handle them? Will these customers consistently demand to deal direct with the factory? (In example 4-2 the first group of customers are very large multinational companies with extremely complex buying requirements. These customers may require some type of major accounts program or a team approach to selling.)

2. Which customers can be handled by a manufacturing or specialized rep in terms of tasks and sales costs? (In our example, the 113 other customers are companies that can be sold by specialist reps.)

3. Which customers buy products that are standard enough to be stocked by dealers/distributors? (In this example there are none.)

4. Which customers purchase in quantities or in order sizes that are below the minimum order size and cannot justify a FTF sales call. (The example shows 13 customers at the end of the list where the total purchase price does not offer enough commission to interest the reps or justify a direct factory sales call. (Might telesales, catalogs, and/or the Internet handle these customers?)

In this example, there was enough difference in customer buying requirements and sales costs to suggest that at least three types of sales channels would be needed:

Major accounts,
Specialized reps,
Telesales and Internet.

Phase II – How to Find General Reps and Distributors

It's one thing to describe the perfect rep or the perfect sales channel solution – it's quite another thing to find one.

In general, here are your first search activities.

1. Ask Other Sales Channels – Reps and distributors who have been in business for many years get to know other reps and distributors personally. They represent some of the same lines, attend the same sales meetings and trade shows, etc. Often they can not only recommend another rep or distributor, they can give you a personal background and referral.

2. Go to MANA – The Manufacturing Agents Association is a good place to begin your search for manufacturing reps. You can purchase their published list of reps by state and you can advertise in their "Agency Magazine."

3. Advertise – Often, trade magazines have an appropriate classified section and rates are usually reasonable. City business magazines may also offer some opportunities. You might even want to run an advertisement in the metropolitan area (or areas) for the geographic area you need covered. Be specific on the type of sales channel you are looking for and the type of products you sell. There are other types of media solutions.

4. Ask Customers – Network. Network. Network. It is very easy to ask your best customers who they think are the best reps selling similar or related lines of equipment or services in a given territory. Best of all, you get a bit of market research as you ask them how they would assess them from the customer point of view.

5. Look at Competitor's Sales Reps – It is also wise to carefully examine all of the competitors annually to see if they are using the same sales channels you use for the same customers and in the same territories. If one of the reps or factory salesmen seems to perform well in an area where you are weak or is possibly looking for a new channel, get in contact with them to see if there is an area of mutual interest.

Finding a rep in a closely related field also makes sense. After all, if you sell syrup, one your best candidates is already selling pancakes.

6. Industry Buyers Guides – Most major publications for major industries offer annual buyers guides. These guides often have lists of reps, distributors, integrators, and engineering firms who are members of the association or subscribe to the magazine. For instance the Packaging Machinery Manufacturers Institute (PMMI) offers a list of reps, distributors, and integrators who are members of the Association.

7. Trade Shows – If you have a booth, it is often productive to put up a sign saying you are looking for reps or distributors in specific areas. Some large trade shows also offer a "matching service" to get channels together with interested manufacturers. Or you can just gather a list of reps that come by the booth and interview them later.

8. Train Your Own – In some cases where the product is very technical and customized it may be in the interest of the manufacturer to develop a special program to train their own specialist reps. This can be done by hiring the person as a factory employee to start the training or to sponsor a new rep just getting started. In the latter circumstance, the manufacturer could provide the necessary expenses and an incentive to emphasize your product line.

Conclusion

Independent reps and distributors complain that their worlds have changed. They say that commissions have gone down, there are fewer exclusive contracts, manufacturers send out fewer leads, and manufacturers want more tasks completed in the selling process for less commission. They say it is harder to make it as an independent rep or distributor. Well, it depends on the type of products and industry but there is truth in all of these claims.

Manufacturers complain that their margins have been eroding, their customers issue more specifications and want more customization at lower prices. They also complain that customers expect more tasks and services done by the manufacturer as part of the selling process, large customers want to deal direct with the factory, and that customers are selecting foreign products over U.S. made products more and more every year. All of these claims are also valid and it is also tougher to make it as a manufacturer today.

Welcome to the new globalized economy. The forces that are driving all of these changes are not going to go away and there is little chance that either independent reps and distributors or the manufacturers have much chance of returning to the good old days when things were easier.

The progressive manufacturers and sales channels simply accept these changes and focus their efforts on how to change themselves to fit the new customer and market demands.

This chapter offers a "step-by-step" process of how to evaluate sales channels, and how to support them. The chapter also describes the basic factors that must be considered when selecting or developing industrial sales channels that can adapt to the demands of the new economy.

Adapting to the change and growing in this new economy will require finding new markets and new customers. Once this commitment is made developing new sales channels and products to fit these new customers is a given. It will also require taking a fresh look at the services you offer, which is the subject of the next chapter.

Key Points

Industrial sales channels have had to change just as much as manufacturers. The sales channels used just a decade ago probably won't work the same today. These changes have all been driven by customer actions and attitudes, such as the following:

- Want to buy at the lowest price
- Demand more technical knowledge during sales
- Want more tasks performed at the point of sale

Manufacturing companies must find a balance between sales tasks performed and commissions paid. This, in most cases, will require a reassessment of sales channels and, perhaps, a creative combination of multiple channels to meet customer needs.

Suggested Action

Print out a list of all of your customers and organize them into general categories as explained in steps 1 and 2 under the heading "Multiple Channels of Distribution" on page 127. Then answer the four questions on page 129 to see if you need different types of sales channels to sell all groups of customers.

Chapter 5
Adding Specialized Services

You've already looked at adding new customers, new markets, and new products. In this chapter we'll examine one more addition you might not have considered as a manufacturer – new services. Here's why.

Globalization has affected customers large and small. By now, larger customers, for the most part, have all gone through a variation of the re-engineering process where they have reduced costs by eliminating, sub-contracting, or forcing many tasks they used to do onto their suppliers. Most of us have seen customer functions such as design, training, spare parts inventory, preventative maintenance, and engineering services, (to name just a few) either reduced dramatically or pushed onto suppliers or outside service firms.

When you think about it, this broad-based trend may offer some specific opportunities for your firm. And that's exactly what is happening.

Many progressive manufacturers have pioneered new ways to grow by capitalizing on these new opportunities for services. They have created additional sales and profits by addressing issues that were problems for their customers and turning them into opportunities for growth. These manufacturers have expanded their approach from product innovation alone to the addition of service innovation

In industry after industry, there are great opportunities for those product manufacturers who can provide product/service packages instead of just products.

There are also great opportunities for job shops who can change their services to fit the emerging needs of customers and globalization.

By carefully examining your customers' problems, it is possible to develop a list of the services that make their jobs easier – and sometimes uncover opportunities to do their work for them.

For example, think about purchasing the things you make from the customer's point of view. Often, the customer must spend time, effort, and money figuring out how to buy your products, use your product, maintain it, store it, train their people on it, upgrade it, and dispose of it.

In each case, there may be an opportunity to provide a service.

As a supplier, it is extremely important for you to monitor these customers closely and develop the kind of communication that helps you know what your customer will do in the future. There are a lot of reasons for this.

The worst thing that can happen to a supplier is to get "blind-sided" and suddenly lose a large customer – one that may be the majority of your business. This is nowhere more obvious than machine shops and other job shops slowly being crushed by the pressures of globalization.

It is hard to fight the fact that things can often be made cheaper elsewhere. But services are another matter.

Services usually need to be delivered and "consumed" much closer to the point of sale. They are not as easy to export and hard to manage at a distance.

Certainly some large scale services can be sent elsewhere. Telemarketing and "back room" services can be sent to India, but smaller, more customized services are not as easy to export.

Let's take a look at how one company expanded their offerings.

EBC Industries – A Job Shop Example

Harry Brown, the President of EBC Industries in Erie, PA, saw these trends even before globalization was a well-known threat to American manufacturing. As a result, he made a conscious decision to change his business to provide unique services that would appeal to U.S. customers and give them additional reasons to keep their business here.

Harry could see that it was becoming increasingly difficult for SMMs (Small and Midsize Manufacturers) to make a decent profit on high volume production work – especially if the customer was a large company with the ability to source products from anywhere in the world.

Harry identified two trends that made him carefully evaluate high volume production work.

First, when the volume gets large enough, the customer is often more able to source from an overseas supplier – often without warning.

Second, there is a relentless pressure from all customers to drive prices down. In many cases, this can eventually erode the suppliers margins to the point where there is simply no way of making a profit. This has become most apparent in the aerospace and automobile industries where customers are demanding cost reductions by contract over a period of 3-5 years.

Harry also knew that his large customers had pressures of their own. They were also being forced to re-engineer their businesses to compete and do their work with fewer employees, fewer suppliers, smaller inventories of parts, and many other problems unique to their own industries.

However, they still had to meet their delivery promises and with everyone running leaner, they often needed emergency parts delivered in a matter of hours not weeks. If they couldn't get these parts they would suffer the costs of lost production time and missed customer delivery dates.

Harry observes "when customers get into trouble and need parts in a big rush, price is not the priority. Time is the priority."

Harry, always the optimist, decided that this new situation being presented by his largest customers could become a business opportunity. He then looked at his own facilities and did a bit of improvisation. He created a "Rapid Response System" in his shop that included special machine cells, heat treating, roll threading, metallurgical testing, and mechanical testing. The idea was to change the nature of some of the services he offered so that he would be able to respond in hours rather than days.

He selected his most experienced journeyman workers to man the Rapid Response part of the company 24 hours a day. These people had job descriptions that required many advanced skills and they were paid more than others in the plant. They had to agree to work at any time of the day or night and on weekends and be "on call" with cell phones. Every worker chosen was also a certified inspector.

Because all of the various processes and materials necessary could not always be supplied by EBC, they also had to enlist other key suppliers into the Rapid Response System.

Each selected supplier had to be ISO 9000 certified and had to have proved that they were also capable of reorganizing to provide the quick services necessary to make this service work. They also had to agree to open up their doors anytime of the day or night and on weekends.

At this same time, EBC adopted Lean Manufacturing techniques. They began the Lean process by talking to their customers about how they could collectively work on reducing waste and cost. The customers became working partners with EBC to drive out waste and reduce costs.

One of Harry's objectives for Lean was to make customers realize that they did not need to buy parts in large volumes from overseas vendors. They could buy parts as they needed them from EBC and not carry inventories. This means, "only making what you have to make."

This "just in time" approach to making parts for his best customers was a key strategy in gaining a competitive advantage over foreign competitors, who can always offer lower costs – if there's enough time.

This is a strategy all job shops should consider.

There was an additional benefit.

Making these changes brought additional improvements to Harry's operation. From his adoption of Lean Manufacturing techniques, he learned to Flow Diagram his processes. By relocating equipment into manufacturing cells, multiple processes were combined into one operation, creating a continuous flow of material.

This allowed Harry to reduce his costs, reduce his and the customer's inventory, improve throughput, and improve quality. As a result, EBC was able to pass on lower costs and shorter lead times to its customers.

Harry also worked with his suppliers to utilize the same Lean Manufacturing philosophy and methods he had implemented at EBC. For example, he would only buy from his key suppliers on a just in time basis. So the component had to be in his shop at a given hour of the day.

Early in the company's history, Harry developed a complete quality program that included a handbook that all of his suppliers also used.

As part of the continuous improvement process, he eventually went through the process of becoming ISO 9002 certified. He then went on to become ISO 9000-2000 certified and he is now involved in helping his suppliers get certified.

Harry says that while you don't necessarily get any new business from being certified, it is simply expected by most customers.

Many Fortune 500 customers, like Caterpillar, expect all of their suppliers to be ISO certified. This commitment to total quality has resulted in the compliance with a broad range of specifications including Military SAE, Commercial Nuclear and other demanding standards.

As it turned out, all of these changes were successful and profitable; and Harry then went on to reorganize his whole company into a Rapid Response Manufacturing System. Other workers saw these new jobs as premium jobs and wanted in on the new system. The Rapid Response jobs had more work, more overtime pay, and more security.

The change in manufacturing philosophy at EBC also changed the organization in an important way.

Many current employees did not have all of the skills necessary to operate in a Rapid Response environment. Harry evaluated each employee in terms of skills and developed a training program for anyone who wanted to improve and advance to the next level. He brought instructors into the plant to conduct both classroom and on the job training.

Rapid Response is now a way of life for EBC.

Rapid Response in Action

A customer recently challenged EBC's Rapid Response System with a classic emergency requirement. The customer operated large power-generation turbines in Texas. A very special stud for the turbine had broken and the turbine had to be shut down. This was a generator type turbine so every minute it was down it was not generating power.

The customer called Harry on a Friday night and requested the part be delivered the following Sunday. This would mean utilizing his new Rapid

Response System 24 hours a day, but he confidently said he could do it. The part was so important to the customer that they promised to send a Lear Jet to Erie to pick up the part on Sunday morning.

The stud was made of very special materials. Harry called the steel supplier on a Friday night to go in after hours and pick up the material. They started work on the parts on Saturday morning and Harry notified two other vendors that he would need their services immediately. The Rapid Response Team worked straight through Saturday night and the wee hours of Sunday morning, and the job was completed on time. On Sunday morning the customer's Lear Jet arrived with an inspector. They picked up the part and flew back to Texas.

This had been no easy task. This part was difficult to make. It required many operations as well as heat treatment and hardening. However, the Rapid Response Team was able to respond to the emergency needs and had the part manufactured, inspected, and ready to go in 32 hours.

Your Customers Have Problems, Too

The whole point is that your customers (even large ones) also have many pressures and problems. They also have to lay people off, "farm out" systems that were integral to their manufacturing, and reduce inventories – so there may be no spare parts for emergencies.

Harry says the key is to "go to the customers and find out what you can do to help them solve their internal problems." Once again, we see the value of external information as a source for new ideas, growth, and guidance. Harry acknowledges that globalization will cause a huge cultural change in manufacturing but he believes there will always be opportunities for manufacturers that can change with their customers and continuously offer innovative services."

Harry Brown personifies what the managers and owners of small and midsize manufacturers must become in our new world of globalization.

An engineer by education, Harry spent much of his adult working career with Bethlehem Steel as a sales manager before buying EBC and becoming an entrepreneur. His unique experience gave him an unusually good understanding of customers and markets as well as how to work with people at all levels. The fact that he came out of sales may have given him better than average abilities to connect with customers and understand their needs. But he still had to satisfy those needs as a manufacturer, not as a sales person.

We can view Harry Brown as the prototype for the owner/manager who is going to succeed in the new economy.

- He sees opportunities in the chaos caused by globalization
- He doesn't make excuses – he looks for solutions
- He is cognizant of all problems faced by manufacturing and volunteers to help everywhere he can
- He always asks why not – instead of why.

Perhaps his most unique ability is his knowledge of marketing and sales. For, as we've said from the beginning, intelligent marketing from a manufacturer's point of view will be critical for success in today's tougher-than-ever global marketplace.

Some of the key reasons for Harry's success are his abilities to:

- Make sales calls
- Monitor customer needs
- Evaluate market trends
- turn customer problems into new products and services.

Harry is a Renaissance man in the new age of manufacturing.

Now let's look at a very different example.

Ashland Inc. – A Product Manufacturer Example

There are many opportunities to add services to your product offering. But a manufacturer shouldn't just add services that they think the customer might want. That commitment has to be based on genuine customer knowledge. It requires visiting the customer and finding out their problems. Ashland is an example of a manufacturer that has become excellent at monitoring customer needs.

The U.S. appliance industry is a multi-billion dollar business dominated by a few large manufacturers. It is one of many American industries going through massive change because of the pressures of globalization. The big four appliance manufacturers are Maytag, General Electric, Whirlpool, and Electrolux. All of these companies are continuing to cut costs by moving plants and sourcing from offshore competitors.

Here are some examples:

A Maytag plant in Galesburg, IL, moved to Mexico. Frigidaire shut down their Greenville, MI, plant to also pursue Mexican production. Whirlpool closed a plant in Canada and, while consolidating that plant into other U.S. facilities, has established additional facilities in Monterrey and Celaya, Mexico. GE formed a venture with a Mexican firm and is producing ranges in San Luis Potosi, Mexico. Maytag has a plant in Reynosa, Mexico. Haier is a Chinese manufacturer of appliances that is becoming more and more active in the U.S. market and has opened a factory in South Carolina. The Korean firm LG has built a refrigerator manufacturing facility in Monterrey.

This may sound like a "last man standing" scenario where there won't be any suppliers left in the industry. But, fortunately, this is not true. There are U.S. suppliers that are not only surviving but also thriving in this competitive global industry. One of them is Ashland Inc.

A Brief History

Ashland was founded in the 1930s as a contract metal finisher. In the mid-1950s they expanded into metal stamping and fabricating. In the 1980s they further broadened their capabilities into the fabrication, assembly, and distribution of mechanical components for the appliance industry. Throughout the 1990s, they've continued to grow by meeting the customer's requirements for quality, cost-competitive components, and on-time delivery.

Focusing on Customer Needs

The real secret to Ashland's success is a unique ability to monitor their customers' needs and come up with unique solutions. They do this by calling on each major account regularly and also by doing competitive intelligence on what their competitors are offering in terms of products and services.

Ashland builds many parts for the appliance industry, but they are specialists in making functional metal products such as latches, drawer slides, hinges and other hardware. In the past, the OEMs designed and manufactured their own subassemblies. But as these large OEMs re-engineered themselves, they looked for better, more efficient, and lower cost ways to manufacture the subassemblies that went into their products.

Ashland was close enough to their major customers to recognize that changes in their production processes and needs could become opportunities if they could be flexible and willing to take the risks of expanding their services.

Building subassemblies and assemblies – Originally, Ashland and other suppliers provided the components going into the subassemblies – items such as die castings, stampings and moldings. Gradually, as new products were introduced, Ashland began doing subassembly work. As it turned out, their new subassemblies were so good that eventually they got the chance to manufacture and assemble the complete modules.

> **Lesson #1:** If you're going to take on a new task, work to be an exceptional supplier in terms of quality. Ashland's performance moved them up the consideration ladder.

Improved internal systems – To get a chance to do this type of work, however, Ashland had to show their customers that they could improve their systems. They willingly spent the time and money to become ISO 9000 certified. (Remember, Fortune 500 firms expect it.) They also improved their production control system and developed a 98% on-time delivery reputation, which included the ability to handle emergency deliveries.

> **Lesson #2:** Delivering to today's demanding customers may mean you have to invest in upgrading your capabilities.

Shipping and drop shipping – Ashland's systems evolved to an efficiency level where they could ship just-in-time to the customer's assembly schedule. In fact, many customers would send their trucks to pick up parts at specific hours on specific pick-up days. The parts had to be ready – and they were.

Lesson #3: One thing leads to another. Becoming a high quality manufacturer of unique products may mean improving your ability to ship those products.

Aggressively lowering costs – Since the appliance industry is global, the major OEMs can source parts anywhere in the world. They continuously compare Ashland's prices to those of foreign competitors. In response, Ashland spends considerable time finding ways to redesign parts and change their manufacturing processes to lower their costs.

Lesson #4: Quality can get you in the door, price can keep you in the game. In general, it's better to start with quality and then squeeze out costs. It's hard to start cheap and then dial up the quality. Though, of course, these days we have to do both – deliver the highest possible quality at the lowest possible cost.

Providing design services – As the OEM's customers have re-engineered themselves, part of their cost cutting was to reduce their own "in-house" engineering staff. Ashland responded by hiring engineers and offering to take over the design work for these modules.

Lesson #5: Once you become a true partner, adding necessary complementary services becomes a natural part of the process. In this case, becoming an extension of the OEM's design department. Once this kind of organic growth builds in partnership with key customers, the relationship undergoes an important evolution.

Prototypes and testing – At the same time Ashland offered to both design new prototypes and test them at their factory. They developed a testing lab and the procedures to test and build many types of designs.

Lesson #6: Keep looking for new ways to add services and value to the relationship. One thing leads to another.

Reduce complexity – Part of Ashland's success in reducing costs is to reduce the complexity of the designs and to reduce the complexity of the manufacturing processes. This is a true value-added service that serves both the customer and supplier. This service also led to doing more of the assembly and turnkey products.

> **Lesson #7:** Simplify. Simplify. Simplify. Don't forget that you can add by subtracting. With the need for cost reduction also came the requirement for faster design cycles and shorter lead times. You might say that cost reduction, faster design cycles, and shorter lead times are all fundamental requirements of supplying large American OEMs in the future. Ashland responded so well that they continue to get more work from their OEM customers.

Local customer service and geographic proximity – Another key point of the Ashland success is their location near their customers. Any supplier company who can make headway in all of the services and requirements described above will have a natural edge over foreign competitors because of their location in the U.S. and their geographic proximity to the customer. Since many OEM plants want parts just in time and often have needs for emergency services, American suppliers will always have a competitive advantage. But, geographic proximity is only a competitive advantage if you can also offer short delivery times, fast design cycles, and competitive costs.

> **Lesson #8:** Location still counts if you can stay competitive. All the problems of distance – communication, shipping, understanding customer and market needs – remain advantages if you can continue to deliver.

Ashland continues to grow because they focus on the issues surrounding the customer's products. Besides developing new products Ashland creates unique services that solve their customer's internal problems. It is a full-service company that handles all of their customers outsourcing needs and is focused on creative problem solving for their customers.

> **Lesson #9:** Keep it up. This is a whole new way of doing business. Top performance doesn't necessarily mean long-term success – now, it just keeps you in the game.

How to Get Started Adding Services

The key is to figure out new ways to help your customers do their jobs better by assisting them with special needs. The easiest way to get their attention is to help them lower costs – either by allowing them to out-source some relatively expensive (for them) function to you or by finding some other way for them to eliminate a cost of doing business – such as carrying inventory.

Figure 5-1 is a User Benefit Checklist with thirteen questions that can help you get started in this process.

To begin, pick out a favorite customer, one you know fairly well, and ask yourself these questions – all with a simple goal. Can you offer a product or service that will reduce their costs or provide some kind of realizable savings?

For instance, if you can offer services that will improve their products, lower their capital needs, lower their costs, or improve production capacity, then you have the beginnings of some new business with them.

Remember, at this stage, products and services can become very inter-twined – building a subassembly involves a bit of both.

Figure 5-1: USER BENEFIT CHECKLIST

How will the new product or service save the customer money or reduce his costs?

1. Reduced labor cost   _____
2. Reduced downtime   _____
3. Lower inventory costs   _____
4. Less storage expense   _____
5. Saving time in a service job   _____
6. Increased productivity   _____

Is the product or service higher quality?

7. More reliable   _____
8. More dependable   _____

9. More durable (lasts longer)   _____
10. Improved product performance   _____

Does it offer more or better services?

11. Easier to maintain and service   _____
12. Improved production capacity   _____
13. Better technical support   _____

Here is another way to evaluate and explore innovative services. It's a "brainstorming" checklist to help you start thinking of the things you can do for your customers.

Services such as design services, start-up services, training and education, maintenance and repair, emergency services, financial services, trade-ins, remanufactured and used products, and consignments are just a few of the service categories that can be offered.

Don't be afraid to do some creative thinking in your brainstorm meeting. At this stage, ideas are cheap, though, as we all know, they can get expensive once we decide to make the commitment.

But for now, open up your mind to new creative services, even if the initial idea or suggestion seems inappropriate. Use this list to conduct a "brainstorming" session with your key managers.

Figure 5-2: New Service Brainstorming Checklist

Here are some examples of things to think about.

1. **Design Services** – Such as plant layout drawings, pre-sale service and advice, proposal drawings, vendor consultation, programming help, and machine layouts or sketches.
2. **Start-up Services** – These may include project coordination and management, installation, assembly, inspection, product testing, debugging, and start-up of equipment.
3. **Training and Education** – Customer guidance and training in the application and adaptation of products, on-sight demonstrations, user workshops, in-plant service training safety advise, library services, and technical literature.

4. **Maintenance and Repair Services** – Cleaning, repairing, reconditioning, loaning equipment, maintenance services, trouble shooting services, and parts stocking.

5. **Emergency Services** – 800 support numbers, 24-hour-a-day service contacts, production down time emergency service, overnight part shipping, and 24-hour hot line.

6. **Marketing Services** – Joint or co-op promotions, sales engineering services, new product or application development, joint market research, program updates, and sales aids.

7. **Financial Services** – Credit, leasing, renting, factoring, discounting, etc. Is there something you can do to make it easier for your customer, or your customer's customer?

8. **Miscellaneous Services** – Think of things like trade-ins, dismantling, newsletters, application news, just-in-time delivery, consignment, and on-line information.

Product/Service Packages

There's another trend that may provide an opportunity. Customers are moving more and more to purchasing complete product/service packages.

In capital equipment, this trend is very obvious because customers want "turnkey" contracts with all services included in a fixed price.

A manufacturer of robot material-handling systems is a good example of this in the material-handling industry. Fewer and fewer customers want to buy just a material-handling robot arm. They want a robot system designed to their specific standards, and they want the specialized services that keep it operating. The services to deliver this type of product/service package include:

- Engineering design customized to their plant specs
- Layout services showing the machine installed in their building
- Special engineered options and parts
- Testing of the machine handling their products
- Customer inspection of the machine operating in the factory
- Special shipments to their plant with cell phones to follow driving progress

- Turn-key installation of the machine
- Start-up and testing services
- Training of all operators
- Spare parts for the machine
- 24-hour emergency services
- Factory connection to the machine program by modem
- Purchased preventative maintenance services
- Field service for 20 years.

Conclusions

Now we're going to change gears in our transformation process.

We've examined new customers and new markets. We've discussed the development of new products and new specialized services.

Now let's look at how we can develop the kind of organization best able to accomplish all of these activities. Let's see how we can transform ourselves.

Key Points

If you have reached the end of what you can do to lower your product costs and you do not currently have unique advantages over your competitors, then new services may be the only way to compete in the future. Here are four reasons to explore adding new services:

1. The most compelling reason to offer specialized services is that they can differentiate you from competitors. They can give you a competitive advantage that is very difficult for foreign competitors to emulate.
2. In addition, new and innovative services are ways to increase sales volume, and provide the growth needed in stagnant industries.
3. Creating new services can help SMMs keep customers who are considering switching to low-cost foreign suppliers.
4. New services can also help capture new customers in new markets.

Suggested Actions

All manufacturing companies in stagnant or declining industries need to explore services that they might offer to improve sales growth and profitability. Look at the list of services as described in Figure 5-2. Then get the sales team together and list all customer problems the group can think of collectively. What kind of new service solutions might help to solve your customers' problems?

Chapter 6
Changing the Organization to Compete

Once the manufacturer has focused or re-focused in the marketplace, in itself a major series of tasks, the second big change must occur – a change in the organization.

Besides the obvious organizational structure, these changes are also about behavior, culture, and leadership.

Customers, particularly new customers, will want quicker response, more customization, new products, new services, and more flexibility – all at reduced costs.

For the most part, the traditional manufacturing organization, known as a functional organization in textbooks, is not up to it. In fact, it hasn't really been working since globalization changes began.

So your second major challenge is to re-organize your company into a new entity that will work in the new economy. This chapter is all about how to go about changing your organization to be able to compete in this new marketplace.

You might want to think of this necessary change as strategic renewal because for many companies it will be like the Phoenix – a new company rising from the ashes of the old organization.

It is perhaps best to begin with two recent examples of manufacturers who have made this change. They have evolved to new organization models that they feel will better serve the needs of their customers. The first example is our friends EBC Industries in Erie, PA. As you may recall, they are a machine shop who saw that their customers were demanding specialized service with much shorter lead times. In response EBC developed a Rapid Response Organization. The owner, Harry Brown, changed the organization completely to meet these new demands.

The second example is a product manufacturer called SEMCO. Their owner, Ricardo Semler, took many chances in developing a new type of organization that could respond better to both customer needs and employee needs. He experimented with what would be considered "radical organizational concepts" that were featured in his book, *Maverick*. The new manufacturing organization he created pushes the very limits of organizational change.

Both stories exemplify the fundamental changes that are needed in most modern manufacturing organizations.

I know that many of you are hoping that just "getting lean" will get it done. That's just part of the job. Successful 21st Century manufacturing organizations must do three things:

1. Get "lean."
2. Improve marketing capabilities – the subject of our first chapters.
3. Evolve to a more responsive type of organization.

I know that seems like a lot, but you will find that, like so many things, it just means taking one step after the other. So let's go!

A Job Shop Example

Let's look at EBC Industries of Erie, PA, to see how a job shop manufacturer changes their organization in response to the changes in its customers and markets.

Remember, they had already changed their services to Rapid Response Manufacturing. The President, Harry Brown, believed that he would also have to change the organization if he were to provide the quick response and flexibility he had promised.

Because of that commitment, he made a conscious decision to change his organization from the bottom up. His objective was simple – to make it easier for customers to contact the company and to get quick decisions. The implications were clear. He needed to share decision making down to the people who were doing the work and connect these people to the customer. In fact, the machine operators in the work cells were even allowed to call the customer if they didn't understand part of the job.

In addition, Harry decided to flatten the organization's pyramid structure and eliminate middle levels of supervisors. He felt this would improve communication and improve the speed of responses. In addition, it would eliminate overhead and force the teams in the work cells to make their own decisions.

EBC has a sign over their door that states "Eliminate all activities that do not bring value to the customer." That sign means the company operates very lean and has an absolute minimum of accounting, data processing, production control, and human resource employees.

Seen from the perspective of EBC employees, getting "lean" actually meant enriching jobs in terms of involvement and responsibility. Done right, when you evolve your organization, everybody gets a promotion!

Product Manufacturer Example

A good example of the new type of manufacturing organization is SEMCO, featured in the book "Maverick" by Ricardo Semler.

Ricardo took great risks to remake his company into a new organization – one that was driven by the customers and employees. In his preface, Semler says "you will see in this story of an admittedly peculiar company and its people a new way of running an organization. It is not socialist as some of our critics contend. It isn't purely capitalist, either. It is a new way. A third way. A more humane, trusting, productive, exhilarating, and, in every sense, rewarding way."

The organizational pyramid is the basic structure of the functional organization. The people at the top of the pyramid control many levels of people and departments below them. It is a pyramid of boxes, like traditional military organizations. It is not uncommon to have seven levels of management in an SMM and as many as thirteen levels in large manufacturing companies.

Communication and decision must flow up and down the levels of this pyramid. This process is inherently inflexible, slow, and isolates the people at the bottom doing the work.

Semler decided that there was no way to get his employees into the decision-making process as long as they were a centralized, functional manufacturer. He said, "The only way to change is to make each business unit small enough so that people can understand what is going on and contribute accordingly."[1]

He continued, "I wanted our people to have more contact with one another. I wanted less clutter. I wanted fewer levels. I wanted more flexibility. I wanted a new shape for our organizations."

So Semler scrapped the pyramid organization and organized the company into three circles.

As a matter of fact, they abandoned all organization charts. Ricardo said by breaking the company down into smaller units it made the employees "feel human again," feel involved, "feel that they belong."

He adds, "even the most cynical observers were astonished to find that things were better off once we got rid of the pyramid and all its rungs and roles."

In fact, SEMCO went ahead and began eliminating all types of structures, rules, and top-down policies. They also fired the entire information technology department when they found out it had become a priesthood of people who made systems more complex, harder to use, and was very expensive to boot.

Semler says "we no longer have all those programmers or keypunch operators; we have dismantled our information systems department and thrown out the systems master plan."

Well, did all of those radical organization changes really work? When Ricardo started the project to remake SEMCO into a new company, sales were down to $4 million per year, each employee produced about $10,800 worth of goods per year, the company had a lot of debt, and productivity was terrible. With the implementation of Semler's changes, SEMCO grew at a rate of 40-50% per year to $35 million in sales. At last report, the goods produced per employee was $92,000 per year, productivity had risen 6.5 times (by the value added method), and the company had no outstanding loans and six months of working capital in the till.

The Advantages of Strategic Renewal

Both companies developed organization models for manufacturing companies that will survive and prosper in the new century. Both scrapped the old pyramid type of organization. And both "promoted" their employees – giving them more challenging, rewarding, and productive roles within the organization. It is a lesson that should be taken seriously by all manufacturing companies. They found their path to change. You will have to find yours.

Four Organization Types

Professors Raymond E. Miles and Charles C. Snow are the preeminent thinkers on the changes in organizational models. Their 1972 research is regarded as the seminal work on organizational theory. Their original research is important because it describes an enterprise's organizational structure, process, and strategy mix holistically.

This research has stood the test of time for twenty-five years as one of the major research instruments in the field. Their classic book is *Organizational Strategy, Structure and Process.*

In Miles and Snow's view, there are four basic organization types that populate the business landscape:[2]

1. **Defenders:** Defenders are businesses that prosper through stability, reliability, and efficiency.
2. **Prospectors:** Prospectors prosper by stimulating and finding new product and market possibilities.
3. **Analyzers:** Analyzers prosper by purposely being more innovative in their product/market initiatives than defenders, but doing so more cautiously and selectively than prospectors
4. **Reactors:** Reactors vacillate in their approach to their environment and, as a result, don't prosper at all.[3]

The Analyzers and Reactors are not appropriate to SMMs. The two models that best fit manufacturing are the Defender and Prospector models. Let's take a look at them.

The Defender Model

This organizational model describes most small and midsize manufacturing companies. It is very important to examine the profile of a Defender company because it describes in detail why many defenders are in trouble in the new and changing economy.

Defenders, according to Miles and Snow, are described by the following:

- **Domain.** The Defender's success comes from a narrowly defined and relatively stable market.
- **A few primary markets and customers.** Defenders typically direct their products or services to a limited segment of the total potential market.
- **Market and competitor intelligence.** Management has a tendency to ignore developments outside of their domain. They allocate only a small amount of administrative time and personnel to monitoring other organizations, events, and trends. In addition, environmental scanning is performed only by a few top executives or their staffs.
- **Functional organizations.** Defenders tend to rely on functional organization structures that group specialists with similar skills.
- **Formalization and administration.** Defenders develop a relatively high degree of formalization, the codification of job descriptions, and operating procedures which specify appropriate behaviors for organization members.
- **Deviancy intolerant.** The Defender cannot afford deviation from prescribed behaviors. They view conformity rather than deviancy as a way of reducing uncertainty.
- **Centralized command and control.** The characteristics of a functional organization structure require the Defender's control system to be centralized.
- **Centralized decision making and communication.** Defenders normally restrict information flows to vertical channels: directives and instructions flow down the hierarchy and progress reports and explanations flow up.
- **Baton passing.** A functional structure creates great interdependence among organizational sub units because each is engaged in only a portion of the entire technological process. The output of one sub unit is the input of another.
- **Efficiency rather than effectiveness.** The Defender's fundamental emphasis is on efficiency (doing things right) rather than on effectiveness (doing the right things).

- **New product and new market weaknesses.** With few resources devoted to scanning the environment, the defender possesses little capability for locating new products or market opportunities. (We focused on this area in previous chapters.)

The primary disadvantage of the Defender model is that it relies too much on one market or a few large MVC customers and requires steady demand. The organization makes money when its heavy investments in capital equipment and technologies are totally utilized. It has little or no defense for a stagnant or declining market (or the loss of a large MVC customer), and does not have the people or systems to locate and exploit new markets. To the extent that the world of tomorrow is similar to that of today, the Defender is ideally suited for its environment.

In fact, the Defender model worked for a long time because we did have long-term stability. For decade after decade, from the end of World War II, market demand was fairly stable – there were few competitors and customers relied on loyal (and relatively local) suppliers. A manufacturer didn't have to monitor customers or be a good industrial marketer.

Most Defender organizations are now faced with a much different world: new competitors, changing markets, more demanding customers, and erratic margins. To make matters worse, Defenders do not have the people or systems to monitor the external customer and market changes. The organization, by definition, is generally inflexible, slow to react, and requires a lot of overhead to operate. Unfortunately, in these types of organizations, the priority of important things to do always favors the internal, tangible, and process-based things, rather than the external, intangible, and customer-based things.

But, as most of us know all too well, the Defender model is not working very well today – except where a Defender can still dominate a small market niche with little competition and stable or growing volume.

The Prospector Model

It is my belief that succeeding in the new global economy will require an organization that is some variation of what Miles and Snow identify as a Prospector organization. Miles and Snow's definition of Prospectors describes a type of manufacturing organization that works well in a changing environment. As they note, the Prospector's prime capability is that of finding and exploiting new product and market opportunities.

Prospectors, according to Miles and Snow, are very different than Defenders and are described as follows:

- **Domain.** The Prospector's domain is usually broad and in a constant state of development.
- **Multiple markets.** Unlike the Defender, whose success comes primarily from efficiently servicing a stable, primary market, the Prospector's prime capability is that of finding and exploiting new product and market opportunities.
- **Market and competitor intelligence.** Prospectors maintain the capacity to monitor a wide range of environmental conditions, trends, and events. The Prospector, therefore, invests heavily in individuals and groups who can scan the environment for potential opportunities. Prospectors have the ability to find new customers and markets on a continuous basis.
- **Market driven.** This ability to do external surveillance, of customers, markets, and trends makes them market driven
- **Product organization.** In focusing on new products and new markets, the logical extension of this approach is the product organization in which all resources needed to research, develop, produce, and market a related group of products are placed in a single, self-contained organizational sub unit. Hence, the company is decentralized into many divisions and sub units. This decentralized organizational structure is a flat organization with many units, cells and teams.
- **Formalization and administration.** Prospectors develop only a low degree of structural organization, since it would not be economically feasible to codify job descriptions and operating procedures in an organization whose tasks change frequently.
- **Deviancy tolerant.** Indeed, formalization is a means of reducing the probability that deviant behavior will occur but, in many instances, this is exactly the type of behavior the Prospector is attempting to encourage.

- **Centralized command and control.** Control is decentralized because the information needed to assess current performance and to take the appropriate corrective action is located in the operating units themselves, not in the upper echelons of management.
- **Decentralized decision making and communication.** Prospectors prefer short, horizontal feedback loops. Therefore, when a deviation in unit performance is detected, this information is not channeled to higher management for action, but rather is fed directly back to the unit for immediate corrections. This is truly an example of pushing responsibility and authority down to the people who do the work. This type of organization gives them the ability to quickly respond to customer demands.
- **Effectiveness rather than efficiency.** The Prospector's fundamental emphasis is on effectiveness (doing the right things). Prospectors usually define organizational performance in terms of outputs or results. They appraise effectiveness by comparing past and recent performance with that of similar organizations.
- **Production.** Prospectors often use flexible production systems and adaptable machine tools.
- **Weaknesses.** A Prospector often cannot maximize profitability because of its inherent inefficiency. In addition, the Prospector may grow in spurts. Prospecting is gambling and experimenting, but when an organization strikes gold, the results may be spectacular.

While these characteristics are useful in general, there is no one "right model." In fact, there are many variations of a Prospector-style organization in a wide range of industries and sizes.

What Is Driving Organizational Change?

To make the necessary changes that will retain profitable customers and find new customers, the SMM will have to become market and customer driven. Simply put, they will have to become Prospectors. This is easy to say and hard to do because, for most of us, this requires both organizational and cultural change. There are Five primary considerations:

1. **Monitoring Customers.** This is the old question "Do you know what customers want and need?"
2. **Response Time.** Customers up and down the supply chain are demanding quicker responses to everything from quotes to phone calls.
3. **Decision Making.** The old dodge of having to ask the boss or get approval from the production committee doesn't get it anymore. Customers want faster decisions from whoever answers the phone.
4. **Communication.** Customers want better communication between their people and the manufacturer and don't want to get transferred around to phone messages. Manufacturers also have to improve on their own internal communication to be able to offer faster responses and decisions.
5. **Order Processing.** Customers want faster deliveries and they don't care about the manufacturer's organization difficulties. The process of passing an order between departments (even though very accurate) is too slow and bureaucratic. The walls and barriers inside the manufacturer directly affect the customer's order.

Issues for Your Organization to Consider

Now let's look at each of these issues as organization questions.

1. Monitoring Customers: Does your organization have systems to gather and analyze information on customer wants and needs?

Defender-type manufacturing organizations are defined by their lack of emphasis on monitoring customers, competitors, and markets. Why? Because they haven't had to in the past. But today, most SMMs need external information to understand where to find new opportunities in the marketplace. In other words, where to prospect. Today, monitoring customers and markets is a matter of survival. To survive in the new economy, SMMs need to be able to change their products and services as fast as the customers demand.

All the progressive manufacturers I've studied have developed ways to gather competitor and market intelligence. They seem to accept that putting a process into place that continually gathers competitor and market intelligence is the only way that a manufacturer can change fast enough to retain good customers. They prospect as a matter of course.

All departments and, in fact, any employees who deal with customers in the organization are involved in monitoring customer wants and needs and gathering a lot of specific information on a day-to-day basis. What is needed is a method of collecting and sharing the information and acting on the problems. (This was discussed in Chapter 2.)

2. Response Time: Does the organization respond as fast as customers demand?

Customers are demanding fast response to phone calls, quotations, service requests, parts sales, and every communication that has to do with products and services. Fast response time is almost a contradiction to the traditional functional manufacturing organization because the very structure of the Defender organization inhibits response.

It is not a matter of working perpetual overtime; it is simply a matter of designing systems to respond in an efficient and timely manner. If your company is forced to find new customers and markets, organizing for improved response time will be absolutely necessary to succeed.

Manufacturers should consider promoting multi-tasking in all areas, doing tasks in parallel (not serially, so there is less baton passing) and creating teams wherever possible. But the real answer to improving response time is to change the very structure of the organization.

3. Decision Making: Think about it. Is decision making controlled from the top or the bottom of your organization?

Decision making in a hierarchical (pyramid) organization can be a real problem because it takes too long to make decisions. Decisions must travel up and down the hierarchy and top managers are often too far away to understand the real problems.

One answer is to continuously work at shortening decision-making times by pushing authority to make decisions closer to the people receiving the calls. In addition, success in delegating authority and decision making down to the work levels will drastically improve response time

– providing the decisions are good ones. This is a difficult task for many owners of small manufacturing companies who built their companies by keeping their hands on all of the control levers. It takes a combination of courage, self-confidence, and good employees to give real power to the employees and watch them make mistakes as they learn to accept their new responsibilities. Pushing decision making down the organization to the people who are doing the work is absolutely essential in improving response time.

This was a primary objective of Harry Brown and his re-organization of EBC Industries. He even allowed the machinist working on the plant floor to call the customer anytime for clarification.

4. Communication: Does communication between departments need to be improved? Yes and yes.

There are two different kinds of communication problems. The first problem is the employees communicating with the customer. The second problem is communications inside the company itself.

Communicating with the customers was discussed above in terms of response time and decision making. But this won't solve customer problems if the communication problems are not solved inside the organization. Following the acceptable chain of command in a hierarchical structure is time consuming and there is usually not enough horizontal communication or feedback between work cells or business units to react as quickly as is often needed. Remember, when a customer is on the line with a problem, your relationship with that customer may be on the line.

Ricardo Semler decided there was no way to improve communication in a centralized organization where communications went up and down through layers of management. So he decided to eliminate levels of management to shorten the communication distance and give more people the freedom to make their own decisions.

5. Order Processing: Do you have a problem with the time it takes to get an order through your system? "Serial baton passing" is a term I use to describe the process of following orders through a manufacturer. For instance, when an order is received it goes through the system department by department in a serial order and is checked and re-checked for accuracy. This method worked for a long time. But in the new marketplace, where customers want customized products, shorter lead times, and change orders, serial baton passing can become a serious organizational constraint.

This problem is always exacerbated in midsize manufacturers who can afford separate overhead departments like accounting, human resources, information technology, credit, etc. Overhead departments can create automatic barriers because these people are generally not on the same page as the business group finding the orders. In fact, they are often physically separated and there are often other built-in obstacles and barriers to communication that slow response to the order. If allowed, these separate departments will always want to resort to command and control techniques that slow the process down.

Strategic Renewal: Getting Started

Getting started is a serious challenge because it means moving from an "operations-oriented" company to becoming an organization that can find (prospect for) new customers and markets. The demand of finding new customers and markets requires flexibility, rapid response, quick decisions, and an orientation on external market opportunities.

There is no universal model to use. The reason is simple but complex. Manufacturing organizations have different kinds of products, services, customers, markets, etc. In fact, these specialized differences are an advantage for the survival of the company. But one common thread running through all manufacturing organizations is that they will all have to move away from a centralized organization. Each in their own way will need to flatten the pyramid.

If you are not convinced that you need to move towards a decentralized or Prospector-type of organization, you need to do some investigation.

Begin by defining customer needs and working backwards.

Perhaps a good way to proceed is to trace an order through your organization and determine the problems encountered at every level of the organization. I often like to do this on butcher paper because you can show the whole process from the first request for a quotation to the final customer service problems.

Another simple way is to do a brief survey of people in each department about the customer problems using these five basic questions:

1. **Monitoring Customers.** Do they feel they are doing a good job finding out what customers want and need?
2. **Response Time.** Do they feel they are responding to customers with quick responses in all customer communication?
3. **Decision Making.** Do they have the authority to make decisions on customers problems most of the time?
4. **Communication.** Do they feel that communication between all departments and functions is excellent?
5. **Order Processing.** Do orders get hung up in the process because of rules and policies?

Strategic Renewal: Evaluation

The following methodology will help you evaluate your current organization.

It's designed to help you think through the problems unique to your organization, and begin to visualize how you might initiate the process of restructuring what is probably more of a Defender organization and help it evolve into some kind of Prospector organization.

The methodology makes the case that the new organization must be decentralized and flattened to improve decision making, communication, and response time. The idea is to break the pyramid down into as many self contained and self-managed sub units as is practical. Some of the basic principles that will define this type of organization are:

1. Decentralized Structure.

Most progressive manufacturers are decentralizing their organizations and getting rid of its vertical hierarchies. Prospectors are generally decentralized and much more agile than Defender companies. Decentralization almost always requires flattening the hierarchical pyramid, and creating self-governing units, teams, cells, or divisions where possible.

Figure 6-1 shows the typical Pyramid or traditional manufacturing organization with many levels and structured decision making.

Figure 6-1: The Functional Production Organization (Pyramid)

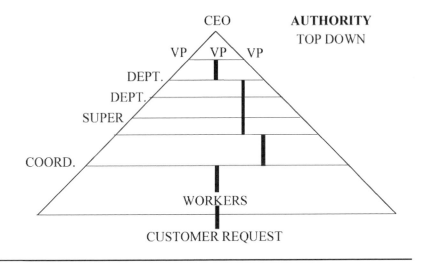

Figure 6-2 shows a flattened organization that is decentralized and broken down into many sub units.

Figure 6-2: A New Decentralized Organization Model

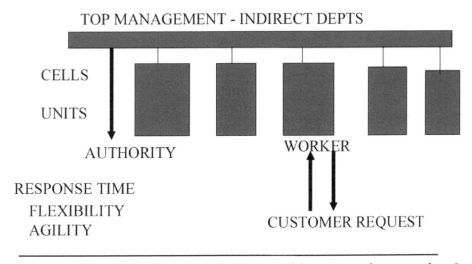

How can you flatten your organization and begin to decentralize?

2. Reduce reliance on command and control function and systems.

Top down management in a centralized organization using command and control techniques is too slow, too inflexible, not fast, and not responsive. Layers of management, departmentalization, centralized decision making, and specialist jobs all create functional barriers that slow response time and communication.

The other problem is that the more command and control the less freedom there is for employees to make day-to-day decisions. Ricardo Semler saw this as a killer of employee motivation. He went about eliminating all kinds of structure, rules, and policies. The new organization should move away from the old command and control method of management, which requires delegation of authority.

What have you done to reduce command and control functions and to push authority down to the people who do the work?

3. Minimize bureaucracy and administration.

The very structure of an organization designed to develop specialization, efficiency, and cost control will always lead to some kind of bureaucracy. This type of organization and, in fact, any manufacturing organization that is bureaucratic is not going to be flexible or agile enough to respond to new market demands or find new customers. Eventually, it will cost too much in overhead to maintain.

Reducing bureaucracy that does not bring value to the customer, reducing the cost of systems, and improving the speed of systems should be a primary goal.

Ricardo Semler's termination of the entire information technology department was a radical approach to eliminating bureaucracy. But, it makes the point that manufacturers cannot afford departments and technology that are too complex, difficult to use, and too expensive when compared to the results.

Look at every indirect function and evaluate carefully if it is costing more than the benefit of using it. In short, stamp out bureaucracy everywhere you can.

4. Reduce emphasis on rules, policies, and handbooks.

Well-managed Defender organizations love tight job descriptions, rules, policies, and HR handbooks. This seems like a precise and efficient way to handle problems and manage employees.

But more rules automatically lead to more administration, more over-head costs, less flexibility, and less freedom. Many SMMs will not be able to afford these administrative luxuries in the future. Why not get rid of them now?

EBC does not have a human resource manager or a human resource handbook. Harry believes that trying to codify all problems into a policy handbook is an impossible task – one that will never be completed. He observes "you will never have enough pages in the handbook to have policies for all problems."

In addition, Harry observes that SMMs cannot afford the human resource people it takes to write and enforce the rules. He wants the managers and employees to communicate about their problems and not use handbook intermediaries

SEMCO decided that it could create order or progress, but that they are, in some ways, contradictory terms. Semler notes, "policy manuals are created with the idea that if a company puts everything in writing, management will be more rational and objective."

He came to the conclusion that too many rules, policies, and manuals were a contradiction of the type of company he was trying to build. SEMCO noted the following, "With few exceptions, rules and regulations only serve to:

1. Divert attention from the company's objective.
2. Provide a false sense of security for the executives.
3. Create work for bean counters.
4. Teach men to stone dinosaurs and start fire with sticks."

SEMCO threw away the policy manuals and handbooks because they wanted people to think, innovate, take responsibility, and make their own decisions.

If you are going to become a Prospector organization with increased response speed and flexibility, you won't have the luxury of spending a lot of time on rules, policies, and handbooks. They are becoming mutually exclusive. You need to spend your time and energy prospecting.

5. More generalists. Fewer specialists who can only do one job.

The Defender organization depends on specialists. Having the luxury of refining the work down to specialists who are experts at a specific part of the system worked very well in the early assembly days. But today's manufacturers can't afford many specialists. They need people who can be moved around and do multiple tasks. This may, of course, require significant training and education, but the organization must be able to move people around to different projects and different sub-units, and do multiple tasks.

Think about the training that would be needed to increase the skills of specialist employees to allow them to do more jobs in the organization. You can't just hope it will happen. Set up a program to cross train.

6. Emphasize employee motivation.

The most progressive manufacturers work at fostering an atmosphere of trust and security – a key ingredient missing in most large companies in recent years. They also believe that a motivated employee is always more creative and productive than the typical worker. Without some trust, security, and motivation, most attempts to get employees to buy into change will fall flat. There may even be strong resistance.

As SEMCO evolved, Ricardo Semler came to believe that the true driver of productivity was motivation and genuine interest, not predetermined routines and tight job descriptions. He says, "I believe that Frederick Taylor's precise job descriptions limit workers' potential and constrain the possibility of job enrichment, which dampens their motivation."

Interview the hunters in your organization. Find out what motivates them. I bet you will be surprised. It is going to take very motivated employees to make the changes that will transform the company.

7. The leader as change agent.

In the past, manufacturing company leaders tended to organize around their own needs or model their companies like the organizations they worked for in the past. The natural tendency is to favor reporting arrangements that make sense to the leader and are based on his or her personality. Natural though it may be, this can be a very bad thing if the company is in a fast changing industry and the company is already stuck with a Defender style organization.

In most cases, the leaders of these new organizations will take on the role of becoming change agents (not administrators). The ideal leader will accept change as inevitable and look for the opportunities. They will be people who have a way of inspiring their employees by continuously showing them that the benefits of change outweigh the costs. They will be people who foster the notion that change can make jobs fun and exhilarating. They will be people who can operate with a low degree of structure and move people around as the market changes. (There is more about new leaders and the need for emotional intelligence in Chapter 10.)

Like it or not, the leader (usually the owner) has a big role to play as a change agent to transform the company. If you or the CEO are not "change agent" types, hire one.

8. Participative decision making.

It stands to reason that the more you can push authority and decision making down the organization, the faster you can respond to customers. One can also make the case that empowering employees can make a big difference in employee motivation. But the big question is what kind of employee can handle the responsibility?

Actually, you might be pleasantly surprised. The simple IBM mantra, "Every problem is an opportunity to demonstrate service," is one that every employee worth having can understand.

Participative decision making and accepting the responsibility of authority is not for every employee. Though the basics of courtesy and common sense are within the reach of most. Begin the process of finding out who can and who cannot handle it.

9. Getting the best employees – hunters vs. meat eaters.

Progressive manufacturers always seem to attract more than their fair share of the best people with the right skills. The best managers are not afraid to hire employees capable of replacing them.

Another problem for many SMMs is the tendency to hire people who fit their comfort zone rather than a high performance employee who may make waves while getting the job done. But in this new era of continuous change, the high performance person who will always push the organization and challenge the rules can be an asset. I call these people "hunters."

On the other hand, there are employees I call "meat eaters." They do their job, always play by the rules, do not take risks, and are good conformers to the company culture. These people are the eight-to-five group who need a job, and their job is not the most important thing in their life. We need the meat eaters along with hunters, but the critical factor is the ratio between the two groups.

The new leaders must be ready to restructure their organizations and go "on the attack." This means they will need more "hunters" and may not be able to afford as many "meat eater" type employees. To improve the ratio of hunters to meat eaters requires an open-minded leader – one who can function as a change agent and focus on hiring performers rather than conformers.

This may be easier said than done. It requires a progressive management who is *deviancy tolerant* to accept the idiosyncrasies of people with unusual personalities who use creative methods and break some rules to get things done, but who are dependable in crisis situations.

The question is, do you want people who fit the "organization profile" or do you want people who can get things done? Often, that is the choice.

Ricardo Semler, knowingly or unknowingly, used these principals to invent his new manufacturing organization. Harry Brown matched his new organization to the Rapid Response business model he had created.

You may not have to change your company organization as radically as

SEMCO or EBC, but all SMMs are faced with inventing new organizations that are more flexible, more agile, and more responsive than what has gone before.

The Special Case of the Family Manufacturing Business

There are 340,000 manufacturing companies in America. More than 80% of them are family owned. Even if both numbers are shrinking, in terms of numbers of manufacturing companies, it is fair to say we are a nation of predominantly family owned businesses.

This may describe your business situation. Let's examine this very common "special case."

The Classification of Manufactures shown in Chapter 1 illustrates the tremendous differences between Type 2 family-owned manufacturers and Type 3 professionally managed manufacturers, particularly in their different approaches to organization.

Small, family-owned organizations do not operate with the cold logic and efficiency of large manufacturers. But herein lies their virtue.

Family-owned companies are often labors of love and, in this day of downsizing, they can offer employees the communication, care, dependability, and security that is all too often missing in companies that owe their day-to-day existence to stock prices and corporate ownership much more removed from the human beings who work there.

Family-owned companies can also offer their customers:

1. Uncommon integrity and commitment.
2. Speed and flexibility in getting things done.
3. Communication directly with owners.
4. A personal touch to quality and service.
5. A willingness to customize, and innovate.

This is very good news. These inherent characteristics can give family-owned companies strong competitive advantages in a fast changing marketplace dominated by changing customer needs and niche markets. By their very nature, many family-owned manufacturers are combinations of Defender and Prospector models.

I have found in my consulting work that if you don't understand the family agenda, and if you don't have the patience to deal with family members at their speed, all of your good advice will be to no avail.

The organizational challenges facing Type 2 family-owned manufacturing companies are much different than those facing the Type 3 professionally managed companies, who have evolved into larger functional organizations to gain efficiencies.

Family-owned Type 2 companies have two unique problems.

Problem #1: Delegating Authority

Delegation, or "letting go," is a big problem for virtually every family business owner, both for psychological and practical reasons.

Many owners need a lot of help in letting go. There is an understandable psychological fear of losing all that they have built because the company's success has so much to do with their personal commitment, strengths, skills, and leadership. And there is an understandable reluctance to change the habits and behaviors that "got you there."

Still, most family owners know that the challenges their companies face are severe, and it's "change or die."

It also tends to be true that the family-owned company has already changed dramatically – even though the change may have been gradual. What worked for the start-up company when the owners had four employees really doesn't work any longer for the fifty-employee company.

Change will demand a lot from everyone. Most will need help to address their fears and develop a plan to push decision making and authority down to the employees.

Problem #2: The Family Agenda

Whether it's stated or not, virtually all family-owned manufacturers have a family agenda. Most professionals who work with family-owned businesses are mystified by the anomalies of this family agenda.

Many of the complaints are entirely valid. Three examples are promotion of non-qualified family members, business decisions based on emotion, and the domination of the business by the family agenda.

Be that as it may, the real question is how will the family agenda affect the company's ability to change with the customers and market? One ongoing aspect of this problem is that family agendas almost always seem to affect the organization's ability to get the right people into the right jobs.

Many Type 2 manufacturers will also need help in separating the family agenda from the realities and necessities of creating a new and more efficient organization.

Communication among family members and non-family managers and advisors is a critical factor in managing this change. After assessing the family agenda, any professional advisor will have to understand how the company communicates.

I have clients who are very verbal, clients who like memos and reports, clients who must visualize problems on a blackboard, and clients who can only be reached through their emotions. The bottom line is that they won't make decisions or accept change unless you communicate with them on their terms.

If you are part of a family-owned operation, one key issue you will have to address is how truly effective communication and persuasion works in your own company. And, of course, what is your own particular role in that family dynamic? The good news here is you know the players and, as we noted, you already have some inherent characteristics that will help you implement change.

Family-owned manufacturing businesses will need help with the issues of delegating authority, communication, and defining the practicality of family agendas. They will also need help in improving many of their systems (e.g. cost accounting) if they are going to try and get business in supply chains or from larger customers.

Finding solutions to each of these issues may mean the difference between future success and failure. But change we must.

Now, we're going to change gears and examine another key dimension of strategic renewal – where competitors may even become partners.

One problem of the SMM – whether family-owned or not – is one of size and resources.

We'll outline the principles and forces behind this trend and then show you three examples that demonstrate how three companies in three different parts of the country developed new organizations through alliances.

Team Concepts
A Look at Manufacturing Networks and Business Alliances, Corporate Partnering, Joint Ventures, and Marketing Partners

As you can see by the subhead, there are many valid ways to describe this cooperative process. These are terms that have been around a long time. They all define symbiotic business relationships between companies.

I will use the term business alliances as a generic term. This simply represents any alliance that is:

- Invented by entrepreneurs seeking unique business solutions
- Formed around specific market opportunities or contracts
- Focused on sales and profits
- Designed for self sufficiency
- Funded by personal investment rather than government grants
- Defined by a specific organization with a written agreement.

A brief word on "soft networks."

These business alliances have nothing to do with "soft networks" or inter-firm collaboration. Soft networks are the U.S. version of a model from Northern Italy. Public policy people transferred this idea to the U.S.

Hundreds of these networks were created by government grants in the early '90s with the hope that they would stimulate business and create jobs. However, very few networks had income that ever exceeded costs.

The "soft networks" idea emphasized social interaction and learning and is not the subject of this chapter.

Up and Down the Supply Chain

Business alliances can be formed up and down the supply chain. For example, on the market or customer side, many SMMs simply do not have the resources or the staff to develop new products, explore foreign markets, and acquire other companies and product lines, or even to find and capture new customers in new markets.

Upstream: In the "upstream" or customer side of the supply chain there are many opportunities to form business alliances such as:

- Finding new markets and customers
- Developing new products
- Creating unique or specialized services
- Using special sales channels
- Exploring foreign markets
- Getting outsourcing contracts from larger customers.

Downstream: On the "downstream" or vendor side of the supply chain, manufacturers are struggling with costs and finding new customers and markets.

There are opportunities such as:

- The need for cost reduction of professional services
- The need to compete against foreign competitors
- The need to form a vendor alliance to improve efficiency
- The need to subcontract parts of their work to low cost countries
- The need to join a customer's vendor supply chain.

Now let's take a look at three case studies. They are each an excellent example of how these business alliances can work. I've written them as comprehensive stories to show how they were formed, how they operate, and why they achieved results.

Case #1 - Prime/Sub Alliance – EBC Industries
Creating a Manufacturing Network with Key Suppliers

Let's take another look at our friends at EBC – this time with a business-alliance perspective.

Back in 1986, Erie Bolt in Erie, PA, was an old, low-tech supplier of nuts and bolts, landlocked in the inner city. As the defense and other major markets declined, their customer base dropped from 300 to 140.

Erie Bolt had no new products or services and nothing resembling innovative technology. It had generated no profit, only red ink for the previous three years. At the same time, the industry began demanding higher quality, which required new capital equipment. Also, local banks were tightening access to credit.

When Harry Brown, an engineer by training and a former Bethlehem Steel sales manager, purchased the Erie Bolt Company (renamed EBC Industries) in 1986, it was losing more than $100,000 a year.

Today, EBC Industries is a manufacturing alliance consisting of Erie Bolt and about a dozen collaborating small manufacturers. It is profitable with sales having more than tripled to over $10 million. The alliance shares technology, inventory, proprietary information, marketing, sales, and quality systems.

EBC has evolved from the old, low-tech supplier to a highly flexible, Rapid Response manufacturer of critical application fasteners, forgings and machined parts.

As part of the Rapid Response strategy, Brown formed a manufacturing alliance, now known as a flexible-manufacturing network. Today, the EBC Network comprises about 12 small manufacturers who have helped each other improve sales, enter new markets, offer new products and provide better customer service.

The impetus for these changes came from a focus on marketing, starting with a complete assessment of network members' capabilities, and an effort to match customers' needs with the network's capabilities.

That assessment also included a determination of customer profitability and sales potential to provide focus on the best customers and market niches, development of customer profiles to help the sales force find more good prospects, marketing support, and a focus on making the changes needed to support the customer.

The changes included the following:

- Organizational restructuring
- Information sharing
- Development of rapid response manufacturing
- Implementation of lean manufacturing methods
- Implementation of ISO 9002
- An ongoing employee training effort.

The key to EBC's success is the leadership and vision of the CEO. His unique experience in both manufacturing and sales gave him an unusually good understanding of customers and markets as well as how to work with people at all levels.

This unique set of "people skills" helped make the connections necessary to form the alliance. It also helped that everyone was pretty much "in the same boat," which made others receptive to the alliance message.

Before and After

Before 1986, there had been, Brown recalls, an established rigidity of thinking among the company's managers and workers alike that almost assured continued red ink.

In an organization with only 63 employees, there were five management layers separating the president from the shop floor. This distance helped aggravate another problem. On the floor, inflexible union work rules virtually guaranteed poor productivity. Says Brown now, "we looked like a mini-GM."

According to him, employee morale, even among 20-year veterans, was so low you couldn't measure it. Quality control had been eliminated to cut costs; the pension fund was under funded; payables were overdue; and if you can think of any other ailments that could afflict an old rust belt manufacturer, Erie Bolt probably suffered from those as well.

In the last three months of 1986, Erie Bolt's loss jumped to $138,000.

Brown had spent 15 years with Bethlehem Steel Corporation, the last three as assistant sales manager for their Lebanon, PA, plant – an operation that competed with Erie Bolt in making precision metal parts.

When word got out that Bethlehem was going to close Lebanon, the chairman of Erie Bolt's board contacted Brown to find out if anyone would be interested in buying Erie Bolt? Brown asked, and no one was interested – except himself, and he didn't have the asking price.

Nonetheless, he drafted a business plan and presented it to the board, which invited him to join the company as vice-president of special projects. His "special project" was to turn the business around.

While he was starting to turn the business around, he was also looking for the financing needed to buy it. In six months, he raised the money needed to buy 51%.

Forming a Manufacturing Alliance

In an unconventional move, Harry, now the new owner, turned to his competitors for help. He suggested pooling resources. The basic reasons were to cut costs, improve quality, and provide faster turnaround. Harry also added one more unique ingredient – vision.

At first, Brown says, "They were reluctant even to discuss the idea. They thought I was up to something and wasn't telling them the whole story." Years ago, says EBC's Brown, "small business had enough business. If I have this coming through the door, why should I look at alternatives?

"We did it because we didn't have any choices. We were looking just for survival." Over a period of several months, Harry got them to agree to collaborate because it meant more business for everyone. EBC also brought a national marketing capability to a group of companies that otherwise couldn't afford to do it themselves. Let's be clear. One of the things that Harry was selling was Harry – an experienced go-getter in a mature industry.

Along the way, he had inadvertently formed a manufacturing alliance, now known as a flexible-manufacturing network. The network is also able to provide better customer service.

There have always been prime/subcontractor arrangements in the industries EBC serves, but the unique idea behind Harry's flexible network was to share proprietary business information and to have employees from all companies collaborate at all levels.

For example, Brown wanted to know how the vendor was going to execute his part of the fabrication process, whether the vendor could think of a way that he, or Erie Bolt, could improve or simplify the process or make it cheaper.

Brown wanted to be able to send his engineers to the vendor's shop with suggestions or to try something new. They were going to collaborate. Employees, after all, work better when they know how their jobs fit into the whole project. If they know the process, they can often figure out ways to improve it or shorten it or make it faster or cheaper. Why, Brown reasoned, wouldn't the same psychology work with vendors? Besides, reducing outside processing costs was a significant part of the EBC turnaround plan.

EBC and its "collaborators" also share some expensive technology. One example is a full set of calibrated gauges and manufacturers' specifications maintained at EBC and shared with local manufacturers.

EBC also shares engineering support, sales advice – even manufacturing equipment. For example, EBC gladly shares its electronic data interchange (EDI) expertise and inventory database with team members working on the same job. EBC also helped members with other technology problems such as installing computer numeric control systems on their machine tools.

Another reason this worked – besides Harry's powers of persuasion – is that small manufacturers are not large manufacturers. For obvious reasons, decisions and behaviors are often driven by resource limitations.

Brown reasoned that by banding together, the group could do more research and development, purchase materials at lower prices and share training costs.

Other advantages of forming a manufacturing alliance include better access to financing, shared marketing costs, increased distribution, quicker production, sharing cutting edge technology, and wider market penetration.

The team approach has helped each member reach independent goals in ways otherwise not possible. In Brown's case, his goal was big contracts that were beyond his reach.

Each year, sales at the now-profitable EBC Industries company grow by 10 to 12 percent. But Brown adds that young companies joining the network have sometimes seen even greater sales growth – as much as 50 to 80 percent. EBC has grown from less than $4 million in sales to more than $10 million annually.

Marketing/Sales

EBC Industries developed a marketing plan for the network.

They had an experienced marketing manager in Norman Strandwitz, who had already recruited five independent rep firms to explore new market opportunities around the United States. In representing all network companies, they needed to focus their marketing efforts on those accounts that best fit the network members and gave them a chance to improve profitability as well as sales.

To do this, they developed a marketing plan with the following steps:

- Assessment – Network Member Capabilities
- Customer Needs/Market Opportunity
- Customer Profitability and Sales Potential Profiles
- Marketing Support
- Strategic Focus.

While this is a lot of work for one company, it was not twelve times the work – since there was a great deal of overlap and synergy. Here are the results of each of these steps described in more detail.

Step 1: Assessment

The marketing program began with a complete assessment of all members manufacturing capabilities, machine tools, and core competencies of each company.

Step 2: Customer Needs/Market Opportunity

VP Norman Strandwitz examined customer needs through trial and error selling with the objective of finding contract opportunities that related to network capabilities.

Step 3: Customer Profitability and Sales Potential

They examined each new customer in terms of profitability, sales growth potential, and the cost of support. This information allowed them to focus on the best market niches and customers.

Step 4: Customer Profiles

They developed customer profiles in terms of NAICS codes, company size, and other factors that would help the sales department find similar prospect companies. All of the customer information was installed in a database after every quote or order.

Step 5: Marketing Support

EBC (as the prime company) provided all marketing and sales support. It offered the network members the sales coverage of their independent reps. It also developed promotion programs that generated leads for the reps and sales literature, which described the capabilities of the network. Its sales engineering department responded with prompt quotations and samples, and developed profiles of the best customers.

Step 6: Strategic Focus

This was a major task. EBC needed to make changes in internal operations and business strategy.

The marketing program and a commitment to satisfy all of their customers drove many internal changes to both EBC and the network companies. The changes were focused on areas where improvement could be seen and mattered to the customer.

For EBC, the areas of change included the organization's structure, Rapid Response Manufacturing, Lean Manufacturing methods, implementation of ISO 9002, and employee training.

Organization

The organizational model used for this network was not new. It was a typical prime contractor/subcontractor arrangement, common in the aerospace and other industries. In the typical prime/sub relationship the prime handles all customer contact, marketing, administration, project management, and contractual issues.

What is uniquely different about this network is how the members shared proprietary information and the quality and manufacturing standards EBC imposed on all members. All subcontract members had to pass a quality and manufacturing audit once a year to continue as members of the network.

Case #2 - Outsourcing Business Alliance
Anson Stamping Company
Forming a Business Alliance with Three Competitors

John Anson, having established himself as a leader for 30 years in the business of metal removal and equipment rebuilding, launched an ambitious new venture into the business of metal forming.

He started Anson Stamping Company, Inc. (ASCO) in Louisville, Kentucky, in January 1994. What is unique about ASCO is that it has become a partnership with John's competitors – described in economic development circles as a flexible manufacturing network or supplier alliance.

Anson had been calling on the General Electric plant in Bloomington, Indiana, for 30 years. One day, he decided to ask for the opportunity to bid on the pre-painted steel blanks and stamping used in GE side-by-side refrigerators, as well as stamping the unfinished galvanized blanks for their profile washer.

GE's reaction to this brash request to bid on this business, was a resounding no. In fact, the answer was no the next two or three times John asked to bid on the business. GE felt that John's company was simply too small to take on this kind of commitment and business.

John, however, is not a person to give up easily. He went back to Louisville and decided to talk to his two largest competitors about forming a network. He recruited Stauble Tool and Die and Spaulding & Day Tool and Die to become partners in a new company that would become a manufacturing network.

At first, both companies were reluctant to even discuss a partnership. Then John told them the contract potential was $10 to $15 million a year.

Anson then set to work developing a formal proposal to convince GE that the new company could handle the business. The proposal included details on how they would jointly handle production, contract management, and quality standards. The proposal included proprietary information on the company labor rates, machine capacities, and plant capacity.

John also developed a formal agreement that described how they would do business and share profits and the specific tooling they would need to purchase from GE. All companies were required to share proprietary financial information in order to put together this proposal.

After several meetings and a thorough analysis of the proposal, GE awarded ASCO the job. At that point, John had to find the equipment and people to get the work done immediately. John's company, Anson Tooling, acted as the prime contact for the network, and handled all administrative, contractual, and marketing calls.

The New Manufacturing Plant

John formed ASCO in June 1994 and moved into a separate building with 150,000 feet of manufacturing space. As part of the agreement, he had to transfer 275 specialized tools from GE ($7,000,000 worth of tooling). He moved, reconditioned, and installed more than 30 stamping presses. He put in one cut-to-length line and one slitter line.

It took six months for them to set up the tooling and get the plant operational but they were totally ready to produce orders by the end of 1994.

ASCO now runs three shifts. On a typical day they process more than 500,000 pounds of metal. More than one million pounds of material is cut to length on a weekly basis.

In months, the network was producing 400 different blanks and stampings. Some blanks are up to 16 feet long with tolerances as tight as 0.005 inches. Moreover, panel flatness was essential.

With demands such as this, purchasing the correct processing equipment was an absolute must. According to Anson, "We have done a significant amount of large blank development, which, to my knowledge, has not been accomplished at this size and gauge of metal while holding the flatness that we do. Furthermore, we are stacking and shipping orders 105 miles on a just-in-time basis. Any flaw in this expensive pre-painted material and it has to be scrapped, so our equipment has to perform."

ASCO has never shut a customer down. What's more, they can't. Customers have come to count on his company as an integral part of their just-in-time supply chain.

Bottom Line Outcomes

The ASCO network is a perfect example of an opportunity driven network. John Anson first focused on the opportunity for the GE contract, and then designed the organization, purchased the equipment, and hired the people to carry out that contract.

The network was financed exclusively with private money, and did not use state or federal grant money for any activities.

Here is a brief summation of some of the outcomes from this network:

1. The partners invested $27,000,000 into the new network partnership including $7,000,000 of tooling purchased from General Electric.
2. The network has created 200 new jobs and has a payroll of more than $5,000,000 per year.
3. The network has a vendor base of more than 300 supplier companies and there are other informal networks among ASCO's vendor base.

4. Finding and hiring skilled people is a problem for all manufacturing companies, but John Anson aggressively tried to solve the work force problems. The company started its own apprenticeship program to train both machine shop and tool and die employees.

5. John also formed a separate network that created a daycare and adult education center. The adult education center uses touchtone screens to help people with literacy problems and to help people get their GED certificate.

6. Anson uses a human resource specialist who does a skill analysis on all employees in the network to help determine skill efficiencies and job interest.

7. The network has been a phenomenal success in terms of revenue. The original forecast was for $13,000,000 in sales. When the dust settled, the network had achieved more than $60,000,000 in sales revenue the first year. In the second year ASCO reached $120,000,000 in sales and successfully negotiated contracts in other GE divisions in Norwalk, Ohio, and Erie, Pennsylvania. John Anson's long term goal for the network is to do $500,000,000 in five years.

Advances in Technology

Among other things, the ASCO network has proven that it is possible for competitors to collaborate and share information and cooperate on joint projects that would lead to improvements in technology.

For instance, the network spent more than a year obtaining an ISO 9002 certification and the company started another program to achieve the QS 9000 certification in 1996.

Being a customer- and market-driven company has also forced many other changes by ASCO to stay up with customer needs, such as:

1. Offering solid modeling capabilities to all of their customers.
2. Using pro-engineer software to do rapid prototype modeling.
3. Using composites to reduce the cost of metal dies and to have low cost "throw away" dies for short production runs.

4. Developing a specialized production software program that tracks steel coil, controls the inventory, has a cost accounting package, and keeps track of machine times.
5. Using the University of Louisville facilities. They can offer stereo lithography to create paper molds.
6. They have designed a new blanking press operation.

Strength in Marketing and Sales

ASCO is truly a market-driven network looking for market opportunities. This is largely because of John Anson's sales and marketing skills and his knowledge of the marketplace; you will find "Kentucky's number one salesman" printed on his business card.

The phenomenal success of the ASCO network is not only a tribute to his aggressive and persistent sales efforts, but it makes a strong case that the inscription on his card may be an understatement. Yes, John Anson is a terrific salesman, but it's more than a one-time sale. He focuses on building long-term relationships with customers and he knows that real sales success is built on repeat business.

Being able to focus in the marketplace and uncover contract opportunities is the expertise missing from most U.S. manufacturing networks.

John Anson feels there are many other opportunities out there to create networks like ASCO, but that it requires persistent selling and market focus to find them.

The Spawning of Other Networks

Anson is fond of saying that he found the original contract opportunity from outsourcing and that his network is now "outsourcing the outsourcing to other vendors."

"Outsourcing the outsourcing" suggests that there may be many other network possibilities within the vendor and supplier base.

At this point, ASCO has informal network relationships with a variety of key vendors, but there are also opportunities to form an international network now that they have ISO 9002 and are working on Six Sigma certifications. The networking idea with sub networks allows ASCO to offer value added services in stamping, tooling, fixtures and gauges, equipment rebuild, design engineering, consulting, new equipment, parts, assemblies, finishes, and an information bank.

In addition to the vendor networks, ASCO is a member of a Michigan network called Decorative Castings. This is a network of 12 different vendors formed to manufacture door handles for the auto industry.

They have a contract to handle Buick door handles, which will produce $25 to $30 million in sales per year. But the network is after more business and is looking for contracts with Ford and Pontiac. All members of this network have to be ISO 9000 certified and all of the companies are in Michigan – except for John's company in Louisville, Kentucky.

Results

ASCO may be the best example of a manufacturing network in the United States. It's certainly the best example that I know of. But if you have some examples you think I should know about, please share your knowledge and experience. (I can be reached at mpcmgt@att.net.) Clearly, good networks require excellent marketing/sales, investment, technical innovation, training, skilled people, and visionary owners. The type of network that can generate this kind of revenue and can become self-sustaining without government funds has all the opportunities and problems of other start up companies. But even though the ASCO type network requires a great deal of effort and investment, the payoffs can be phenomenal.

In terms of true economic development, ASCO created 200 new jobs in the first year without any government assistance. When you think of how much state economic development departments are paying to attract foreign companies in terms of tax abatements and other incentives to just locate a plant that would create 200 jobs, it makes creation of an ASCO manufacturing type network perhaps one of the great economic development bargains of all times. Perhaps the success of ASCO will also make the venture capital community and other investors sit up and take notice of what can be done with manufacturing networks.

Case #3 – Exploring Foreign Markets
Western Canada Marine Group
Mission Development: An Alliance of Six Companies Building a Ship for a Foreign Country

In the early 1990s, the ship building industry in Vancouver was declining – as in most of North America. Shipyards, naval architects, and manufacturers of marine equipment were all wondering how they could survive and stimulate their businesses, and where they could find new customers and markets for their products and services.

Dave Longdale, a person familiar with shipbuilding in many parts of the world, decided to do something about the problem. In 1992, he approached the British Columbia Trade Organization to do a market assessment and to act as a facilitator (with BC Trade) to get interested companies together to look for new market opportunities.

Longdale understood that no one small company was going to be able to solve this problem but he reasoned that a consortium of companies might be able to pool their resources and find new markets. They invited more than 30 local marine companies to a meeting to discuss this alliance idea and to examine the possibilities of export markets.

After many meetings and a practical selection process, the group was first reduced to twenty-one companies, and finally to five marine equipment firms and a design house. Each of these companies was committed to investing the necessary time and money to form this network.

The original strategy of the network was to concentrate on the marketing of two vessel designs and to construct and outfit the hull of the ship in a developing country. The network was only interested in contracts for new vessels and the spare parts business they could get over the long term.

Their specific objective was to find new markets and new opportunities for contracts in smaller countries around the world, which could bring each of the network members increased sales and profitability.

They wanted to use government assistance only for the initial market assessment and to help organize the network. They specifically wanted to develop a network that was self-sustaining and would operate on internally generated funds without government subsidies.

Market Assessment

Perhaps the most critical step in developing any network is spending the time and money to assess market opportunities. BC Trade sponsored part of the market assessment project and put up most of the money to do the preliminary market research.

Dave Longdale, however, did most of the field research himself, and explored contract opportunities in Indonesia, Malaysia, Korea, South Africa and Chile during the original market assessment and sales prospecting campaign.

The networks decided to focus exclusively on two main products – offshore patrol vessel and ferry designs. These vessels had already been designed by one of the network members, and Dave felt that they could find a very specific market niche in smaller developing countries.

After completing the market assessment they projected market potential for these specific products around the world as $300 million. 40% of this would be Canadian content. Longdale traveled extensively during the first four years, including four trips to Asia in 1996, establishing personal contacts and relationships with the prospects.

Organization and Management

The group was called Western Canada Marine Group and it was organized as a for-profit corporation. Dave made sure no competitors were in the network. They didn't want to have to deal with the tensions and proprietary information problems that are inherent in having competitor companies in the same organization.

The six companies selected were all committed to developing export markets, all had some previous exposure to export markets, and each was willing to invest $5,000 to buy stock in this new corporation.

Dave Longdale acted as president and as a board member, but he was not an investor. The president of each member company was also a board member of the network company. All shares were equal, and some decisions required a total consensus of all shareholders.

However, in most cases, a simple majority would rule. Each member then made another investment of $10,000 four months after the corporation was originally started.

The corporate charter included a business agreement between members that spelled out bidding processes, production, and other legal issues involved in contracts. The agreement also included a code of ethics for the network and all of the boilerplate usually involved in defining shares of the corporation including member termination and addition.

Their plan was for the corporation to accept the first major contract from the customer and sub contract to each member. Each member had to submit a bid and a budget for their share of the work, and there was an administrative process to oversee the budget results from each member company. The five primary network members (one company was eventually dropped) sub-contracted their work to smaller suppliers. Ultimately, more than 100 local suppliers in the Vancouver area benefited from the contract.

The corporation began with a budget and sales forecast. The budget was reevaluated every two months. All dividends flowed through to members. Initially, the corporation did not retain any of the profits.

Each member company made money on their bid part of the project, and all members shared any excess profits left over when the contract was complete.

Securing the first order required an overall budget of more than $160,000. This financed sales trips, travel, brochures, administration, and all of the communication expenses involved in large bids.

Going after large ship orders also required insurance from a government agency (the Export Development Corporation) that would protect each member company during the contract against nonpayment by the customer. This insurance cost the companies $100,000.

Results

One of the inquiries they received through the Canadian Government early in the market assessment was from Mauritius, an island nation in the Indian Ocean, off Madagascar. They were looking for an offshore patrol vessel. The network spent $160,000 on the design and the proposal, and finally secured a $20 million contract for the vessel.

Approximately $5 million of the contract was paid to a shipyard in Chile. The balance went through the network and their suppliers in British Columbia.

The relationship with the Chilean shipyard was successful and a separate joint venture to market the shipyard into selected markets was proposed and developed. However, this did not prove to be a practical strategy and was abandoned by the network.

A Summary of What Worked and Didn't Work:

1. **Organization.** Dave Longdale's assumption that a small core group of investor companies was the best organization to create a network turned out to be critical. He was correct. Eliminating the competitors and the companies that did not have a serious interest in export eliminated many of the organization and trust problems seen in similar networks.

2. **Investment Strategy.** Beginning with a $5,000 investment, each member became an investor rather than a member. This was critical to getting the network mission off the ground. Dave Longdale feels that any network looking for a meaningful export opportunity should be ready to invest a minimum of $100,000 per year or they will have very little chance of finding real opportunities. There is little evidence in Canada or the U.S. that export networks with marketing missions can be achieved without serious up-front investment (relying on member dues or grants will not work).

3. **A Good Mix.** One of the six members was a very large company in British Columbia – the Caterpillar dealer, Finning Inc. – that, according to Dave, added both stability to the group and some

professional management needed to help keep the entrepreneur-ial smaller companies moving forward.

4. **Small and Flexible at the Top.** The network organization turned out to be a very flexible and low overhead organization, which works very well for specific project or contract opportunities.

5. **A Clear Agreement.** Spending the time to develop the 21-page agreement that defined all the legal and business procedures turned out to be a very good investment and avoided many of the member disputes and defections that have plagued many U.S. networks.

6. **The Market.** The market assessment was also a critical factor because it allowed the network to do formal market research on many market niches around the world and the field work to also do research/sales prospecting. The market assessment and Dave's field work resulted in a $20 million contract and eventually developed more than $450 million of active bids.

   Note: Using only market research is usually inadequate when you need to find specialized market niche opportunities. Dave Long-dale's field research and sales calls in the target countries were critical to "filling in the blanks," developing the market opportu-nities, and describing the sales potential. His communication of these sales opportunities also kept the network companies inter-ested enough to provide ongoing funding of the project.

7. **Need.** There was a pressing economic need to develop the network. The ship building business was under severe pressure in North America. The incentive to create the network and find new export markets was much greater than it might be with the average U.S. network, which is usually just looking for additional sales.

Conclusion

In 1999, Miles and Snow published a working paper "The Concept of the Corporation in the Twenty First Century." This paper makes the case that a new type of corporation is emerging to replace the old functional and division models. They see four major trends that will challenge and change business organizations in the 21st century:

1. Markets will become more global.
2. The pace of product and technological change will accelerate.
3. Customers will increasingly demand individualized attention and customization.
4. Managers and workers will increasingly insist on participation ownership.

Their prediction is more than prophetic. All of these things have already happened. The need for the new organization in manufacturing is upon us.

Very few manufacturing companies will have the luxury of remaining in their traditional "Defender" organizations – even though this had previously been adequate. Today the real question is how much do you need to change your organization and how fast?

Key Points

If your manufacturing company decides to develop a growth plan based on finding new customers and markets, the decision will require that the company organization must be able to respond fast, be more flexible, explore market niches, monitor customers better, and develop new product ideas. This type of organization is called a Prospector organization. The Prospector model is described in detail on pages 158 and 159. There is no universal model or method for developing a Prospector organization but the obvious goal is to get away from the limitations of the traditional manufacturing organization – the Defender or pyramid model. The specific objectives are to improve the following.

- The way you monitor customers and prospects
- Response time to customers and prospects
- The speed of decision making
- Communication between departments and functions
- Order processing.

Suggested Action

If you are not convinced that you need to move towards a decentralized or Prospector type of organization, then you need to do some investigation. Begin by defining customer needs and working backwards. A good way to proceed is to trace an order through the organization and determine the problems encountered at every level of the organization. I like to do this on butcher paper because you can show the whole process from the first request for a quotation to the final customer service problems. The idea is to determine what you need to change or improve in the organization to solve customer problems and delays.

Notes:

1. Ricardo Semler, *Maverick: The Success Story Behind the World's Most Unusual Workplace* (Warner Books, 1995).

2. Raymond E. Miles and Charles C. Snow, *Organizational Strategy, Structure, and Process* (Standard University Press, 2003).

3. Raymond E. Miles and Charles C. Snow, *Fit, Failure and the Hall of Fame* (New York: The Free Press, 1994), 13.

Chapter 7
Cost Reduction and Continuous Improvement

The 1980s and 1990s marked the initial adjustment and operational changes to what we would come to refer to as "globalization." Most of the solutions were "internal" changes to reduce cost such as:

- Downsizing and flattening hierarchical organizations
- Outsourcing – both locally and internationally
- Implementing Lean Manufacturing and JIT (just-in-time) methods
- Bringing "IT" into the mix – implementing a host of information technology hardware and software.

That was twenty years ago. All of this talk about changing times now seems somewhat dated and a step behind. Times aren't changing – they have already changed and those changes appear permanent. The real question is what are manufacturers going to do to adapt to the new marketplace and the new level of customer demands?

Now that we are into a new century, the pressures from globalization have increased and, in most cases, purchasing power has been centralized. Good examples of this are the mega-chain, "big box" U.S. retailers like Wal-Mart, Costco, and Target. They buy from giant consumer goods manufacturers like P&G, Kraft, Del Monte, Unilever, and Nestle, to name just a few.

In the first decade of the 21st Century only 10 of these "mass channel" retailers at the top of the chain "account for some 80% of the average manufacturer's business. This compares to about 30% for the top ten just two decades ago."[1]

To make it even more interesting, most of these giant retailers are now creating their own private-label brands that are often 10% below the prices of the consumer goods manufacturers. Between these private brands and the products they import from overseas, retailers are forcing big price concessions from manufacturers. As their margins shrink through discounts, the manufacturers look at the overall costs of their products.

Part of the cost of each brand is the capital equipment they buy from their Tier 1 and Tier 2 vendors. They in turn ask for a proportional decrease in prices from the equipment manufacturers.

The equipment manufacturers then have to ask for a discount from their smaller vendors, so the pressure for price discounts cascades down the entire supply chain.

Reducing Costs and Maintaining Margins

Lean Manufacturing techniques are being used by many U.S suppliers to reduce costs and drive waste out of their organizations. Because of the continuous pressure to lower prices, Lean Manufacturing is one of the first methods every manufacturer should employ to be competitive.

First a word of support for all of you manufacturers that aren't familiar with Lean Manufacturing. Over the last 30 years we have had a number of three letter acronym programs that were all meant to save American Manufacturing. Programs like MRP, JIT, TQM, ISO, and ERP, not to mention benchmarking, Six Sigma, and Lean Manufacturing. Each has been sold as a "magic key" answer to all manufacturing problems. Well, the truth is, each one of these programs has delivered some success but none of them are the universal answer they are often touted to be.

The well-meaning proponents of these programs generally ignore the fact that manufacturers are not a homogeneous group and one size will not fit all. Too often, the implication is that every manufacturer must do every part of the process improvement program regardless of their size and resources.

The (Collins) Classification system we discussed in Chapter 1 makes the case that any new program or system must be adapted to the size, resources, knowledge, and type of manufacturing. The Toyota Production System, which certainly works for Toyota, will not work for Sam's Fabrication Shop. In fact, it very well could cause cash flow problems.

A second (and often overlooked) point is that systems that work for the manufacture of standard products do not necessarily work for custom manufacturing and job shops. Later in this chapter, we'll show a good example of the anomalies of custom products.

"One Size Fits All" vs. "Right-Sizing"

The truth is, there is a lot of common sense and useful ideas in every one of these programs. But, you must be careful about adopting generic approaches. The "one size fits all" approach simply does not work. To be successful, the approach must fit the size, resources, and understanding of the manufacturers.

That said, I will try to avoid duplicating the thousands of articles written about Lean Manufacturing by simply summarizing the major parts of the program and supporting them with real life examples that show us how these principles can help.

The Lean Manufacturing objectives are simple:

- Do it right the first time
- Partner with suppliers
- Create a culture of "continuous improvement."

Now who would ever argue against these common sense objectives? Who would not agree with the virtues of these practices? Proponents of Lean Manufacturing say that in 3–5 years, the following overall performance gains are typical of a Lean conversion:

- Defects reduced by 20% per year with zero defects performance possible
- Delivery lead times reduced by more that 75%
- On time delivery improved to 99% plus
- Productivity (sales per employee) increases of 15%-35% per year
- Inventory (working capital) reductions of more than 75%
- Return on assets improvement of 100%.

So with these kinds of results why isn't every manufacturer in the U.S. standing in line for their "Lean Conversion"? As we've discussed, customers are driving cost reduction, zero defects, shorter delivery, on time delivery, etc.

The problem is that while the basic principals may be simple, applying them to hundreds of different industries, thousands of different companies, and millions of different products and services is actually quite problematic.

Just as in the application of industrial marketing techniques, one solution does not fit all. While the principals are valid, the specific application must take the following into consideration:

- Leadership
- Ownership
- Level of knowledge
- Sophistication of systems
- Capital
- Cash flow
- Customization of products and services.

Lean Manufacturing principles are tools. You can't fit the problem to the tools; you must fit the tools to the problems.

This is most easily explained by examining approaches used by some different types of manufacturers. But before explaining these approaches, let's examine the eight primary Lean Manufacturing tools.

1. **Value Stream Mapping** – VSM maps the flow, material, and information from in the door materials and out the door as finished goods.

2. **Five S** – The Five S's of good housekeeping are:
   - Sort – separate out unnecessary things
   - Straighten – arrange things into essential order
   - Scrub – keep machines and work areas clean
   - Stabilize – make checking and cleaning a standard practice
   - Sustain – make Five S's a way of life.

3. **Total Productive Maintenance** – TPM aims at reducing equipment downtime to zero.

4. **Kaizen Blitz** – Lightning-fast continuous improvement. It is an intense, focused improvement to a specific process.

5. **Quick Changeover** – Operators are empowered to reduce "make ready" or "set up times" and increase run speed of machines.

6. **Cellular Flow** – This is combining manual and machine operators to improve the flow of products by reducing wait time, movement of parts, and inventory.

7. **Pull/Kanban** – This means replacing only those parts that have been used in assembly and not using inventories as a backup.

8. **Empowered Work Team** – Lean practices are accomplished by an empowered work team that diagnoses problems, brainstorms, and implements the solution.

So far, so good. There are few if any supply chains or industries that are immune to the pressures for price reduction. Every manufacturer, from the tiniest job shop to large product manufacturers must implement some kind of cost reduction just to "stay in the game."

The problem is that Type 1, 2, 3, and 4 manufacturers are very different in terms of resources, management, knowledge, and financing.

With that in mind, the following four case studies will show you how four different manufacturers approached cost reduction. These manufacturers represent a wide range of manufacturing technologies. All were under some sort of pressure to reduce costs and improve operations.

The four examples are:

- Minster Machine Company
- American Licorice
- Sexton Can
- Jacquart Fabric Products

In each case, you will see how they selected their own "recipe" of Lean Manufacturing tools and techniques to achieve their goals.

Minster Machine Company – Minster Ohio

Founded in 1896, the Minster Machine Company has over 100 years of experience in developing manufacturing equipment and clutch and brake technology for the metal forming industry. Minster built its first mechanical press 76 years ago and has a global reputation for supplying high quality products that are known for their durability, technology and production enhancements.

Minster Machine is an exceptional manufacturer. They have always been the leader in innovation, design, and quality. Their brochures say, "Our competitors may try to claim superior designs or features, but the fact remains that they can't measure up when you compare 'apples to apples.'"

To make this point another way, in the 1950s there were approximately 20 companies manufacturing presses in the U.S. The U.S. was still the world leader in machine tools.

Then, in the 1960s, things began to change, and countries like Germany and Japan began marketing their machine tools in the U.S. The big recession of the early 1980s resulted in many American machine tool manufacturers going out of business. In fact, by 2001, Minster was the only significant U.S.-owned stamping press manufacturer remaining.

Besides quality and innovative new products, Minster Machine's primary competitive advantages include:

- Willingness to adapt machines to satisfy unique customer needs
- Exceptional parts and service support
- An ongoing system that gathers customer, competitor, and market information
- A relentless pursuit of finding ways to assure the success of their customers.

All of these factors contributed to their growth as an international supplier with plants in Minster, Ohio, and Beaufort, South Carolina. Minster also has sales and service facilities in Germany and most recently, in association with AMT, in China.

Minster Machine has survived a depression, two World Wars, seven recessions, and the invasion of foreign competitors and has continued to grow. All of this despite the revolutionary changes in manufacturing.

However, by the '90s, globalization had begun to seriously affect Minster Machine's customers. These customers had to reengineer themselves to compete in the global metal-forming markets and they needed price concessions from their suppliers. No longer was it possible to pass on cost increases to the customers every year. In fact, there was constant pressure to discount prices. This finally led management to the conclusion that they would have to find a way to reduce internal costs and eliminate waste anywhere they could.

Joe Kumpf, Director of Operations, was intrigued by the concept of Lean Manufacturing. He and his staff began by reading many books, visiting other manufacturers and attending Lean seminars. One book of particular interest was "Speed to Market" by Vincent Bozzone. The book was about doing Lean Manufacturing for job shops and made a lot of sense to management.

The Operations staff continued to learn all they could about Lean, including the development of their own in-house simulation exercise.

However, most literature and available expertise on the subject was related to standard products and used examples of the Toyota Production System, which did not translate to the problems with low-volume, custom-designed and -manufactured machines. They knew Lean Manufacturing could work for them, but they could not see how to implement Lean Manufacturing the way it was written in most books.

Joe wanted help from someone who understood the peculiarities of a custom manufacturer. He found that person in Mike O'Donnell, a manufacturing consultant from the CAMP MEP Center in Cleveland, Ohio.

Mike began the process by training 63 people in an overview of Lean Manufacturing principals in a three-hour session.

After this training 18 people were picked from a variety of different departments to attend a five-day boot camp to learn to use the basic tools of Lean Manufacturing. These people became the "Lean Champions" and the backbone of the Lean initiative. In addition, many of these people have progressed to become Lean facilitators and effectively guide Kaizen events to achieve desired results.

Most Lean programs begin with a Value Stream Mapping process. Value Stream Mapping (VSM) is the creation of a material and information flow map of a product or process to identify areas of improvement opportunity. Minster Machine chose to skip this step, because they had already identified key waste projects in the Value Stream.

Instead, they chose to begin with the Kaizen methodology. Kaizen is an intensive and focused approach to process improvement. Kaizen means "continuous improvement." Kaizen empowers teams to rapidly develop improvements to specific problems in the process. Kaizen can employ other lean tools such as Kanban, setup reduction, line balancing and the Five S's.

The Kaizen approach of process improvement defines team boundaries, the sponsor, the project charter, and a method of reporting the results.

Initially, Minster Machine selected six high-priority shop projects for the Kaizen Team. The team achieved savings or improvements of 25-80% on the projects with an average of 35%. Today, Minster does one or two factory Kaizen events every month. Doing these events is seen as the new paradigm for continuous improvement in the manufacturing environment and is considered to be a perpetual activity.

To increase or even maintain profitability, manufacturers can no longer simply raise prices. Instead, like Minster Machine, SMMs will have to lower costs. Lean Manufacturing is a proven method of lowering costs by eliminating non-value added activities, reducing waste and creating flow throughout the company. It is a long-term plan to streamline your manufacturing company for the future.

American Licorice – Alsip, Illinois

A candy manufacturer in Mexico approached American Licorice with a challenge it couldn't refuse. The Mexican manufacturer claimed it could produce the company's candy cheaper than the American plants. Corporate agreed to a trial. The results shook the management teams in the Alsip, IL, and California plants to their core. The Mexican plant produced the candy for "a lot less," says James Marturano, director of World Class Manufacturing at the Alsip plant.

Instead of moving production south, management in Alsip believed that Lean would answer the Mexican offer. Marturano called South Suburban College, an affiliate of the Chicago Manufacturing Center, to assist in staging a one-week Lean brainstorming event at the plant. Ten to 12 associates from across the company – from the shop floor to information technology to maintenance to the controller – attended. The team identified 75 areas to eliminate waste. By week's end the Alsip plant had reduced enough costs to be able to produce the candy at 50 percent less than the Mexican plant. "From the model, we saw it was possible to make candy in Alsip at our current wage and compete with Mexico," says Marturano.

Marturano says a key problem for the plant was the handling and re-handling of materials. Therefore, most of the cost savings came in reducing wasted motions. For example, for the beans, line team members repositioned the packaging machine to where the candy came off the line. Marturano says that made it possible for one team leader to handle both the panning and packaging area.

For management who might have feared a huge capital investment in going Lean, Marturano is pleased to report 80 percent of the changes American Licorice made have come from people and ideas.

Other results in this first year of a multi-year transition process have been just as impressive.

- The cellular processing structure has allowed associates to better view the production process and to increase productivity. For example, in the two-ounce licorice line of candy, productivity is up 30 to 35 percent. The team on the vertical form and fill machine increased productivity 64 percent.
- Scrap is down by 50 percent.
- Increased flexibility means the company can get new products out to market faster.
- Lean is proving to be a good selling tool in demonstrating American Licorice can give customers the best value and the best products.
- Corporate culture has undergone a metamorphosis from an

autocratic structure to one that embraces empowerment. For example, Marturano says one team was investigating new equipment and decided they didn't need $500 of extra bells and whistles. That, he says proudly, was a huge cultural shift.

Marturano is most proud of this latest statistic from American Licorice's accounting department. For every one dollar the company spends on Lean, it gets back two dollars.

Sexton Can Company – Martinsburg, West Virginia

Sexton Can Company also goes back to the 1890s. The company began by selling paint containers to hardware stores and also produced funnels, measuring cans, and caskets.

Over the years, Sexton has developed vital manufacturing competencies such as deep drawing, ironing, and decorating as well as press technology. Sexton has pioneered the use of drawn containers where none were previously used and has the capacity to develop and produce seamless containers specifically designed for each customer's needs.

Sexton has supplied the electronics industry with drawn steel containers since the 1930s and the automotive filter industry since the 1950s. It developed the first drawn and ironed steel aerosol container in the 1970s. Today, Sexton has two manufacturing plants: the filter and electronics facility in Martinsburg, West Virginia, and an aerosol facility in Decatur, Alabama.

Sexton's primary competitive advantage is it can manufacture a huge range of sizes, in small lots, and meet accelerated delivery requirements. The company has been ingenious in designing its own proprietary hydraulic presses and processes and can produce high-quality steel containers at very competitive prices.

Sexton Can has survived several wars, many recessions and all of the changes to their products for many years. A great deal of their success is that they have continued to develop specialized products for niche markets where they could gain a competitive advantage and maintain profitability.

But, in recent years, pressure from foreign suppliers and powerful customers has made life tougher. It was obvious to company management that the plants needed to step up efforts to reduce cost and waste through a program of Lean Manufacturing.

Yurij Wowczuk was assigned as the new plant manager in 2004 to begin the process of change that would lead to continuous improvement. Yurij decided to begin with the Five S's. He selected a cross-functional team consisting of production, maintenance, engineering, and continuous improvement.

The team began by identifying the "low hanging fruit" – areas most in need of attention in terms of clean up that could yield the quickest results.

They immediately found waste in the following areas:

- Sort – tooling and maintenance (MRO) parts
- Straighten – hardware for routine line operation
- Scrub – areas around hydraulic units
- Stabilize – flow of metal blanks to the lines
- Sustain – fundamental housekeeping practices

The next problem they decided to tackle was changeover time. Changeover times were all driven by the type and quality of orders (some in very small lots).

Because Sexton has so many different products with short runs, it was common to change over a production 2-3 times per shift. Most of these changeovers were complicated and could take 6-8 hours to make the changeover, check the tolerances, and test the new final product.

The team brainstormed solutions and adopted a procedure that:

- Called out and labeled all parts required for the changeover, down to the washer
- Assembled parts into kits for storage
- Placed kits on carts that were placed near the machine at the exact time of changeover.

These new procedures and kits reduced changeover time on production lines by one third.

Another obvious issue was downtime on the lines. This was due to a wide range of causes. Since the company runs production on all 3 shifts, downtime meant lost production. The team attacked downtime using a Kaizen Event. They developed a procedure for the operator to record all reasons for downtime. The Kaizen team then met twice a week to discuss the causes and the solutions. Company management had adopted the 80/20 rule where they would focus on the 20% of problems that caused 80% of the downtime. The Kaizen realized immediate benefits and, over time, downtime was reduced by a further 5%.

It is worth pointing out that, for Sexton, some of the most accepted Lean tools could not be used cost effectively.

- Value Streaming Mapping was not useful because each production line began and ended with the same raw materials and groupings of production tools. Additionally, the finished product was individual stampings that did not require assembly or additional processing.
- Just-in-time inventories could not be used because it was impossible to get customer forecasts and the company had to keep large supplies of steel to meet deliveries.

Sexton Can is only at the beginning of their Lean journey, but they are committed to continuous improvement company wide. This case study suggests several conclusions.

One Size Does Not Fit All – An SMM should not try to adopt the same Lean process and tools used by Toyota. All Lean tools do not fit all manufacturing processes and should be adapted to the specific company (see FACTS).

All manufacturers need Lean Manufacturing – All SMMs have waste and opportunities for cost reduction. Finding the problems and solution is only limited by the number of people and their time.

Jacquart Fabric Products – Ironwood, Michigan

The apparel industry has been in the spotlight for the last 15 years as an American industry that is rapidly becoming a foreign industry. In the period from 1989 to 1999, according to the U.S. Department of Labor's Bureau of Labor Statistics, the apparel and other textiles industries lost 383,000 workers – almost one third of the entire industry. Since 1999, it is estimated that another 100,000 jobs have been lost.[2]

Most of these jobs were eliminated because of imported goods now manufactured in Vietnam, China, Pakistan, India, and other Asian countries.

It would appear at this time that we have a "Last Man Standing Scenario" and no U.S. manufacturers will be able to compete in the new century. However, this does not seem to be true. There are small American manufacturers in this sector that are not only surviving, but are thriving in the new economy.

Take, for instance, Jacquart Fabric Products in Ironwood on Michigan's Upper Peninsula. Bob Jacquart took over a small family business in 1971. Bob is proud of the fact that he is a significant employer in the small town of Ironwood and he can pay people a living wage and good benefits. This is at a time when so many small communities are losing manufacturing plants and the people have to rely on retail jobs like those at Wal-Mart and Target.

A Growing Company in a Shrinking U.S. Industry

Jacquart Fabric Products grew from $35,000 to $13,000,000 in 25 years and from 2 to 175 employees in the same time period. Jacquart's current success is based on their ability to quickly customize and deliver products. A good deal of their success has to do with implementing Lean Manufacturing methods.

Jacquart had already started down the manufacturing process improvement path to reduce costs when their biggest customer asked for greater product variety, more customization of that variety, faster delivery, and more services. Sales success in customized products always leads to production problems. The company began struggling with an unwieldy production system, inventories, quality, costs, and deliveries.

They knew it was time to re-examine their manufacturing processes to better handle these new customer and market needs. In the spring of

1998, Jacquart began working with Joe Boyle, a professional business advisor from Northern Initiatives, a Manufacturing Extension Center in Marquette, MI. The changes described in this case took place between early 1998 and Spring 2001.

Joe helped them begin their Lean Manufacturing journey with a Value Stream Mapping project and by appointing a mapping team. They began with a Kaizen blitz, and progressed to the other Lean Manufacturing projects described as follows:

- **Kaizen Blitz** – A Kaizen blitz helps the company quickly identify and implement solutions to bottlenecks. Northern Initiatives' Joe Boyle helped Jacquart through this event. It began with a six-week training program, during which employees were taught how to work together to diagnose problems and devise solutions. Jacquart had started this training because they knew they had to do something about their manufacturing costs. Specific techniques included Five S visual systems, cellular/flow manufacturing, and pull/Kanban systems.

  The mapping committee members quickly devised a compelling argument for changing the plant layout to move toward zero finished goods inventory. Using a modified blueprint of the plant floor with all the work areas, equipment, and inventory racks shown, the committee estimated the distance a dog bed had to travel to get out the door. Their calculations, based on input from other blitz team members, estimated the number of cycles needed to get parts to and from the cutting and sewing areas, and how many times finished goods went in and out of inventory before shipment. This was enough information to begin to eliminate the bottlenecks in production

- **Just-in-Time** – Within seven months, employee teams implemented a Just-in-Time work cell for the dog bed line. The just-in-time production process changed the flow of materials from cutting to sewing and from sewing straight to inspection and shipping.

- **Materials Resource Planning (MRP)** – A new MRP software system was installed to keep track of the thousands of pieces in production on any given day. MRP generates a daily cutting order, which is a task that used to require hours of manual work.

- **Automation** – In order to cut the material into accurate quantities, with little waste, and for Just-in-Time assembly, Jacquart purchased several automated cutting machines. These machines are programmed to deal with a variety of materials and sizes and efficiently cut the materials in small batches.

- **Design Team** – Having a product plan to introduce new products on a continual basis is the key to customization success. It requires monitoring the customers, market, and competitors to find ideas for future products. It also requires a design system that continuously develops ideas for new product prototypes. Jacquart employs a full-time team to develop new products. Their success in new products is due largely to their experience: Bob and his top managers have more than 30 years of custom-sewing and fabric-design experience. This allows them to incorporate a wide variety of sewing practices and skills to create hundreds of new designs. From the beginning Jacquart focused on low-volume, highly customized products and steered clear of the high-volume standard product markets. Those are the products that are going to Asia.

- **Local Service** – Jacquart has a definite advantage over foreign manufacturers when it comes to service. Located in Michigan, they can provide quick response to any customer problems compared to foreign manufacturers.

- **Special Services** – Besides customized products in a wide variety of colors and materials, Jacquart also offers embroidered names and special printing. You can buy a dog bed with the dog's name and breed embroidered on it and have it delivered in 48-72 hours. Now that is customization.

Let's quickly review some of the unique aspects that made Lean work for these companies.

- **Minster** hired a consultant to help translate the Toyota-style principles to their needs.

— As they got up to speed, they were able to skip certain steps, such as Value Stream Mapping, due to having gathered that data earlier.

— It was a company-wide effort, and a strong company culture helped get everyone to "buy in."

- **American Licorice** faced a shock to the system – foreign production that was much cheaper. Though they thought of themselves as a "relatively efficient" operation, their first efforts managed to beat the foreign price significantly.

  — This has inspired a cultural shift in the company, resulting in additional efficiency.

- **Sexton Can** skipped two major components that were not appropriate.

  — Sexton achieved the bulk of their improvements through application of Five S Guidelines.

- **Jacquart Fabrics** had a more traditional set of problems and value stream mapping was at the initial point of improvement.

  — Despite being very different from Toyota, here was a case where standard Lean techniques achieved good results almost across the board.

Clearly, one size does not fit all. And, just as clearly, intelligent application of the principles will almost always yield significant improvements.

Costs and Margins [Written by Charles France]

In the list of Six Essentials described in Chapter Two, Question #6 is, "Do you know if you are making adequate margins on each product line, model, or job?"

This question is extremely important because competing in any industry or supply chain where the customers are relentlessly forcing price reductions, will require better costing systems than most SMMs have used in the past.

This is particularly true if the customer wants a price quote on a large volume order or when the customer compares your prices to foreign competitors. In the auto and aerospace industries the larger customers are dictating the prices they want from their suppliers.

For a start, suppliers must have good enough cost information to know whether they should participate or drop out of the bidding process. Here are six typical examples:

1.   **How will SMMs establish prices and discounts?**

   Example – A tiny machine shop with fewer than five employees. The owner is a gifted toolmaker and leaves all of the accounting to the local CPA firm that also does his taxes. The owner has been in business for five years and only looks at the income statement every month to see if he is in the black. (He has no idea what to say about the balance sheet so he ignores it.)

   He has been setting prices by using estimated material costs and estimated hours per job. His hourly cost, or shop rate, is a number used by his friends in similar shops. For example, $40 per hour to cover overhead. Then he multiplies the estimated hours per job times his shop rate per hour, adds to this the amount of direct materials and an estimated profit margin to arrive at a price he thinks will sell the job. He doesn't know the true profit at this price because he's used estimates for direct labor and overhead.

   Thus, his price has more to do with whether he needs work (sales volume) than attaining a sufficient margin. He hardly ever goes back to check his operation sheet to see if his estimates were correct because he doesn't have time.

   But now, customers are asking him to discount his prices and he doesn't know what to say or do.

2.   **How can manufacturers determine a reliable pricing strategy that will allow them to estimate margins on each quotation or bid?**

   Example – A Type 2 machine shop with 50 employees that has annual sales of $5 million. This company has a work order system that captures direct labor, material costs, set-up times, and tooling.

However, they had purchased a generic accounting system when the company was founded and they use another software system that is supposed to estimate prices. But, the accounting software system is not designed to cost out "one-off" products and services and the estimating system has no real relationship to actual costs.

However, they keep using it because it is easy to use and up to this time they have managed to make some profits.

There is no way to establish either a pricing strategy or a target margin to examine each job without first establishing a "contribution margin." But what is a contribution margin and how do you determine it?

3. **How will manufacturers know if the company is breaking even each month based on the prices they are quoting?**

    Example – A small manufacturer of custom machinery that quotes every job with a custom price. The sales and shipments were never stable. They shipped machines in bunches every 2 –3 months. The boss never knew if he was breaking even or losing money- until the income statement finally came out. They couldn't determine breakeven because they had not separated fixed from variable costs and didn't know their contribution margin.

4. **How will manufacturers compete against foreign competitors who know their costs?**

    Example – A small niche manufacturer of wooden bar stools. This company had a good business selling high-quality bar stools to restaurants and bars in a local market. One day a customer told him that he could now source a similar bar stool from China for a price 50% less than his price. Because the American manufacturer did not have detailed costs of the components in his bar stool, he didn't know what to say or how to react.

5. **How will SMMs participate in supply chains without good cost/ margin information?**

Example – Large aerospace machine shop. Several years ago, I was conducting a workshop on finding new customers and markets on the West Coast. One of the participants was a high tech machine shop doing $40 million of work per year for a large aerospace customer. He had been doing the work for more than 20 years, and had made a large investment in special machine tools, quality systems, and employee training just for this customer.

One day the customer came to him and said that he needed an immediate reduction in U.S. supplier prices. After a few minutes of chitchat, the customer purchasing agent announced that he wanted a 20% discount to current prices for 3 years. If the supplier could comply, the customer would send him a contract immediately. The supplier was stunned and asked about the alternatives and what would happen if he couldn't offer the discount. The buyer said "either you take the deal or the work goes to Asia."

The small manufacturer wanted badly to take the deal because the customer's business was 65% of his total volume. But, he didn't know his costs well enough to make a good decision, and a bad decision might put him out of business.

6. **How will SMMs know what and when to outsource?**

Example – A manufacturer of packaging machinery. This is a Type 3 midsize manufacturer of packaging machinery that has been in operation for 50 years. They sell to large Fortune 500 type customers who are relentlessly pursuing price discounts and comparing their supplier prices to foreign competitors. One of their largest customers came to them and demanded a 50% price reduction on their equipment based on similar equipment built in China. They strongly suggested that at least 50% of the machines should be sourced from China or India.

But, the problem was that they did not have good enough cost information for any of their manufactured parts or weldments. Hence, the company couldn't ask for bids on their parts or weldments until they knew their own costs.

Each of these examples is based on a very real situation. And, in each case, it is pretty much a life or death situation. The conclusion? You and your company need to get a better grip on your own version of the cost/margin issue.

How to Get Started

Many SMMs have avoided having to deal with the cost/margin problem for a long time by using "rule of thumb" pricing or by using aggregate information from the income statement. But, playing in the new game of price reduction is much more serious and there is less room for error. Developing an improved cost system will be key to helping you find the right new customers and, most important, not taking orders that can put you out of business.

The research that led to the Collins Classification of Manufacturers shown in Chapter One revealed big differences in costing systems between Types 1, 2, and 3 manufacturers. The following solutions to these costing/discounting/pricing problems take into consideration the size, experience, and sophistication of the company. For Type 1 and Type 2 firms, there are seven things they should do.

1. Hire an advisor.
2. Reformat the income statement.
3. Implement procedures to capture actual direct labor and actual labor costs.
4. Prepare a budget.
5. Determine the margin/profitability of the firm and of products, work orders, or jobs.
6. Determine the minimum level of sales to generate a profit (breakeven sales).
7. Establish pricing policies.

Let's review these steps one by one.

1.   Hire an Advisor.

Hiring an advisor who has worked with manufacturers and is familiar with manufacturers' cost structures is usually very helpful. A bookkeeper or accountant would be preferable, since CPAs tend to be more focused on taxes and do not specialize in manufacturing cost accounting.

2.   **Reformat the Income Statement.**

Reformatting the income statement is needed to put costs into their appropriate place for subsequent cost analyses. My experience is that many small manufacturers' income statements do not break out cost of goods sold into direct materials, direct labor (typically "hands-on" labor), and manufacturing overhead (salaries and indirect labor for production employees, depreciation, etc.).

Frequently, these costs are commingled with other expenses, making it impossible to see them individually on the income statement. Reformatting the income statement will get all costs related to cost of goods together and all other expenses separated into sales and administrative expenses and will provide a more accurate picture of overall cost of goods and gross margins.

The benefit to revising the income statement is to properly report production and SG&A (sales, general, and administration) expenses so that effective cost analyses can be conducted on production, products, and manufacturing overhead – which are where most cost reductions and efficiency improvements occur. SG&A costs are less of a target for cost reduction because they're considered generally as fixed overhead.

3.   **Implement Procedures to Capture Actual Direct Labor and Actual Labor Costs.**

Good pricing requires a method to capture actual material and labor costs. Typically, Type 1 and Type 2 firms do not implement systems and procedures to capture actual material and labor costs needed to produce a work order, product, or part. Rather, these costs are aggregated on the income statement.

Implement procedures to capture the actual direct labor hours incurred to produce the job or work order, which will entail being able to record direct labor hours per operation, work station, etc. Many manufacturers are reluctant to do this because it is a tedious job that takes time and effort and they do not see the immediate value of accurate costing to determine a selling price. This is one of the major shortcomings of small firms – not seeing the need to know actual costs or wanting to pay to get them. Nevertheless, it's the foundational step to survival.

4. **Develop an Annual Budget That Separates Fixed Costs from Variable Costs.**

Ask the accountant or advisor to help you develop an annual budget, using last year's income statement as a basis. This budget should show total material, payroll, and all other manufacturing and operating expenses.

Fixed costs do not vary with sales or production volume and typically include factory depreciation, rent, salaries, taxes, insurance, licenses, dues, subscriptions, advertising and promotion, etc. ($215,500 in Figure 7-1). Variable costs do vary with sales and production volume and typically include direct materials, direct production labor, and commissions

Figure 7-1 presents a simple annual budget for this firm. Sales are budgeted at $1,000,000 with a 25% gross profit stemming from $750,000 in cost of goods sold, and SG&A expenses budgeted at $180,500, leaving a pre-tax profit of $69,500.

The budget will be used subsequently to calculate breakeven sales and to establish pricing policies.

5. **Calculate an Accurate Contribution Margin.**

Contribution margin is a fundamental concept of cost accounting that can be an effective means of establishing not only pricing policy, but also developing basic marketing strategies. It is defined as sales less variable costs (in Figure 7-1 this is $1,000,000 less $715,000 = $285,000). It is the amount of revenue from operations that remains after a firm pays for direct materials, direct labor, and commissions (in this example) to contribute to overhead and profit.

FIGURE 7-1 Traditional Income Statement

Sales	1,000,000			100%
		Fixed Costs	Variable Costs	
Cost of Goods Sold				
Materials	550,000		550,000	55%
Labor	150,000		150,000	15%
Mfg OH (Depr., Salaries)	50,000	50,000		5%
Cost of Goods Sold	750,000			75%
Gross Profit	250,000			25%
SG&A				
Salaries	75,000	75,000		8%
Rent	75,000	75,000		8%
Commissions	15,000		15,000	2%
Taxes, Dues, Sub.	10,000	10,000		1%
Office Supplies	3,000	3,000		0%
Adv. & Promo	2,500	2,500		0%
Total SG&A	180,500			18%
Pre-Tax Income	69,500			7%
Total Fixed and Variable Costs		215,500	715,000	
Contribution Margin $			285,000	
Contribution Margin %			29%	

Breakeven Sales

$$\frac{\text{Total OH (Mfg. OH + SG\&A)}}{\text{Contribution Margin \%}} = \frac{215,500}{29\%} = 756,140$$

Think about this on a single product basis (Figure 7-2). Assume a unit selling price of $100, direct material of $55, direct labor of $15, and a commission of $2. After these costs are paid, $29 remains to contribute to factory and SG&A overhead and profit. This equates to a 29% contribution margin ($29 contribution margin /$100 unit selling price) and is an excellent measure of the inherent profitability of the single product. The higher the contribution margin percent, the more margin to contribute to overhead and profit – the greater the profitability of that product.

Figure 7-2: Single Product Contribution Margin

Unit Amounts			%
Selling Price		$100	100
Direct Materials	$55		55
Direct Labor	$15		15
Commission	$2		2
Total Direct Variable Cost		$72	72
Contribution Margin		$28	

This is a fundamental and critical concept: firms should want to sell products that have as high a contribution margin as possible. Pricing policies and marketing strategies that focus on high contribution margin products and services will generate more profit for the firm.

Knowing CM$ and CM% is important to Type 1 and Type 2 firms because it:

- Shows the inherent profitability of products and customers
- Shows the winners (more profitable) and losers (less profitable) in the firm's product and service offering
- Can be used to develop pricing policy
- Can be used to develop sales and marketing strategies.

6.   **Determine Breakeven Sales.**

Breakeven sales is the amount of sales volume that equates to total expenses, both fixed and variable, inclusive of cost of goods sold and SG&A. Since total sales equals total expenses, there is no profit; hence, the firm "breaks even." The formula for determining breakeven sales is fixed costs divided by CM% (contribution margin percent).

In Figure 7-1, the firm's fixed costs are $215,500 and its contribution margin is 29%, resulting in a breakeven sales of $756,140. This means that at sales volume of $756,140, the firm's expenses are completely covered and there is no profit.

Knowing breakeven sales is important because it:

- Shows the lowest volume of sales needed to turn a profit
- Can help the firm establish sales goals/objectives for inside/outside sales, reps, and distributors
- Can help management determine if there is too much investment in overhead
- Can direct management to seek efficiency/productivity improvements to lower direct materials and labor costs
- Serves as a basis for establishing minimum pricing policies.

7. Examining Work Orders

Examining production or work orders can apply to either a firm that produces a product or a service shop. If the former, assume that a production order or work order is equivalent to producing a complete product.

This examination looks only at direct costs for materials and labor and purposely excludes overhead allocation; thus it focuses on contribution margin. This is not to say that overhead should be ignored in profitability analysis, but that to look at pure profitability, contribution margin is a better measure. Examining overhead should be done separately.

Since the firm has implemented procedures to capture actual direct materials and labor, it can use its work order system to list each work order's invoice amount (selling price), direct materials and direct labor, and calculate each work order's contribution margin. This information will form the basis for establishing a pricing policy to determine target margins, for accepting or rejecting jobs, and for setting prices. Figure 7-3 presents this information sorted in descending order of percent of contribution margin.

FIGURE 7-3: Basic Work Order Analysis

Invoice $	Actual				Contribution Margin	
	DL Hrs	DL $	Matl. $	Total Labor & Matl.	$	%
640	6	97		97	543	85%
865	20	360		360	505	58%
984	5	90	321	411	573	58%
582	16	272		272	310	53%
3,040	12	216	1,444	1,660	1,380	45%
1,875	60	1,080	76	1,156	719	38%
1,104	40	720		720	384	35%
1,750	2	34	1,250	1,284	466	27%
10,840	161	2,869	3,090	5,959	4,881	45%

The weighted average CM% is 45%. Note there are three work orders whose CM% is below the 45% average and that they are among the largest invoice dollars; their relatively higher dollar amounts weigh the CM% down. From a profitability perspective, this firm should not want more high-dollar-volume work orders with less than a 45% CM because they would decrease the overall profitability of the firm.

However, as Peter Drucker noted, "Volume solves a host of problems." Higher volume at a lower percent of profit is common. The key is knowing primarily, if the business is profitable, and, secondarily, how profitable.

Maintaining the profitability of your largest accounts is an ongoing challenge. Having good data is key to helping you manage.

Managing the Business Using Three Basic Numbers

Now that the firm has developed an annual budget, it will need to convert it to monthly to be able to manage the business on a month-to-month basis. This can be done by simply dividing the annual breakeven sales number and the annual overhead amount each by 12 to get monthly forecasted numbers for both. The third number to use to manage the business is the historical weighted average CM%.

On a monthly basis, the manager should monitor sales volume to see if sales are tracking at least at the monthly BE level and that monthly overhead expenses do not exceed the budgeted amount.

Lastly, he should calculate the monthly cumulative weighted average CM% to see that it's at least equal to the historical weighted average CM%. Figure 7-4 shows the budgeted annual figures from Figure 7-1 converted to monthly. If sales are not tracking at the monthly BE ($63,012), or monthly OH expenses ($17,958) are higher than budgeted, or the monthly CM% (45%) is below historical, the firm risks a net loss for the month.

Figure 7-4: Monthly Breakeven Sales

	Annual	Monthly
Breakeven Sales	756,140	63,012
OH Expenses	215,500	17,958

A lower monthly sales volume requires sales and marketing attention. Higher monthly overhead expenses require belt-tightening, and a lower CM% requires attention to production efficiencies, productivity increases, and/or higher prices.

Actual Costs – It is also vital that all work order actual costs be compared to quote prices or price estimates. This forces the sales department to evaluate pricing mistakes and investigate errors in estimates. This helps refine the pricing policy on a continuous basis.

Summary

At this point, our firm has established all of the ingredients for a pricing policy. Price setting then becomes a function of determining the direct material and direct labor content and calculating the selling price (SP) that will produce the target CM. If the market will bear a SP resulting in a CM higher than the target CM, the firm is OK.

Conversely, if the market won't accept a SP with the target CM, the firm will then know how far down it can negotiate SP as long as it doesn't go below the CM minimum – or negotiate increased volumes to offset the loss in contribution margin. Likewise for proposed discounts, the firm will be able to calculate the amount of discount it can accept and still remain within the pricing policy.

A common belief held by manufacturers is that price discounts can be justified because even at lower prices, the additional volume covers overhead. A review of the CM explanation earlier will show that this is true only if (1) the firm is operating above its breakeven sales levels and (2) that the proposed discounted project in fact possesses a positive contribution margin. If these two conditions are not met, the firm's acceptance of a price discount will result in a net loss because overhead is not being covered – the contribution margin is insufficient to contribute to overhead and profit.

Subcontracting

Subcontracting is an area where I have found that virtually all small and midsize manufacturers can do more to be competitive.

There is a tendency for SMMs to hold onto work that can be done at lower costs by smaller suppliers. This resistance to the "farm-out" idea is a natural one for manufacturers who have been very successful at controlling the entire manufacturing process because they are vertically integrated. Vertical integration is the ideal situation for manufacturers who want to maintain word class quality standards and 99% delivery commitments.

But, today's problem is that many SMMs can no longer afford to keep all those processes under one roof and to control costs, they simply must farm out work that can be done at a lower cost by other suppliers.

There is understandable resistance to subcontracting because SMMs do not want to close down processes, tear down buildings, and get rid of expensive machine tools. They see the trade-off as giving up control of quality, cost, and scheduling to another vendor to get lower costs.

In their view, the primary question is "do the cost savings outweigh the risks?" Certainly this is a good question. But it is not the only one that should be asked.

Another view is, "Can I afford not to be tough-minded in examining every option to reduce costs and improve efficiency?" Another related question is "Are there areas where I can increase my business doing things I'm good at?"

When all Lean Manufacturing practices have been tried, all internal cost reduction efforts have been implemented, and you have subcontracted work out to local suppliers; but the company still cannot meet the price demands of certain customers – there are two options:

- You can fire the customer and try to find different customers to replace it. Remember, every customer is not worth keeping. And, with the techniques covered in Chapter Two, there may be a lot more bad customers out there than you realize.
- You can subcontract part of your work to smaller manufacturers in the U.S. or overseas. Part of Saving American Manufacturing is figuring out what parts you can keep and what you must out-source to stay in business. This is an area we will now examine.

Offshoring – Subcontracting To Overseas Suppliers

Outsourcing to low cost countries is in vogue in America.

Responding to pressure, the outsourcing initiative began when multi-national companies began building facilities in the low cost countries. Now, small and midsize manufacturers are participating in the process to reduce costs. SMMs use a variety of approaches:

- Some SMMs are developing relationships or partnerships with foreign suppliers
- Some SMMs are investing in building plants in foreign countries.

Here are some examples.

Eastman Machine Co. of Buffalo, NY had to face up to this decision in 2001 because Chinese competitors had copied their machines. Their CEO, Robert Stevenson, said "Up until 2001, we were nearly vertically integrated; we manufactured most of our products right here in our Buffalo factory. We brought in the forging, the raw material, we cut the metal, stamped the parts, formed parts, and assembled them into finished products."

Because of price pressures, however, Eastman decided that to increase their retained earnings and improve their profit margins, they simply had to subcontract some functions to lower cost countries. He explains, "At that point, we put in a plan to outsource most of our metal cutting operations or machine shop operations."[3]

Some SMMs are establishing foreign suppliers because their customers are comparing their costs to the unit costs of overseas suppliers, something that is easier to do every day.

Boyd Corporation of Modesto, CA makes a wide variety of tiny parts for large customers like Dell, Hewlett Packard, Freightliner, Intel and Boeing. Boyd, increasingly undercut by competitors with Asian manufacturing outlets, determined that it had no choice but to join the trend. Boyd opened its first plant in the city of Shenzen China with 20 employees and expects to recoup their investment in three years.[4]

Other U.S. manufacturers are outsourcing to foreign countries because they have been given an ultimatum by their customers to find a foreign supplier and lower costs, or lose the business.

Youngers & Sons Manufacturing of Viola, KS, found that some of their business wasn't in Kansas anymore.

Wayne Youngers was one of those people who had no choice. His customer said Youngers' small $6.00 shaft used in hydraulic machines could be bought in China for $2.00 or less, and at comparable quality. Youngers & Sons is now reviewing their entire product line to see which items can be made in China. They figure eventually 50% of them can be made overseas."[5]

Planar Systems is a high tech manufacturer in Beaverton, OR. It makes flat panel LCDs. Doug Barnes, VP of Manufacturing said, "Many of our customers now have a metric they're applying to us, and to other vendors. They want to see 65 to 85% (of content) produced in low cost countries – primarily Asia, with some in Eastern Europe."[6]

As well as this has worked out for Boyd Corp. and Youngers and Sons Manufacturing, many other manufacturers have found that there are many hidden costs and risks associated with outsourcing to foreign suppliers.

A report from the New York based Conference Board suggests that outsourcing is not living up to its expectations. The report says, "With an estimated half of all offshoring operations destined to fall short of expectations, companies are under increasing pressure to calculate the risks – not merely the rewards – that offshoring entails."[7]

The report goes on to describe the brand, regulatory, social, geopolitical, human-capital, and legal risks that companies may not anticipate and how they can "turn a once attractive potential savings into a costly endeavor."

Many manufacturers rush to China because of the proposed low unit prices. But they don't do a good job of trying to determine total cost and the risk factors.

Figure 7-5 is a checklist to help you through the analysis. At a minimum, review these topics before signing any type of offshoring agreement with a foreign supplier.

It makes sense to outsource standard components like CNC (Computer Numerically Controlled) parts, if you have already written the CNC program and the operator only has to place the part in the fixture and wait for it to be completed. A foreign operator can also place the part in the same type of machine without much training.

Figure 7-5: The Outsourcing Checklist For Standard Components

Yes   No

1. **Freight** – Do you have a reasonable quote for landed costs of your components F.O.B. a port near your plant? ___ ___

2. **Expediting** – Does this include the cost of expediting and /or airfreight charges if the supplier can't make the ship date? ___ ___

3. **Logistics** – Logistics can include the costs of crate forwarders, consolidators, customs, regulatory agencies, carriers, ports, and more. Are all of these costs covered in the freight costs? ___ ___

4. **Duties, Fees, and Taxes** – This is a moving target because countries like China reserve the right to change or add special duties, fees and taxes at any time. Have you discussed who will pay the unknown future duties, fees, and taxes with the supplier? ___ ___

5. **Inventory** – Many manufacturers decide that they must have an Inventory of "safety stock" to ensure uninterrupted supply. Have you evaluated the costs of labor, warehousing (rent, utilities, insurance), taxes, etc.? ___ ___

6. **Delivery** – Have you considered the costs of lost sales due to "stock-outs" or unreliable delivery? ___ ___

7. **Cost of Quality** – This can include customer scrap or yield rate, rework, warranty claims, costs of debugging, and costs of finding defective product in a long pipeline. Will your agreement define who will absorb these costs? ___ ___

Sending assemblies or complete products to a foreign supplier is considerably more risky and complicated.

The problems, investment, and risks tend to increase proportionately with the amount of options and customization. For instance, manufacturing a small pallet jack that uses the same bill of materials on every order and can be built in quantities has low risk and a short learning curve.

On the other hand, manufacturing special packaging machines where the engineering and bills of material change on every order is extremely difficult to do in a foreign country. The project management on every order is complex, and the chance of making mistakes that will lead to quality and installation problems is high.

The following is a checklist that will help you think through the most important issues that can lead to mistakes and hidden costs.

Figure 7-6: The Outsourcing Checklist for Complete Assemblies

All the checklist items in Figure 7-5 also apply to assemblies.

	Yes	No
1. **Standard vs. Custom Assemblies** – Have you determined where your products are in the product range shown in Chapter 4?	—	—
2. **Intellectual Property Protection** – Do you have a plan to protect your intellectual property and trade secrets?	—	—
3. **Retaining Proprietary Technology** – Will you be able to protect your proprietary engineering and technology by retaining the most important trade secrets or by outsourcing the product in modules?	—	—
4. **Legal Hassles and Protection** – Have you located a law firm in the target country who can help you with disputes?	—	—

5. **Project Management** – Have you anticipated the investment costs in people and systems necessary to project manage an overseas project?   __ __

6. **Communication, Language, Customs, and Business Practices** – Have you considered who and how you will communicate with the foreign supplier?   __ __

7. **Training** – Can you estimate the costs of training for the first two years of operation?   __ __

8. **Taxes, duties, fees, and tariffs** – Do you understand all taxes, duties, fees, and tariffs that could be levied onto your products, and have you calculated them in your total cost of operation (TCO).   __ __

9. **Warranty and Service Obligations** – Have you specified the responsibility for warranty and service as well as any warranty limitations?   __ __

10. **Sourcing Strategies** – Do you know which sourcing strategy would work best for your company?   __ __

Now let's take a look at why you must ask these questions and what information you will need to answer them.

1. **Standard vs. Custom Assemblies** – There is a huge difference between standard assemblies and products that can be built for inventory and "one-off" or engineered products. The costs of off-shoring can go up logarithmically with customization.

2. **Intellectual Property Protection** – Intellectual property is a big issue when dealing with China and the Asian Pacific region in general. Copying, reverse engineering, and even counterfeiting products is not an unusual business practice in these countries. It is now obvious to most U.S. companies that the Asian view of business ethics is much different than the U.S. view of business ethics. Even a signed contract may be no protection. There are many variations on this theme.

Columbia Machine Concrete Products Division of Vancouver, WA, had been manufacturing and installing complete concrete block plants for China for many years. In less than five years from the first installation, they found that many of their most popular machine models had been copied and manufactured by local Chinese manufacturers. In many instances these local manufacturers sold copies of the machines at one-third of the American prices.

Hayward Pool Products of Elizabeth, NJ, markets their line of heaters, pumps, and other swimming pool equipment all over the world. They inadvertently found that a Chinese firm had copied some of their products right down to their logo and part numbers. They were trying to sell the counterfeit products to an existing Hayward customer at a 25% discount. "That jeopardized more than $20 million in sales to this one customer," said Paul Aderberg, their VP of Technology.[8]

Brett Kingstone of Supervision International of Orlando, FL, is a manufacturer of fiber-optic and LED lighting products. They have been honored as one of the top 500 fastest growing technology companies in the U.S., and they market their products internationally. A Chinese company set up an office in Orlando and paid a Supervision employee to steal Brett's engineering drawings and technology secrets. Brett began to lose various markets to the Chinese, including the Asian market. He was finally able to prove that the Chinese company had stolen his technology and subsequently won a $43 million lawsuit in the Florida courts.

However, Supervision International has not received any payment from the renegade Chinese company, and the U.S. Government has, to date, not been willing to help prosecute the case.

3. **Retaining Proprietary Technology** – Many manufacturers protect themselves either by retaining the most proprietary engineering and technology or by outsourcing only sub assemblies such as frames or modules. Another useful strategy is to outsource different parts of the product to different vendors or even different countries. This makes it difficult for one vendor to reverse engineer

the whole product. Other manufacturers have chosen to only out-source their high-volume, low-value products, or products that are at the end of their life cycles.

4. **Legal Hassles and Protection** – Statistics show that "roughly 50% of all Sino-Foreign relationships result in some form of dispute."[9] Many manufacturers do not understand that they will need third party representation in most Asian countries to enforce their agreements and contracts. In China, the law states that you must have Chinese legal counsel. Many U.S. law firms that do business internationally have offices in Asia. It is practical and wise to seek a U.S. law firm that can help you determine the best counsel that can help you with your agreement and your unique product requirements. A good law firm in the country can also help identify tariffs, taxes, special fees, and other regulatory issues.

5. **Project Management** – The product range discussed in Chapter 4 is useful in defining risk and project management. It is not too difficult to transfer the manufacturing of a standard assembly to a foreign manufacturer. The process is repeatable and the learning curve short. But transferring a highly engineered product where the engineering and bill of materials changes on every order is logarithmically more difficult. The process is difficult to do profitably in the U.S. and any mistakes can render the product unacceptable or a loss.

Many American manufacturers are simply unprepared for the amount of project management required – including late night phone calls (it's the middle of the day there), last-minute travel, and the supply chain monitoring needed to bring an outsourcing relationship up to speed. It may take months, or even years, of heavy travel with key employees living in the foreign country to ensure that projects are correctly managed and both parties understand one another.

The cost and complexity of project management is proportional to the complexity and customization of the product. One rule of thumb is that if the product is difficult to manage in the U.S.

plant, it will be ten times more difficult in the foreign country with customs, language, and other barriers.

6. **Communication, Language, Customs, & Business Practices** – Even if the U.S. manufacturer forms a joint venture with the foreign company, where they will share in profits and risks, there are still communication barriers that must be overcome. Faxes, e-mails, memos, and engineering information can be misunderstood or misinterpreted because of differences in culture, business practice, and language. Often it is necessary to establish a translator on both ends of the communication lines to interpret the meaning of the many communications that are necessary to manufacture the products. The communication difficulties increase with the complexity of the product.

Max Mize learned this lesson in Taiwan in the early 1980s. He had gone to Taiwan to negotiate an outsourcing deal with a Taiwanese company. They met in the World Trade Center in Taipei and spent all day discussing how they would work together. At the end of the day, a man in the next room, who had been listening to the conversation, came into their meeting and announced that they were not communicating and neither party really understood what the other party wanted. At that point, Max hired an interpreter and quickly found out that the visitor was right. They had to start completely over using the interpreter to reach an agreement.

Later, Max decided that he wanted some of the parts he was having manufactured in Taiwan shipped in a protective bubble-pack. The Supplier Company readily agreed. In his instructions to the supplier he put a little note on the sample bubble pack to "Place Sticker Here – Made in Taiwan." When the first of the new shipments of products began arriving in the U.S. packaged in bubble pack, all of the packages had a sicker that said "place sticker here – Made in Taiwan." Max makes the point that you have to be very careful and very explicit in your instructions and communications when working with foreign suppliers. And even then, miscommunication can occur

7. **Training** – Another cost factor that is usually not taken into consideration or added to the total cost of offshoring is training. The question is how much training will the foreign plant need to understand how to produce an equivalent product. A good example is the Boyd Company of Portland, which makes a wide variety of high precision parts from specialized materials. Boyd opened its first plant in Shenzen, China with 20 employees. "To ensure that Boyd's China plant works just as well as its U.S. ones, the company took production workers in Portland off the factory floor and put them on a plane for China to teach workers there the tricks of the trade."[10]

Boyd is making certain small parts in China, but to manufacture a complete assembly or a customized machine could require in-country training from every department in the U.S. plant. It could also require bringing some of the foreign plant's employees to live and train in the U.S.

8. **Taxes, duties, fees, and tariffs** – It is very important to understand all taxes, duties, fees, and tariffs that could be levied on your products and to calculate them in your total cost of operation (TCO). Legal counsel inside the country may be necessary to understand and anticipate all fees and duties before an agreement is signed. For instance, in China, there is a 17% value added tax on any product sold within its borders. Also in China various government agencies can change regulations that can lead to additional costs or barriers to entry at any time. However, the Chinese government says that any foreign supplier can apply for special permission to eliminate these duties and taxes by following the protocol of the local government. The problem is that the Central government designs the rules and regulations, but every local government has its own rules as well. Navigating this maze of bureaucracy is difficult – yet critical to success. You must have knowledgeable and trustworthy Chinese on your staff to succeed.

9. **Warranty, and Service Obligations** – Many U.S. customers are pressuring their suppliers to outsource their manufacturing to

low-cost countries. But, at the same time, the customers would like to continue buying through the U.S. supplier so that the supplier is still responsible for local service and warranty. This is "the best of both worlds" scenario for the customer. They don't have to manage a foreign supplier and they get local service and protection from any problems that might be caused by foreign manufacturing. This is a serious problem if the outsourced product is a complete assembly and is customized or special in any way. The more complex and specialized the product, the higher the risk is of quality problems or some aspect of the product not being correct at the time of installation or operation.

The answer could be to only outsource the standard parts or subassemblies of the product. Or, perhaps, to negotiate a special agreement where the service and warranty is proportionate to the risk. For example, warranty could be limited depending on customization, or full warranty could be applied to an agreed on standard design.

10. **Sourcing Strategies** – There are many different types of sourcing strategies. Selecting the best alternative depends on how much money you can invest, and how much control you need over the manufacturing process. The most popular methods are:

- **Broker/Agent** – for small companies that do not have much money to invest and cannot afford multiple trips to foreign countries, the broker/agent method may be the answer. This type of representation works best on commodity or low cost parts and components where the risk is lower. But because the brokers/agents are paid by commissions or fees, they have a built-in bias for completing a transaction – even if it isn't the best supplier relationship for your company.

- **Direct to Vendor** – If you can take the time to visit the country and evaluate vendors, this strategy will allow you to do your own due diligence and negotiate your own agreement. This is a better approach when you need more control over the process and have low-volume, high-value products.

- **Contract Manufacturing** – Contract manufacturing means allowing a foreign supplier to build the complete product under a contractual agreement. It works best if the product is very standard or a commodity product with a stable demand and very few changes. Contract manufacturing has worked well for the electronics industry on standard products such as printed circuit boards, computers, cell phones, medical devices, and other electronic products. "Contract manufacturers have grown and evolved quickly, expanding from one-service shops that assembled printed circuit boards in the 1970s to supply chain specialists offering services such as product design, supply chain management, repair, and global distribution and logistics in addition to assembly and manufacturing."[11]

- **Joint Venture** – If the products are complex or require customization and a lot of project management, forming a joint venture may be the best approach to offshoring. This gives the U.S. company much more control and reduces the risk of contract problems, service and warranty issues, quality issues, and delivery problems. Joint ventures put the American and the foreign supplier in the same boat with the same risks and opportunities. However, the joint venture by design requires considerable supplier oversight and depends a great deal on the type of joint venture partner you choose. Sometimes it is necessary for American employees to live at the foreign plant to manage the operation until it is up and running.

The Eastman Company of Buffalo, NY, found a partner that would invest with them to build a factory in China. "It took two years to get the right people to do it. We didn't want to go to the first guy who came in the door who says, 'Yeah, I can make you a part in Taiwan, China, or Korea,' because our parts are technically complex and held to fairly high tolerances. It was important for us that if we were going to do this, we would have a quality process in place." They noted, "the key thing you have to have is the ability to identify a good partner – because we certainly couldn't afford to send management over there on a full time basis to supervise and organize."

Eastman says, "Three years later we have accomplished that and we have managed to reduce our direct costs of manufacturing products here in Buffalo by about 35%. This is a significant savings when you add this together over the course of the year and will put more than $1 million down to our bottom line, which we couldn't have been able to do if we had not outsourced. Most of what we outsourced was the CNC machine parts where the operator puts a part in a fixture and then waits until it is finished."[12]

Keeping the Work in the U.S.
Epson Portland Inc – Hillsboro, Oregon

So far America is experiencing a virtual stampede of American manufacturers going to Asia – primarily because of the great attraction of perceived low unit prices. Nowhere is this more apparent than with manufacturers of computers, printers, and electronics.

But the attraction of low unit prices does not tell the whole story. Some manufacturers are finding that increasing production efficiency and output of U.S. plants and keeping the work in the U.S. is a better alternative than cost reduction strategies.

Epson Portland opened in 1986 in Hillsboro, OR, as an outsourced venture by its parent company Seiko Epson Corp. (a giant company that makes everything from watches to printers). In 2001, the parent company decided to move printer manufacturing to Indonesia and China. 850 employees lost their jobs when the printer operation went to Asia.

However, the printer cartridge part of the printer business was not immediately moved to Asia and the Portland operation was given a fighting chance to keep the business in Portland, if they could prove that manufacturing would be cost effective.

At the time, Dave Graham, who was vice president, took charge of the Portland operation along with local employees and made a vigorous push toward reforming the manufacturing operation. Dave began by setting benchmarks on improving throughput in terms of cartridges manufactured per employee and improving quality by decreasing the defective cartridges per million. This meant improving throughput and decreasing the scrap rate.

Dave began by having all management in the plant read a book called "The Goal" which was very helpful in showing the employees the value of increasing throughput as well as motivating the employees. He also studied the Toyota Production system and the Kaizen methods used by the Epson overseas plants. This helped him formulate a common sense plan, which used many lean manufacturing techniques but was customized to his operation.

Graham knew that to keep the cartridge business in Hillsboro, OR, he would have to drastically improve operations. He couldn't rely on just reducing costs because talented production workers made an average of $15 per hour, including benefits, compared to Chinese workers, who earn one-sixth as much. This seemed like an impossible goal because the total cost of a Chinese worker (including wages, housing, meals, transportation, and medical benefits) is about $2.50 per hour. But Dave reasoned that he could offset the low costs of labor in Asia by focusing on automation, throughput, and production efficiency.

They would survive by boosting the number of cartridges made per worker, ultimately doubling the factory's production. "More throughput – that shows we can compete with developing countries," Graham says.

Epson's people studied the Lean Manufacturing methods used in the Toyota Production System, and began to implement their own system of continuous improvement that would reduce defects, lower costs, and improve quality

Dave's new plan was focused on his people and the culture, and it included the following:

- **Hiring Highly Skilled People with Talent** – After the printer manufacturing was lost, Epson Portland tried using temporary workers to reduce costs – like many other manufacturers in many industries. This did not work out because operating and maintaining the new production lines required exceptional people with many talents. Dave reasoned that one excellent worker was probably worth two average workers and would ultimately be more productive.

- **Posting Metrics** – Dave learned from other companies that all employees had to understand the exact cost of operating each line by the minute, including the cost of the line not operating every minute. To accomplish this he posted reader boards on the production lines and scheduled regular meetings with all employees.

- **Improved Communication** – Dave also knew that to accomplish any of his goals communication had to be improved. This was particularly true between production and engineering people. He accomplished this by getting both groups of people in the same meeting and essentially seeing problems as their collective problem. He also made sure that all people participate in production meetings regardless of their function, to be able to understand the problems facing the company. For instance a delegation of office people attends the weekly production meeting every week regardless of their title or function.

- **Open Door Policy** – He emphasized his commitment by having an open door policy and allowing any employee to discuss any problem.

- **New Training Programs** – Epson wanted to upgrade their production lines and needed talented people with strong technical skills. They hired many people and had to implement new training at all levels in the plant. From the lowest paid production worker to the president, everybody went through various levels of training.

- **Improving Automation** – One of the causes of production line downtime was that the automation of these lines was out of date and not properly maintained. Epson Portland invested in a new program for preventative maintenance and began to upgrade the equipment in the lines. The training and dedication of the people also allowed them to make their own improvements to both speed up the lines and prevent downtime. Eventually some of these lines were replaced with more modern automation.

- **New Leadership** – Dave Graham also came to the conclusion that the traditional way of managing a plant was probably not going to work in the new global economy. His study of Toyota Production Systems and other Lean Manufacturing techniques convinced him that most of what he had to accomplish was a cultural change with the people. He decided to devote much more of his time to people management than to the technical sides of management. He took a lot of risks and tried many new ways of understanding and managing people.

It all paid off very quickly

- His "turnaround" process was in no way less dramatic than "The Goal." Dave achieved all of the original goals within 3 years and was appointed president of Epson Portland – the first local president of an overseas affiliate of Epson manufacturing company. Dave becoming president brought the morale of the local employees up, in turn increasing production
- In 2001 defects forced the plant to scrap 12,000 of every million cartridges produced. Under Graham, the defect rate plunged to 300 per million.
- The cartridges per employee increased about 40% (slightly better than other plants in the world). The Portland operation now manufactures about 50 kinds of cartridges and the production is up 200% from 2001 levels.
- Graham feels pressure to improve further. "It never lets up," he notes. "Continuous improvement is our constant mantra, because everyone else is trying to do the same thing, whatever the country."

The Epson example makes five points.

1. U.S. manufacturers shouldn't just look at the estimated unit costs in Asia. These unit costs are not the whole picture. There are many hidden costs in sourcing from Asia and manufacturers

should work hard to assess the total costs of manufacturing a product overseas.

2. Increasing throughput and reducing scrap and quality problems can often result in a more efficient existing production operation and a better alternative than pursuing outsourcing to low cost countries with all the uncertainties and potential problems.

3. There are many advantages in manufacturing close to your markets in terms of costs, efficiency, customization, and customer satisfaction.

4. Asian companies are realizing that Americans and local employees can learn to manage their own manufacturing operations. And, it makes the U.S. plant more competitive if it attains some level of self-sustainability and independence.

5. A great deal of the success of Epson Portland had to do with people management and cultural change.

The Bottom Line on Offshoring

Offshoring to foreign countries looks very attractive when projected unit costs are initially examined. It is easy to multiply labor rates of 18-35 cents per hour in your head and see the immediate cost reduction opportunities. It is particularly attractive when one of your best customers is pushing you and your company to manufacture in a foreign country.

But to be realistic, there are some big problems with offshoring.

The first problem is that most companies and customers are focused on the initial cost per unit. The initial quoted costs are so low and so attractive that these savings blind people to the possible problems. More work needs to be done by SMMs to determine the hidden costs and eventually determine the Total Cost of Offshoring (TCO).

If you do a comprehensive job, you may find out that it is better to keep all or a good part of the work at the American plant because you can come close to matching the TCO costs.

The second problem is the "herd mentality."

Offshoring is so well publicized that it creates the illusion that all manufacturers must get into the stampede or they will be left behind in a non-competitive position. The herd mentality suggests that if other companies in the same industry are into offshoring you must follow suit. This "leap before you look" impulse has resulted in many manufacturing companies rushing into relationships with foreign suppliers without truly examining all of the costs and potential problems.

Many SMMs have found that, promises and contracts notwithstanding, the foreign supplier simply cannot deliver the products on time, at a quality standard, or within the costs originally projected.

Others have found that there are many other hidden costs that make the "total cost of outsourcing" too high. It is very important to understand all of these hidden costs and potential problems and to negotiate a written agreement with all of the terms up front. This agreement could be as simple as a two-page supplier agreement to purchase a simple low cost bracket or as complex as a joint venture agreement to build complex systems. Then, of course, you have to hope that the agreement will be upheld legally if that becomes an issue.

Perhaps a bigger danger over the long haul is that offshoring may eventually make the American manufacturer more vulnerable because of the loss of direct control of the manufacturing process.

There are many examples of reverse engineering and counterfeiting. Together, they do more than suggest that today's supplier may well become tomorrow's competitor.

Another way to look at potential problems is from the customer's point of view. What loyalty will some of your large volume customers have to your company in the future? If you spend years investing in a foreign supplier to manufacture your products to suit a specific customer's needs, what will prevent that customer from simply cutting you out of the supply chain and buying direct from the supplier at an even lower cost.

All of these are definite threats when considering offshoring. But if you are in a position where you must take the risk of outsourcing from a foreign supplier, then concentrate on calculating the total costs of offshoring and getting an agreement that gives you a chance to make the relationship work and make some money.

Supply Chain Management

An additional concern is the subject of supply chain management. Unlike many other industrialized countries, the U.S. manufacturing supply chain is not usually a partnership between large customers and their key suppliers – it is at best an adversarial relationship with few partnering attributes.

In fact, being a supplier to many of America's giant companies, who can source products anywhere in the world, can probably be better described as the "chains to lock their suppliers into cost reduction."[13]

A good example is the auto industry and what the giant auto companies demand of their suppliers. In 2003 "Ford Motor said it expected price cuts of 3.5% from its suppliers by January 1 with more to come. Ford says these moves are part of a broader effort to slash purchasing costs and improve the automaker's profit by the middle of the decade."[14]

Whether this is simply a necessary step for long-term survival or an example of "soulless capitalism" is irrelevant – mandated price cuts are a fact of doing business with Ford and the other U.S. automakers. If you want to play in this game you had better sharpen your pencil and be employing Lean Manufacturing as a way of life.

There does seem to be a big difference in the way Asian and American auto manufacturers work with their suppliers.

A study of tier one suppliers in the auto industry, conducted by Planning Perspectives of Detroit, "confirms that the U.S. and Japanese auto OEMs approach customer relationships differently." This study shows more specifically how the Japanese OEMs are benefiting. Among other results, the study found that:

- Suppliers are shifting resources (capital and R&D expenditures, service, and support) to Japanese Big Three, while reducing these resources for the domestic Big Three.
- Suppliers are increasing product quality at a greater rate for Japanese companies while merely maintaining quality levels for U.S. automakers.

- Suppliers, by a wide margin, prefer working with Japanese OEMs. Many would even like to drop U.S. automakers if they could.

"U.S. Companies tend to take a transactional, even adversarial approach toward working with their suppliers, while the Asian companies approach the relationship more as a partnership."[15]

These adversarial relationships have taken a turn for the worse in most industries because of the pressures of globalization.

After the Type 4 companies re-engineered themselves in the early '90s the pressure to reduce costs was pushed down the supply chain onto the smaller suppliers. This pressure has manifested itself in terms of offshoring, plant closures and relentless pressures on U.S. suppliers to match foreign supplier costs or lose the business.

The Facts of Supply Chains

Many small manufacturers built their businesses by bidding on "farm-out" work now being outsourced by the large companies. However, times are changing. These outsourced contracts are becoming less profitable and more competitive.

Large companies now look for suppliers all over the world in their unending quest for lower prices. Some of these companies are not worth pursuing. In fact, some of the large companies can put a supplier out of business if they do not have the basic systems and information to compete in the supply chain.

To be able to participate in supply chains, the smaller Type 1 and 2 supplier companies need to develop better cost accounting, production control, and quality systems to even have a chance to get this kind of work. Having an accurate cost system that provides immediate feedback on price decisions is a basic necessity of participating in supply chains. The more adversarial the customers are, the more extensive and accurate that cost system needs to be.

Meanwhile, the pressures continue. In the rush (it's really a stampede) to get lower costs and source from anywhere in the world, The Type 4 manufacturers could inadvertently be throwing the "baby out with the bathwater."

They may be creating problems for themselves in the future by not maintaining a strong U.S. supplier base. But the short-term pressures are so intense that it's hard to take the long view.

Some of the more progressive Type 4 manufacturers are beginning to realize this. Robert Lane, Chairman and CEO of Deere and Co. of Moline, IL, said in a speech at the Kellogg School of Management at Northwestern University, "Just like any customer, we had traditionally expected more or at least the same, for less. In most companies, ours included, relationships with suppliers have often been adversarial. But, we discovered that didn't work for either party. We are moving away from those us vs. them supplier relationships. Instead we are teaming up with our suppliers and linking them into our supply chain. We can only hope that this new view of suppliers spreads to other industries."[16]

What we really need is supply chain cooperation not supply chain management. To really achieve the efficiencies and effectiveness that everyone wants in supply chains will require cooperation between suppliers and customers. This means not just cost reduction in a one sided adversarial relationship, but cooperation that is creative and collectively works continuously at trying to find the best methods to bring products to consumers.

This kind of cooperation based on American ingenuity can only happen if all the parties in the supply chain can realize economic gain. And if the suppliers get the type of commitments to really invest in the equipment, people, and systems to provide world-class products and services.

But, for the time being, the real security for SMMs is not putting their faith in large companies but, rather, to prospect in other markets to find customers who really want to be business partners as described in Chapter 2. The challenge is to find those manufacturers who want to have close relationships based on collaboration and the unique product/service package you can bring them.

If supply chain relationships and partnerships are not possible with some of America's premier companies, then the answer is to fire them and find customers who value your products and services. I know it is hard to fire a customer who provides huge sales volume, but huge sales volume at little or no profit will not help you. In fact, it can drive you into cashflow problems or insolvency.

There are still many American companies who value their suppliers and examine the total cost of using their products. It is a matter of finding them.

In the final analysis, the supplier answer to supply chain management is to not allow adversarial customers to manage your margins and put you out of business.

Conclusion

This chapter has covered realistic approaches for achieving cost reductions and efficiency improvement in manufacturing operations.

There is no question that internal process changes such as Lean Manufacturing, ISO 9001, and Six Sigma are necessary and vitally important.

Even though many of these programs seem to eventually fall out of favor like other management fads, methods to reduce costs will be needed for a long time.

This chapter is not about whether SMMs should use Lean Manufacturing methods, participate in supply chains, or outsource some of their products. Rather, it is about recognizing the practical limitations of these strategies and developing the right "recipe" for your company.

"One solution does not fit all." Solutions need to be customized to fit the type of manufacturer and the type of products. This chapter also argues that every solution should acknowledge resource limitations described as "FACTS." Simply put, solutions and strategies adopted by Toyota will not work for Sam's Fab Shop.

All of these process changes in manufacturing will not in and of themselves save manufacturing from the pressures of globalization. It is the market and customers who are driving all of these changes and some of these customers are adversarial and not worth these investments.

It is important to also address the external issues of finding good customers and getting rid of bad customers as well as improving internal processes.

This means beginning an effort to establish a diversified list of customers and a portfolio of markets as a parallel effort to improving internal processes. This is a holistic approach to managing the company that is described as a Growth Plan in chapter 9.

Key Points

The most important point of this chapter is that it is absolutely necessary to know your costs and margins in this new era of price discounting, particularly if you have to find new customers and markets. Accurate cost accounting and pricing are described as indispensable tools for survival in the new economy. As unappealing as cost accounting may be to most manufacturers, it is vital to being able to measure every process improvement that is implemented. More importantly, accurate costing and pricing are underscored by the following six questions.

1. How will you establish prices and discounts in finding new customers?
2. How will you determine a reliable pricing strategy or a solid basis for doing quotes?
3. How will you know if the company is breaking even each month?
4. How will you compete with foreign manufacturers who offer unit prices up to 50% lower then American unit prices?
5. How can you participate in a supply chain where you are expected to offer discounts
6. How will you know when you have to outsource?

Suggested Action

If you cannot predict a monthly break even sales figure, follow the simple procedures in item #4 on page 216 to develop an annual budget that separates fixed costs from variable costs. This process will give you an accurate contribution margin, break even sales figure, and the foundation of developing an accurate pricing system

Notes:

1. Matthew Boyle, "Brand Killers," *Fortune* 148 (8/11/2003): 89.
2. U.S. Department of Labor, Bureau of Labor Statistics, Occupations with the largest job decline, 2000-2010, 4.23.03.
3. "Executive Viewpoint, Q and A: Robert Stevenson, CEO of Eastman Machine Co," *Start*, January 2005, 18.
4. Mike Rogoway, "Moving Abroad to Grow at Home," Business and the Economy, *Oregonian*, E-4, December 2004.
5. Timothy Appel, "Small Firms Outsource Abroad By Tapping Offshore Producers," *Wall Street Journal*, January 7, 2004.
6. *Business Journal of Portland*, May 26, 2003.
7. John S. McClenahen, "Outsourcing Reconsidered," *Industry Week*, May 2005.
8. Traci Purdum and John Teresko, "Smart Outsourcing," *Industry Week*, October 2004.
9. Gloria Kamph, "Eight Key Steps to Sourcing in China," *Hardwares*, January 2004.
10. See Note 4.
11. Katrina C. Arabe, "Outsourcing Manufacturing Spreads," Thomas Net Industrial Newsroom, April 25, 2005.
12. See Note 3.
13. Matthew Coffey, "State of the Industry." Paper presented at the National Tooling And Machining Association, 2004 Fall Conference, Park City, Utah, October 8, 2004.
14. Norihiko Shirouzu, "Ford and GM Put the Squeeze On Parts suppliers for Price Cuts," *Wall Street Journal*, 2004.
15. Pat Panchak, "Supplier Partnerships Provide a Competitive Edge," *Industry Week*, September 2004.
16. John Buell, "Saving American Manufacturing," *Start*, July 2003.

Chapter 8
Workforce Education and Training

One of the keys to improved performance and a more responsive and efficient organization is better people.

Pressures from globalization and the advances in technology are putting a high premium on the skills needed to be competitive in manufacturing.

A study published by the National Association of Manufacturers and the Manufacturing Institute titled "Keeping America Competitive" states that "today's manufacturing jobs are technology jobs, and employees at all levels must have the wider range of skills required to respond to the demands of an increasingly complex environment."[1]

The report goes on to say "The Baby Boom generation of skilled workers will be retired within the next 15-20 years. Currently, the only source of new skilled workers is from immigration. There is a projected need for 10 million new skilled workers by 2020."

This may seem contradictory, but despite the fact that the U.S. has lost 3 million manufacturing jobs since 1999, America is faced with a growing need for more skilled workers in manufacturing.

However, manufacturing doesn't need more unskilled workers. We have more of these than we have jobs for them.

We have a shortfall of highly educated and trained manufacturing employees even though there is no shortage of employees overall. We need workers with specific education and training skills. One of the biggest issues in trying to maintain a viable manufacturing base in America is not outsourcing or foreign competitors, it is training the manufacturing workers we need for the 21st century.

"The Skills Gap"

A study by the Manufacturing Institute, "2001 The Skills Gap," revealed that "80% of the surveyed manufacturers reported a moderate to serious shortage in qualified job applicants."[2]

The report shows that shortages of skilled workers are most serious for machinists, craft workers, technicians, electricians and engineers. How big is that shortage? One estimate is 10 million!

Obviously, 10 million jobs is a huge opportunity, particularly when it is getting harder and harder for people to find "family wage" jobs in the service industries.

So why don't we just announce the opportunity? Tell parents, community colleges, universities, high schools, and grade schools. Then, get industry and the government to support a massive education and training initiative? Unfortunately, it is a very complex problem with many challenges that must be overcome before such a program can be launched.

Problems and Challenges

Here are some of the problems and challenges we face.

Manufacturing's Image

A 2002 study sponsored by the National Association of Manufactures (NAM), and the accounting and consulting firm of Deloitte & Touche was commissioned to see what people think about manufacturing's image.[3]

The respondents were students, parents, and teachers, manufacturing employees, and manufacturing executives.

The study showed that manufacturing's image was " found to be heavily loaded with negative connotations and universally tied to the stereotype of the assembly line." It was also viewed by most people to be a dying industry that was quickly moving offshore.

If these perceptions remain dominant, it will be a self-fulfilling prophecy.

Many citizens still see manufacturing as a world of dark, dirty sweatshops offering long hours and low pay. Actually, the opposite is true.

The control panel on a modern CNC machine looks like the control panel on the Starship Enterprise. The area around the machine is cleaner than a college classroom.

In addition, most people do not realize that the term manufacturing is not a definition of exclusively blue-collar jobs. There are also many white-collar jobs in sales, product marketing, accounting, industrial engineering, CAD design, service, supervision, and general management. All of these jobs are also included in the definition of manufacturing and they are included in the 10 million job shortage. These jobs pay well but they require education and training.

How Students View Manufacturing

The negative view is also shared by students. They use adjectives like boring, repetitive, assembly line, and dangerous to describe their idea of manufacturing. Most young people and teachers have never been inside a modern manufacturing plant and do not realize that most of the dirty, dangerous, and repetitive jobs have been automated, or have already gone overseas.

Perhaps the biggest challenge for the future of American manufacturing is to convince students seeking careers that they should invest in a manufacturing career. The perception by high school and college students is that there "seems to be no sense of loyalty from the manufacturing companies, and this keeps students turned off to the career path." Students see no advantage in the manufacturing career track, and many are looking for more security.

How Parents View Manufacturing

Parents have not viewed working in a factory as an acceptable career goal for at least 30 years. Manufacturing has become synonymous with not getting ahead. Working with your hands became "uncool," and the answer to getting ahead, as viewed by most parents, was getting a college degree.

Regardless of the emerging manufacturing job opportunities, most parents still want their kids to go to college and get a white-collar job, and they still see a college degree as the key to getting their sons and daughters a piece of the American Dream.

Part of the reason for this bias is that many parents (or grandparents) have had factory jobs and have stood in employment lines wondering what to do next. The news of manufacturing's decline compounds the problem. They don't want the same thing to happen to their kids.

How Teachers View Manufacturing

Most teachers and career counselors have never been inside a modern manufacturing plant. Many of them see manufacturing as a dead-end career path – one that may also be risky and dangerous. They hear reports on the news all the time about plant closures, layoffs, and out-sourcing. Both teachers and counselors are in a position to recommend career paths at an early age and at key decision points. Most would not recommend manufacturing because of their perceptions.

For instance, Nancy Perry, executive director of the American School Counselor Association in Alexandria says "it is impossible to swim against the tide of this 'college is the only thing' mindset."

Even blue-collar workers, who are earning a good income for their family say, "I want my kids to go to college." Perry explains that many school counselors are frustrated because suggesting an alternative to college is putting the kid down and trying to keep him down. Somehow, vocational training and working with your hands has become synonymous with failure. She adds, "We know a whole lot of good jobs in the future are going to be jobs that don't require a four-year college education; we've allowed a mass deception to take hold in our schools."[4]

Perception is, in many ways, reality. Today's perceptual bias is severe. Even though there is a real need for workers with technical skills and training, the bias against manufacturing jobs in general combined with very real news about jobs being lost adds up to a very real problem.

It is one more problem that we will need to solve.

We must "sell" America's children, parents, teachers, and counselors on the idea that working in a complex manufacturing job can be, in many cases, not only as good as a college degree, but that often times it will pay more, with better benefits, and be extremely satisfying.

But who is going to do the selling?

Service Industry Jobs

Every authority figure from the President on down continues to proclaim that the future belongs to knowledge workers with computer skills and college degrees. Generally speaking, it is true that there is a connection between more eduction and earning more money over the long haul. But that connection is often misinterpreted as *any* college degree being the ticket to a good job. This is simply not true, and you have to look at specific job categories and specific degrees to find the real answer.

One thing that helps keep this myth alive is the possibility of finding a dream job in the services industry. After all, it was only a few years ago (before the dot-com bubble burst) that young software programmers were making $100,000 per year in their mid twenties.

But, alas, what has happened since the late 1990s? It's not all dreams come true. A wide range of service jobs are being outsourced to India, China, and other Asian countries – from low-paying jobs like call centers and transaction processing to high-paying jobs such as software programming, engineering, design, accounting, actuarial expertise, legal, medical advice, and a wide range of consulting activities. Many of these "dream jobs" are leaving the country. In fact, any job that is "rules based" and involves data that can be transmitted over the Internet is, to some extent, in jeopardy.

Nobody, as far as I can tell, saw this coming. Though you can read a very cogent and thought-provoking analysis in Thomas Friedman's *The World Is Flat: A Brief History of the 21st Century*. He shows how a number of trends all came together to create a dramatically different world. Friedman didn't see it coming either. But now it's here. The fact that the government and the educational community put all of their eggs in the "knowledge worker" and "college degree" basket is regrettable. For these jobs simply won't employ enough of the people who will need family wage jobs. The irony is that millions of parents have funded expensive degrees in areas such as theatre arts and mass communications, and the graduates with these majors are not getting jobs worthy of a four-year degree. Well, there's always Starbucks.

The Impact of the Skilled Worker Shortage

The shortage has had an additional effect. Manufacturers are not moving production to low cost countries just because of costs. They are also moving because of the U.S. skilled worker shortage.

In the report "Keeping America Competitive," the authors state that, "The potential exists that manufacturers will increasingly move their production operations overseas to get the technological talent that is being strategically and purposefully prepared in places like the European Union and the Pacific Rim, including China and India, if they cannot find this talent here."[5]

Government's Role in Training

The Workforce Investment Act (WIA) was passed in 1998. Its objective was to give new skills to current and future employees. The results of this act are mixed. There are good results in some states and none in others. It is difficult to say whether this act is really going to help small and midsize manufacturers.

One aspect of the program is that industry has allowed the bureaucrats to run the system, and this has created a kind of "social worker mentality" that is not focused on meeting employer needs. Critics say there is insufficient money to really build a long-term skills program and there is no money available to keep the current employees up-to-date on new technology. So what's going on here?

There is money available for childhood development programs, for the disabled, and for healthcare paraprofessionals, but why is there little or no money available for training for new manufacturing skills or apprentice programs? The Clinton Administration, which launched the Workforce Investment Act, allowed the individual states to manage the funding through one-stop centers.

There are many examples, going all the way back to the 1950s where the money for training workers was given to the states or local governments to carry out a retraining mission. In my own state of Oregon, we had the collapse of both the logging and the aluminum foundry industries in the

1980s. The state was asked to retrain loggers and highly paid workers from the aluminum smelters into another career. With few exceptions, most people moved to lower paying jobs and never recovered.

Another good example in Oregon is Bill Ruggles, who was laid off when the plastics injection plant he worked for moved to Mexico. In this case, Bill was able to get assistance from the Trade and Adjustment Assistance Program, which helps manufacturing workers who are losing work to foreign competitors. Originally, Ruggles was interested in earning a degree in industrial management.

He figured that he could get a four-year degree, use his course work hours from the community college and end up in a field that would pay up to $75,000 per year in manufacturing. But his employment-training counselor turned him down. Why? Because the degree was going to be too much like his previous job – in manufacturing.

Ultimately, the government allowed him to enroll in a community college natural resources program. This landed him a six-month job surveying spotted owls for $10.90 an hour. He couldn't make a living doing the job and eventually went through all of his savings and filed for bankruptcy in February of 2004. There's a bias against manufacturing – but not spotted owls.

Bill comments that the retraining programs "are a great thing for politicians. They can point to a program and say, 'Hey, we're taking care of all of these people.' And they gloss over the fact that it's really not helping anyone."[6]

Again, this story makes the point that government programs as they are currently set up do not seem to be the answer. Government is supposed to fund the projects and cannot be expected to retrain workers. They will seldom have the people who can select the right jobs for training, develop the training curriculum, or do the training. There has to be another way. We'll show you some examples in a few pages.

On a positive note, however, the Labor Department is beginning to increase government funds for manufacturers on programs that work – like Lean Manufacturing. This is a good start. But only time will tell whether money will be used for skills training and the restart of apprentice type programs. In any event, industry (particularly large manufacturers) needs to take the lead and say what training programs we need.

Automation and Technology

There is very little anyone can do about certain kinds of jobs being transferred to low-cost countries. However, most of these jobs are routine assembly and manufacturing jobs that can be done anywhere in the world. Most of the products being outsourced are high-volume, low-cost parts (for example, consumer goods like you would find at Wal-Mart). This kind of manufacturing will be very difficult to "save."

We have to quit blaming this natural trend on poorer nations or manufacturing management, and focus on what we can do to keep the rest of manufacturing in the U.S.

There is also another factor we can "blame." Simply put, it is technology and automation. Technology and automation have eliminated many non-factory jobs. For example, elevator operators, bank tellers, and service station attendants. In the factory, automation and technology have eliminated millions of jobs in the assembly, process, and production by using automatic machines like palletizers, robots, and packaging machinery. But they've also saved jobs because of productivity increases.

What this means is that routine (rules-based) jobs will probably eventually be eliminated. But, this doesn't mean that new jobs won't be created.

It may seem counter intuitive that automation and technology can create new jobs. But people forget that it also takes thousands of skilled workers to design, install, maintain, repair, and operate these complex technological systems and production line machines. As a matter of fact, we already have a shortage of these types of workers. We need more programs to train them and young people, who want to work in manufacturing, to sign up for these programs.

That is why we will need 10 million additional workers in manufacturing by 2020. But, these won't be routine jobs – they will be a wide variety of skilled jobs.

Apprentice Programs

If advanced skills are what is going to be needed in the next generation of manufacturing workers, getting better at math, science, and English is only part of the task before us.

We also need to train people with the kinds of skills that used to be part of the post-War apprentice/journeyman programs.

Most skill training programs are either dying or dead. With the decline of manufacturing and the loss of jobs, we've seen a proportional loss of the education and training programs for skilled manufacturing workers.

This problem is most obvious in the highly skilled jobs. Most of the journeyman-type programs, the ones that gave us some of the best machinists, tool and die artists, mold makers, and fabricators – workers who were the foundation of many companies and industries – are gone. Meanwhile, large companies like Pratt and Whitney, Blount International, and General Electric have dropped many of their apprentice training programs.

What will it take to get this started again? Well, it could be hard. Or it could be relatively easy. It all depends on how much we want it.

During World War II, America created one of the best manufacturing training programs in the civilized world.

In just a few years, we created all of the skill training needed to take people from farmers to advanced machinists. We created apprentice/journeymen programs for welding, fabrication, pipe fitting, machining, tool and die, and other crafts. We took unskilled workers and trained the greatest manufacturing workforce the world had ever seen to build the arsenal that won the World War. We did it all in just four years. Everyone knows America has the spirit, talent, ingenuity, and resources to do it. So why not do it again?

It seems ironic that training programs for advanced machining, tool and die, and mold making are almost extinct in the U.S. when the eight fastest growing Asian countries are spending millions of dollars a year to train and educate these types of skilled workers.

Richard Walker of the National Tooling and Machining Association says that the 15,000 machine shops across America that employ 450,000 workers are faced with a lack of skilled workers. The NTMA estimates that "20,000 job vacancies will exist in the tooling industry alone."[7] 20,000 jobs!

It's simple. We must reinstitute many of the skills training programs if we are going to meet the challenge of foreign competition and of filling tomorrow's skilled job openings.

Other Obstacles to Starting Collaborative Training Programs

If we have the will and the resources, we can do it. But, there are additional reasons why this is a very difficult problem.

- Many large companies do not want to collaborate with each other for competitive and political reasons.
- There is still an adversary relationship between many suppliers and their large company customers because of their relative positions in the supply chain.
- Unions are only strong in the large companies. Today, there is a definite anti-union bias in most of the supplier companies.
- Most Federal grants are for entry level and rehabilitation type training. To date, the government has not wanted to support the kind of advanced training we will need with grants or subsidies.
- Apprentice-type programs take 8 to 10 thousand hours of instruction and training. Many companies are opting for shorter duration training programs because of their immediate needs and the worsening supply of skilled workers.
- Large companies don't share facilities and training with their supplier companies or other small companies.
- There is no central place or location where all companies can send people for common apprenticeship training or classroom instruction.
- Small and uncoordinated efforts by different government and educational organizations often deteriorate into turf and control issues. And many of their missions aren't defined by specific objectives to increase the number of skilled jobs or training graduates.

- Education usually wants to expand industry specific programs into generic programs that appeal to a wide variety of business and industries, rather than focus on specific industry needs.

These problems can be overcome, but we will need to be smart about it. And adversaries (for example, union and non-union organizations) will have to cooperate. Difficult. But not impossible.

The Crisis in Education

Many different studies sponsored by manufacturing associations have found that our nation's education and training systems are badly mis-aligned with the needs of manufacturing. From K–12 through community colleges and universities, the education and training provided is not meeting the needs of manufacturers, particularly for skilled jobs.

What is going on here?

First, the education system is out of touch with what is going on in manufacturing. Universities are pretty good at giving people a liberal education, but, all too often, they are really not very good at giving them the specific skills that will get them a job.

Even today, engineering schools seem to be out of touch with what is needed by manufacturers. The 2001 Skills Gap report notes that "outside of life sciences, the number of degrees awarded in science and engineering over the last decades has been flat or declining. The impending shortfall becomes obvious when one considers the 50% projected increase in U.S. jobs requiring significant technical skills in the next ten years."[8]

It appears that many people in education (particularly at the college level) have become totally disconnected from manufacturing. Educators have lost track of what is going on in the world of work and most ignore the needs of industry. From my perspective, it seems that many of these education professionals do not want to address or be charged with the responsibility of educating young people to get real jobs. From my perspective, they seem oblivious to the fact that parents cannot afford to pay $100,000 for a four-year general degree and then not have their sons and daughters employable.

The problem is two fold.

First, manufacturers want "first job" applicants who are much better at math, science and writing than are currently being graduated from high school. Mr. Craig Barrett, CEO of Intel, says "Where Americans once viewed the diploma as a common national currency, its value has been so inflated that employers and post secondary institutions all but ignore it in their hiring and admissions decisions today." In the "American Diploma Project," more than 60% of the employers rated high school graduates as poor to fair in English and math."[9]

Second, it is very clear that most kids cannot afford to get "just a liberal education" – one that can't help them find a family wage job. Yet, for the most part, that is what is offered. We need an education system that is open to the idea of including career-oriented classes and skill training into the education curriculum. What is needed is theoretical knowledge combined with practical hands-on experience and up-to-date job skills.

"The Work of Nations" by Robert Reich, and many other books on the new economy make the point over and over again that getting family wage jobs or making a good income in either the service or manufacturing sector is highly correlated with education and skill training beyond high school. Since most of the new jobs in manufacturing require a knowledge of technology, a higher percentage of students will need a much better grounding in mathematics, science, reading, and writing. Here is what is happening in education according to the National Center for Education Statistics.[10]

High Schools – In the 2000/2001 school year, approximately 2,820,000 high school diplomas were awarded as well as an additional 501,000 G.E.Ds. There has been a 5% drop out rate from high school for the last ten years.

Every year, 63% of these high-school grads go on to some kind of post-secondary education, but only half of the 63% who enroll will graduate.

The 2001 Skills Gap Report indicates that "78% of the study's respondents believed that the public K–12 schools are not doing a good job of preparing students for the workplace."

If this claim is even partially true then the 37% of the high-school graduates who don't go on to college and the 50% who drop out of college (another 31%) will not have skills to get a job (not to mention the 5% that are high school dropouts). My rough math says that's about 70%.

Post-Secondary Education – In year 2000/2001 the following education programs conferred degrees.[11]

1. Associates Degree   565,057 graduates
2. Bachelors Degree   1,237,885 graduates
3. Master's Degree   457,056 graduates
4. Doctoral Degree   44,808 graduates

The number of degrees looks impressive until you look at the overall enrollment for post-secondary schools during the same period – which was 15,205,180 people. Many are starting, not that many are finishing.

Community Colleges – Manufacturers rate community colleges as their preferred training providers. The community college problem is that many of the vocational courses are not sufficiently financed, "as a result of community college funding formulas established by state legislatures that limit the number of technical non-credit courses, in only four states do these formulas provide equal per-capita subsidies for all students."[12] This shows the obvious educational and government bias towards the "everyone must have a four-year degree" track.

University – Another problem is the type of degree offered. According to the Labor Department the best-paid jobs in the next 10 years will require associates, bachelor, masters, or PhD degrees in technical or professional curriculums. That said, it is important to point out that just getting a degree in some general, liberal arts subjects like history, psychology, literature, etc., may not get someone a job.

In the study "Baccalaureate and Beyond: a Descriptive Summary of 1999/2000 Bachelor Degree Recipients," the opinions section of the report noted that "the 54% majority of employed 1999/2000 bachelor degree recipients said their job was closely related to their undergraduate major." Is that good news? It means that 46% – almost half – of the graduate's jobs are not related to their majors.[13]

So what is the significance of these facts? Well, let's do the math. Since 1.3 million people received bachelor degrees in 2000, it means almost 600,000 degree holders have general degrees that have little to do with getting a job or starting a career.

Now some of this may be manufacturing bias – I think that factories should turn out functional products and schools should turn out functional people. Some of my friends remind me that those years in school prepare you for the adult world, even if it is with a degree in English literature. Certainly there's something to that, but the statistics still indicate a huge disconnect between jobs and education.

One table in the B and B Report is a "Percentage Distribution of 1999/2000 undergraduates among those with a declared major by field of study." This Table shows that arts and humanities, social sciences, business/management, and life sciences make up 67% of the degrees. The other 33% are in computer science, engineering, education, health, vocational technical, and other technical degrees. In addition, of those entering college, more than half drop out and often flounder for years. "Individuals who already have a four-year degree – or even a graduate degree – "are the fastest growing group of young adults enrolling in two-year community colleges."

To get ahead in the New Economy, the degree, education, or training must be job or career specific. Degrees in engineering, nursing, accounting, teaching and other professional programs train the person to get a job. In the main, these people get the jobs they were trained for.

But at least half of the degrees awarded do not give people the skills to get a good job. This notion runs counter to the higher education system, which claims, "to get a good job, get a good education."

On top of that, as the needs for manufacturing skills and vocational education go begging, there has been a proliferation of "studies" programs: ethnic studies, environmental studies, peace studies, women's studies, etc..

For instance, The University of California at Santa Barbara now has 62 different courses listed under Chicano Studies.[14] It is our view that professors and administrators are taking the easy way out by offering courses that are interesting and easy to teach, but won't help a student get a job. Maybe we should start a major called manufacturing studies.

I certainly feel we should do something to provide better choices. Educational elitists still look down their nose at vocational training and apprenticeship programs that may not be the equivalent of a college degree. But programs such as these can earn a person an immediate job and, in many cases, a much better living than general college degree programs can. It is clear that the U.S. education system in its present form does not match up to the new needs of manufacturing or, for that matter, the information/services sector of the economy.

The bottom line is that all students will eventually need to get some kind of a job. Most of these young people will also eventually get married and have families. They will need family wage jobs. The need for hard job skills is increasing as we move farther into the new "technical economy" which begs the question of why aren't we doing more to provide job skills in grade school, high school, or college.

More importantly, what will we do with the millions of high school dropouts, high school graduates, college drop outs, and general college degree graduates who have no specific job-related skills? And, what about their parents? Parents deserve to eventually have children who are out of the house and self-supporting. Loan institutions deserve to be paid back.

A broad conclusion is that our education system has not kept in tune with the skills needed for our children to get jobs in the New Economy. My big question is, "Can manufacturing help fix this?" Can manufacturing provide its part of the guidance and support to realign the education and training programs to better meet the needs of both individuals and manufacturers – or will they just sit back and point the finger?

Vocational Schools and Training

Too often, vocational programs have become a dumping ground for students who aren't doing well and are at risk. The collapse of vocational programs didn't happen because of counselors, teachers or funding authority. In my view, the primary blame can be laid at the feet of manufacturing itself. Industry allowed the schools and instructors to sell the program to the students instead of participating in the marketing themselves. Industry helped get themselves into the "Skills Gap".

It is ironic that at the same time manufacturers are crying about the need for millions of new skilled jobs and bitterly excoriating educational institutions, vocational education institutions are being closed down.

The message from both the Clinton and Bush administrations has been unmistakable. It is a message to both students and parents that a college education is the only guarantee of success in the New Economy. The Department of Education, and even the federal school to work program, echo this message.

The result has been the elimination of industrial arts training in grade schools and high schools and a decrease in funding for vocational colleges. This reinforces the stigma that getting skilled training or enrolling in a vocational program is a dead-end ticket to a dirty job with no upward mobility.

John Balzar, of the Washington Post, writes "I was disappointed to see a subsequent story – the latest in a decades-long string of accounts – that denigrates what we call vocational education in schools. This curriculum is dying out. Those courses that remain are stigmatized. Boys and girls from the underclass are shunted into them, and their dreams are ruined." Balzar goes on to criticize the current educational program and test scores. He says, "it's single track college prep with some athletics thrown in. Too bad. With specialization crushing in on us we need rounding out; home economics, sewing, wood shop."

I say "Amen." Why not give students something that is interesting and useful. Why not focus on giving them skills and a career?

This lack of foresight is unforgivable in light of the fact that technology and automation are the drivers of future manufacturing jobs. And the evolving truth is that many highly skilled blue-collar jobs may be better family wage jobs than those available to college graduates with general degrees.

This author believes that there is honor and satisfaction in creating things with one's hands. This feeling is true for artists and artisans and it used to be true in manufacturing. I think it still is. In 1953, I took my first shop class in the 7th grade at a public school in Portland, OR. In 1956, as a sophomore in high school I built a birch plywood coffee table with two drawers, for my mother. My mother kept that coffee table in her living room as a centerpiece for almost 50 years, I must say that neither my mother nor I ever got tired of the table or the design.

The joy of building things with my hands led me to pursue auto mechanics, scratchboard art, pencil drawing, and, eventually, building my own woodshop (which has spawned hundreds of projects).

That joy of learning how to create things with my hands both enriched my life and my thinking. In my spare time over the years, I have designed and built furniture, buildings, decks, fences, and hundreds of other home projects. I have learned to work with metals, plastics, and glass, and I have mastered a wide variety of power and hand tools.

As I gained confidence, I learned to lay roofs, make cabinets, thread pipe, install gas lines, tile floors, and a myriad of other skills. I reached a point where I believed there wasn't anything I could not build given time and study. I began to see working with my hands as an art form and that man and tools were made for each other. Along the way, I recognized the true value of the people in manufacturing who were very good at it.

After many years, I came to the realization that making things is not just a matter of interest and hobbies. The skills that are used in working with my hands also served me well in my professional career in manufacturing, particularly as a general manager.

I learned that there is a direct connection between the kind of thinking that allows you to work with your hands and the kind of thinking that helps you make good decisions as a general manager in manufacturing. I was able to combine the subjects I learned in college with my skills as an artisan to better understand technology, manufacturing, and the development of new products.

Being able to make things and work with your hands is a set of skills, which should be honored and supported by more people. These skills should be exploited and supported because they are absolutely essential to manufacturing in America. In addition, these skills should not be allowed to fade out of the economy. It is up to everyone to recognize and honor the importance of manufacturing and making things.

Certainly, making things with your hands will not in and of itself make the U.S. competitive in the global climate. But when you connect this set of traditional skills with the new requirements of mathematics, computers, software, reading, writing and the need to get ahead, you may find that you have created the 21st Century manufacturing worker that we need to save American manufacturing.

Large Manufacturers and Globalization

Perhaps the most difficult problems to overcome are being caused by the Fortune 1000 manufacturing companies and their response to globalization. These are companies at the top of the supply chains – the ones who control both the supply chains and, sometimes, whole industries.

These are the manufacturing companies who are closing U.S. plants, sending work to foreign suppliers, and forcing their U.S. suppliers to lay off employees. They have combined to create much of the basic instability in American manufacturing and have contributed greatly to the poor image of manufacturing and manufacturing management. Sad to say, they have not made a strong case that investing in the time and training to be a skilled worker in manufacturing is a good economic decision.

The obvious question is how are we to get young students to think about investing time and effort in a manufacturing career when it seems that we cannot offer them job security?

A second problem also associated with the large manufacturers is their unwillingness to invest in training. Many studies have shown that manufacturers invest about 2% of their payrolls in training. Both the NAM study, "Keeping America Competitive," and the "2001 Skills Gap" study show that 88% of U.S. manufacturers are already indicating that there are serious shortages of qualified workers and that this problem will get worse as the baby boomers retire. So you don't have to be an economist to figure out that the traditional 2% of payroll is not going to solve the problem. Manufacturers, particularly the publicly traded kind, are not yet increasing their investment in training that will make a difference. In fact, public companies, for the most part, still treat employees as liabilities not assets.

In the past, these large companies have been key players in both organizing and funding training programs in specific industries. They complain often about not having the skilled workers that they need, but they are reluctant to fund or support training programs for supplier companies or even their own employees. Many of them have off-loaded the training function to their vendors as a result of re-engineering and cost cutting.

Most industry critics believe that manufacturing's image is manufacturing's fault. Whatever the root causes, manufacturing must take the responsibility to change its image. In my own view, a major factor is the fact that most manufacturers are focused on what they do – so the need for PR and image building simply never get addressed. But that will also have to change. Manufacturers, particularly the giant manufacturers who control supply chains, are going to have to make much more of an effort to convince current and potential employees that manufacturing is a career worth pursuing. Most manufacturers and their associations like the National Manufacturers Association agree with the studies such as the "2001 Skills Gap," and sound the alarm about the impending shortage of 10 million skilled workers. But they are not putting their money where their mouths are.

Pat Panchak, editor of *Industry Week*, summed the point up very succinctly in her August 2004 editorial "Reversing U.S. Manufacturers Skilled-Worker Challenge." She said, "Could it be that higher pay is not the only reward today's employees seek? Perhaps they are looking for a position that gives them a sense of contributing to a greater cause than the profit line. A sense of self and peer respect that comes with a position that encourages self-management and input into how work gets done? Or perhaps the wages, though good, are viewed as self-limiting.

"Upward mobility is the American dream, and it was once associated with factory jobs. No longer. Indeed they now represent just the opposite – downward mobility."[15]

American manufacturers are going to have to change that perception of "downward mobility." This will require making a strong effort to change minds about loyalty, security, and trust. This is difficult when they lay-off, outsource, close plants, and force pay and benefit decreases. The problem of skilled workers begins with manufacturing's image. So, before we can ask schools, parents, and governments to do their part, manufacturing must take the lead in showing that manufacturing workers are valuable. And that manufacturing careers are viable.

What Can Be Done?

The good news is that there are jobs – a lot of jobs. There is a serious shortage of skilled workers for many manufacturing occupations. This has been true for more than four years.

Parents, students, teachers, and counselors also need to be made aware that this shortage is not just in the blue-collar jobs. There will also be shortages of white-collar jobs that require both technical skills and a college degree. (It is not either/or. Ideally, everyone should have technical skills and a degree.)

Today's blue-collar jobs are generally safer, more demanding, and better paying than they were even ten years ago. In the year 2000, manufacturing jobs averaged $54,000 per year in total compensation. This is 20% higher than the average for all American workers. Here is a short list of some of the manufacturing occupations that we will need in order to meet current and future demands for manufacturing. The salaries listed are from the Occupational Outlook year 2000.[16]

BLUE COLLAR   Salary (median annual earnings 2000)

1.	Machine Operators	$40,000
2.	Machinists	$44,000[17]
3.	Tool and Die Maker	$41,000
4.	Senior Tool and Die Maker	$56,000[18]
5.	Tooling Supervisor	$63,000[19]

6.	Environmental Technician	$35,000
7.	Multi-Tasking Assembly Technicians	$40,000
8.	Electricians	$40-55,000
9.	Multi-Skilled Field Technicians	$75,000
10.	Plant Maintenance	$42-50,000
11.	IT Technicians	$47,000
12.	Robotics Technician	$41,000
13.	Industrial Engineering Technician	$41,000
14.	CAD –CAM Designer	$45,000

WHITE COLLAR

15.	Engineers	$60,000
16.	Electrical Engineers	$65,000
17.	Industrial Engineers	$60,000
18.	Sales Engineer	$57,000
19.	Product Marketing Manager	$72,000
20.	CAD-CAM Designer	$46,000
21.	General Managers	$125,000 plus
22.	Scientists	$100,000
22.	R&D Engineers	$75,000

Solutions to the Skills Gap

This book has set a big goal – saving an entire sector of our economy.

So, we shouldn't be surprised that some of the tasks we must accomplish are also a bit large.

Yet, it still boils down to how you eat an elephant – "one bite at a time."

Each of us has one or more roles to play. And, with a shared goal – providing meaningful training to meet our country's genuine needs for skilled workers – we can get the job done. Piece by piece.

Here are some of the things we must do – group by group.

1. Educating Parents, Teachers, and Counselors

We must sell some of America's parents and their children on the idea that working with their hands in a complex manufacturing job can be a good career alternative. This may be the biggest obstacle to overcome if we are going to get young people interested in manufacturing.

It is not simply a matter of having a "Manufacturing Day" where all the parents and teachers are invited to a local manufacturing operation. It is a matter of continuous, positive publicity and education about manufacturing. This should be supported by both the largest and smallest manufacturers, as well as relevant government agencies.

The first part of the challenge is to help parents, teachers, students, and counselors understand that skilled manufacturing jobs (both blue and white collar) are technology jobs that pay well and can be a good career investment. For some, manufacturing jobs will be a better career choice than most service or "knowledge worker" jobs. We also have to convince them that manufacturing and college degrees don't have to be an "either/or" proposition. That a college degree is needed and helpful as long as the student gets skill training along with the education.

The second part of the challenge is manufacturing's overall image. Specifically, manufacturing is going to have to convince the public that it is not a dying industry that is slowly going away. I believe that America really wants to maintain a diverse and productive manufacturing base. This is really a challenge for the large manufacturing companies who control whole industries and supply chains. They must address the issues of trust, security, loyalty and a long-term manufacturing base if they are going to change the public's mind about manufacturing. They must "walk the talk."

Government/Industry Collaborations That Work

Government can play many significant roles in doing something about the skills gap.

The ongoing problem is to find out the most efficient way of spending the taxpayer's money to get the best bang for our buck. And it won't be easy. As soon as there's money on the table, a host of experts and special interests always seem to show up.

What could be hugely helpful is specific direction from industry on whom to train, how to train, and where to train. And this advice could vary by region. In American manufacturing, "one size does not fit all." Government, in this author's opinion, should not invest any money in training programs unless the manufacturers of a specific state or region can demonstrate that they can work together and with educational institutions to develop comprehensive training programs that focus on genuine needs.

A Program That Worked

A good example of what can be done is the Wisconsin Regional Training Partnership formed in 1992 by 22 charter member manufacturing firms and unions, in a collaboration with several public agencies.

This private/public training consortium is industry driven and worker oriented. It is a training program that worked because industry took the initiative to say what they needed for their workers and how they wanted the training to be conducted.

For this program, the manufacturers are concentrated in metal working, machinery, and electronic controls. They range in size from 85 to 3,000 employees (roughly half the membership is comprised of manufacturers with fewer than 500 employees). Taken together, these companies employ nearly 30,000 state residents.

As of 2003, membership in this program has risen to 125 members.

This organization's goal has been to jointly develop workplace education programs and to improve the skills of their current workforces as well as provide training for future workers. This union/management partnership is unique – and it works. The companies want to improve productivity and implement the most modern manufacturing methods, and the unions and workers want more secure jobs at family supporting wage levels.

Their mission includes the following:

1. **Basic Skills** – The partnership is committed to provide core training and basic skills at both on-site and off-site workplace education centers. These workplace education centers are employee

driven and instruction must match the speed of learning.

2. **Upgrade Training** – The WRTP also facilitates the spread of upgrade training in the workplace education centers. This allows employees to move into advanced positions within their firms – making way for new entry level workers.

3. **Pre-employment and Re-employment Training** – All manufacturers in Southeast Wisconsin report problems in recruiting and training successful entry level workers because of a variety of social and skill problems. The entry worker project developed by the WRTP is designed to make recruiting and training of qualified entry level workers more efficient and to reform the system so that more workers can make the successful transition to long term productive employment. The candidates for this training are permanently laid off manufacturing workers, disadvantaged adults, and young adults with no manufacturing experience.

4. **School to Work** – The main component of the WRTP's future workforce development effort is to strategically assist school to work programs that have emerged in Wisconsin as a response to Federal mandates. From kindergarten to senior year in high school, they provide students with technical training and equally valuable skills of communication, cooperation, and flexibility. The program brings organized labor and companies into partnership with public schools, technical colleges, parents, teachers, and industry sponsors. There has been an additional benefit – a more positive awareness and attitude among the groups mentioned a few pages ago: parents, teachers, and counselors.

5. **Expansion** – The WRTP training partnership has now been expanded to include training for construction, healthcare, and utilities.

The WRTP chose an "open architecture" for the development of their training organization. The partnership is based on the assumption that members must invest in helping themselves and part of the price of membership is a commitment to act upon recommendations once consensus is achieved.

In the original model, the company and union formed a steering committee to design and develop on-site and off-site training programs. The on-site training programs are called Workplace Education Centers. This is a distributed system of on-site education centers, and the Wisconsin Technical College system, one of the best in the country, is able to offer a wide variety of training curricula. This program did not need to build their own technology center. They were able to use the Milwaukee Area Technical College as the core of the system.

External resources from both state government and national foundations were critical during the start-up phase. Then, as confidence in the process improved, companies began investing in the program. For the most part, the companies offered in-kind investments such as donating the training room, equipment, and instructors.

They also donated money for the operation budget. Given how often we read about multi-million dollar boondoggles, we think you'll be pleasantly surprised by the cost of this program.

The average Workplace Education Center has a $70,000 per year operating budget. There are now 70 centers. And the "product' of these centers is employable men and women who become part of the work force.

Some centers that are teaching basic skill training or re-employment training do get Federal and National Foundation grants. These grants are on a "matching basis." Companies have to match government funds on a declining percentage basis. Eventually, the program will be totally financed by the companies and users.

The WRTP program suggests that there are three keys to successfully designing and implementing this type of training consortium:

1. Influential companies and business leaders (including union leaders) need to take charge and lead the initial drive to develop a working partnership.
2. There must be agreement that this program will be driven by industry before going after the money to fund the project. This includes large manufacturers, small manufacturers and their unions. The program must train for real jobs in the region.

3. It is important to keep government agencies from imposing their own agendas during the start up of the program. It must be driven by the region's manufacturing sector in partnership with the region's technical training resources.

Hopefully, there's more good news. Another program in Illinois called the Critical Skills Initiative, which is similar to the Wisconsin program, has also been awarded significant money by the Federal government.

Apprentice Training

The 10 million skilled jobs needed for manufacturing's future are technology jobs. They are *not* unskilled jobs.

Government agencies often overlook or ignore the even more critical need for training beyond entry-level positions – this is the advanced training that used to be called apprenticeship training. This is training that allows workers to move up into higher pay ranges, and gain the skills needed for promotion in a manufacturing operation.

Most apprenticeship is a combination of occupational training, on-the-job experience, and classroom instruction that allows the apprentice, under supervision of an experienced journeyman-type worker, to gain crucial skills essential for the occupation. This is the in-depth skill training that is needed to turn a metals industry job, for example, into a high paid career path.

Here's how it works in today's manufacturing environment.

Mech Tech – An Ideal Model

Mech Tech, Inc., in Rhode Island is a good example of a model that could be used to begin apprenticeship or advanced training. The Mech Tech Apprenticeship Company is the result of a group of Rhode Island industry leaders who got together in 1986 and organized a private company in response to the state's shortage and need for qualified workers. Instead of leaving the problem to the government, or to a few large companies, Mech Tech organized an apprenticeship program around a consortium of manufacturers. What is unique about this program is that Mech Tech is a participating private company, and uses a rotational process for training within a variety of companies.

A second distinction of the Mech Tech Apprenticeship Company is that the practical hands-on training is enhanced by a rigorous college-level academic curriculum.

The Mech Tech idea is to prepare the apprentice for a career in manufacturing technology, mechanical engineering technology, or engineering transfer programs. The company recruits some of the best students in the area out of high school, and these candidates for apprenticeships are already sold on the idea of manufacturing as a career that could include a college degree.

Every apprentice is registered with the state apprenticeship council. Then they begin rotating through the participating companies to get their hands-on training. The apprentice programs for machining or tool and die work call for 8,000 to 10,000 hours of hands on training and academic instruction.

Mech Tech takes care of initial recruitment, screening, paying the apprentices, assigning them to the rotation and training, and eventually placing the apprentices in a permanent position in a company.

Unlike academic degrees that may have nothing to do with the actual economic need, Mech Tech apprenticeships are developed with an ongoing connection to the evolving needs of the changing job market.

The Importance of Apprentice-Type Jobs

The advanced training in these types of skilled jobs leads to journeyman status or an advanced position in a plant. These are critical to manufacturers for the following reasons:

1. **Promotion** – The advanced training allows the worker to learn a wide variety of skills that allow them to do a wide variety of tasks and the knowledge to move up in the organization.
2. **Capability** – The wide range of skills and knowledge required to become a journeyman is critical to manufacturing growth. The journeyman-type worker is the only worker with all of the skills to handle the tooling, design, and innovation necessary to develop

new products. Journeymen are also critical because they specify and install capital equipment and are often the key to plant expansions.

3. **New Companies** – Journeymen spawn new companies. Many of the journeymen trained in the '50s and '60s started their own businesses and are now running the new, innovative companies driving many local economies.

4. **Worker Progress** – Advanced or journeyman-type skills are the key to advancement in a manufacturing company and, more importantly, they help the worker progress from entry-level wages to family job incomes.

As of 2004, the Mech Tech program had spread to Connecticut and Massachusetts, and the sponsoring manufacturing companies are as enthusiastic as ever.

The Siemens Example

A terrific example of what a large manufacturer can do if they are really committed to closing the skills gap is what Siemens Energy and Automation has been doing to nurture a skilled workforce in the U.S. since 1998.

This program has commitment from the top down. Thomas Malott, who was then President and CEO of the company headquartered in Alpharetta, Georgia, has been a critical factor.

Since U.S. educational programs do not instill many of the skills required for his workers, Mr. Malott suggests that manufacturers establish their own apprenticeship programs to train their own workers. Malott says, "Siemens long-standing corporate program 'bridges the education gap' created when non-college bound students are given only minimum academic background in math and English."

Siemens's current apprentice program is based on the company's 100-year-old program for funneling people from school to skilled jobs in industry. Siemens has 13,000 apprentices in 20 countries including 25 separate training programs at 13 U.S. sites.[20]

Structured around the basic educational needs, Siemens youth and adult apprenticeship programs provide specific work-related skills, hands-on training, and/or community college–based learning or advanced manufacturing training.

Malott notes that "apprentice-trained workers achieve a 42% productivity increase and 70% fewer product defects than their untrained counterparts. This delivers a total savings of $458,000." He adds, "Not bad for a training investment of only $30,000."

Education – K–12

The headline in my local paper read "Lackluster scores disappoint." The article began "Mediocre achievement in the state's middle and high schools demand urgent, proven fixes to raise teenagers reading and math skills."[21]

What's more, this article came after a 13-year effort in my state to improve test scores in all schools. Our programs for educational reform were similar to many other programs in other states to do something about education – most have the same results.

In my view, programs that focus on improving test scores are a failure in three important ways. First, the objective of the programs – to improve tests scores on math, reading, and science – simply haven't worked, even though many schools are teaching to the test.

Second, there never were many dollars budgeted for the kids who couldn't or wouldn't pass the tests and weren't college bound.

Third, there is little effort to offer the training and skill classes that lead to actually getting a job or finding a career. I know that my frustration is showing, but perhaps one answer is to not leave it up to the educational system to come up with the answers. Now let me get off my soap box and tell you about a program that actually worked.

An alternative approach has been successfully developed in Pennsylvania. It is called the Pennsylvania Global Academy Charter School. It was formed by a group of manufacturers and business people who put their heads together in Erie to try and come up with an alternative approach to K–12 education. The focus of this program is to help students find a career.

The curriculum is not the usual college prep curriculum, although the students are encouraged to go as far as they can in their education.

The idea of this alternative school is focused on a blend of academic classes and job skill or technical training. This alternative school is dedicated to educating children who can't or don't want to go to a four-year college. For those who want to get an associates or four-year degree, the program provides technical classes that can be taken for college credit.

The alternative school approach is simple and essentially based on the concept that kids can acquire career skills along with a basic education. The Global Academy Charter School is also focused on improving math, science, reading and writing skills and is doing better in test scores than the public schools.

Just as there is no "one size fits all" marketing program, there is no "one size fits all" education program. We have trouble admitting that some students just aren't very good at "book learning" even if they have other useful skills and talents. The science of neurolinguistic programming reveals that people learn in many different ways. For example, many people only learn by doing or working with their hands. Sometimes it is not only the best way to teach them, but also may make the subject more interesting.

Most child development experts believe that "hands-on" learning imprints knowledge on a child's brain through different sensory pathways. In her book, *Endangered Minds*, Jane Healy notes, "visual stimulation is probably not the main access route to nonverbal reasoning. Body movements, the ability to touch, feel, manipulate, and build sensory awareness of relationships in the physical world are its main foundations."[22]

An interesting example of this principle is Kris Meisling, a senior geological-research advisor for Mobil Oil. As you might imagine, he uses computers a lot in his job to find oil. However, he also uses a pencil and paper – tools that, ironically, he considers more interactive than the computer, because they force him to think implications through. Kris notes, "You can't simultaneously get an overview and detail with a computer." When asked to explain, he says "It's linear. It gives you tunnel vision. What computers can do well is what can be calculated over and over. What they can't do is innovation."[23]

These examples fly in the face of what is happening in the classroom today, where computer labs dominate teaching, and hands-on learning is either minimized or absent. With so much criticism about education, particularly criticism that students can no longer think for themselves or think creatively, one wonders why nobody supports bringing back "hands-on" learning.

The people who operate the Global Academy Charter School understand this. They allow students to take classes in all kinds of technical or hands-on classes at the Academy along with their usual courses in science, math, reading, and writing. The idea is to not drag every kid through the "college prep knothole" whether they want it or not. The idea is to both provide an education and prepare them to get a job and have a career. In my view, this approach would work very well to prepare kids for skilled manufacturing jobs as well as many other careers.

Vocational Schools and Colleges

In the same geographical area of Western Pennsylvania as Global is CamTech, the Center for Advanced Manufacturing Technology, established in 2001 as a private non-profit educational institution designed to build and rebuild the regional workforce. CamTech's unusual goal is to "help provide qualified workers who can adapt to constant changes in the work environment."

CamTech is a premier technical college that provides:

- Industry specific job training that includes the awarding of diplomas, certificates, and associates degrees
- A curriculum that combines technical education, technical training, and general education
- Industry specific job training for companies, which can be delivered either at their sites or CamTech's
- A combination of hands-on training and work experiences that

will prepare the students for long-term success in the workplace
- Guidance to business and industry in developing and implementing training plans and in sourcing funds for that training
- Career guidance, advisory services for financial assistance, and employment placement services for students.[24]

CamTech offers all of the basic education courses needed to get an associates degree such as English, mathematics, technical writing, communication, and social sciences. But they also offer many specialized technical courses in areas such as welding, machining, visual basic, and other computer related classes. They can offer careers in areas such as industrial safety specialist, maintenance, metalworking, plastics technology, quality specialist, tool and die and mold-making.

NWPA Manufacturing Association

In addition to the charter school and technical college, this region has also created the NWPA Manufacturing Association. Manufacturers created this association to serve the needs of local employers. The Association, "provides a focused educational experience that delivers exactly what your people need to know based on job responsibilities and skill levels."[25] The curriculum lists classes in supervisory skills, management leadership, customer service, Lean Manufacturing, project management, and all of the computer skills necessary in the modern manufacturing business.

In addition, the NWPA Manufacturing Association provides these classes either on-site or in a classroom at any one of four different campuses. Here, the focus is on the skills you need on any type of job, which includes many of the soft subjects not taught in technical colleges and universities.

Now you can see why there may be hope.

The models are in place – and they're working.

The Alternative Global Academy Charter School, CamTech, and the NW-PAMA collectively offer almost all of the skills and classes needed to develop and revitalize our new manufacturing workforce. These successful programs can serve as a model to educators, government agencies, and manufacturing companies on how to solve the educational crisis and the skills gap.

Universities and Four-Year Colleges

Outside of professional programs such as engineering and accounting, universities, for the most part, are out of step with what is going on in the business of manufacturing. As an institution, the university has not changed with the needs of manufacturing. Many universities resist the notion that they are responsible for young people getting jobs. They don't seem to want to address the fact that tuition keeps going up and many parents cannot afford to send their kids to a four-year college that doesn't enhance their chance of getting a family wage job. Likewise, students saddled with a significant student loan burden have their own pressures to be prepared for a viable career. At the same time, manufacturers cannot afford to retrain students with general degrees, with all of the skills needed to begin a career.

One answer to the problem is obvious. Why not combine the academic courses with skill training courses that will help any graduate secure some kind of decent paying job? This means that various educational organizations will have to give accreditation to many schools that don't fit their educational models. It means giving college credits for classes taught in technical colleges and manufacturing associations or by providing the same skill classes on campus. From the perspective of preserving our manufacturing sector, this makes sense. A student graduating with a major in psychology and a minor in machine technology would be a much better job candidate than someone graduating magna cum laude in a general degree.

If you could combine a general degree with 1–2 years of specific skill sets that are taught in associates and other programs, general graduates would have some skills to at least begin in manufacturing. In addition, the white-collar jobs listed above, like product marketing manager, sales manager, or general manager are not necessarily the best jobs for engineering graduates. This kind of training could be much more useful.

American manufacturing needs reinforcements.

Ten million skilled workers can help us compete.

Conclusion

Manufacturing is at a crossroads. Are America's manufacturing companies (large and small), educational institutions, and governments on the regional, state, and national levels going to get together to launch the skilled training programs we need to compete in the world market?

Or are we going to simply run to the nearest low-cost country and take our chances on a future that we might not be able to control?

According to Robert Reich, who was Secretary of Labor in the Clinton Administration, the big challenge is to "bring the bottom 60 to 80% of the working population up to a minimum level of competence, so that they can get the skill sets that are needed and don't have to rely on personal services." Reich is also concerned that four-fifths of the working population's "economic future is growing more precarious."[26]

Manufacturing has shifted toward jobs requiring higher skills. The more skills the employee has, the more flexible they are for employers. We can supply manufacturers with the people needed to fill these skilled and semi-skilled jobs if we commit to providing the education and training. This is something that, in many ways, has been lost over the last 30 years.

We need to bring it back. This country was built on manufacturing. And manufacturing is more than making things – manufacturers made a middle class in the United States. Now, it is up to manufacturing (particularly the large manufacturers) to develop training programs and opportunities to attract some of the best and the brightest back to manufacturing. To succeed in this new world, manufacturing must also convince young people who want to make a difference by making things that this is a career worthy of pursuing.

The National Association of Manufactures (NAM), which represents most of the giant manufacturers in the U.S., has made a commitment to manufacturing training. That commitment is, "to make manufacturing careers a preferred career option by the end of this decade through an integrated awareness, career planning, and public education campaign." To their credit, this is the goal that has been needed for a long time, if we are to help U.S. manufacturing survive globalization.

But right now, this worthwhile goal and commitment are only written words with little meaning unless the large manufacturing companies decide to support it.

NAM has also issued four challenges:[27]

- To the President of the United States:
  Declare U.S. manufacturing a national priority

- To the United States Congress:
  Establish "National Manufacturing Day" to recognize this priority

- To manufacturers in the U.S.:
  Open your plants and facilities to young people, teachers and parents on National Manufacturing Day

- To educators in the U.S.:
  Bring your students and guidance counselors to a modern manufacturing facility on National Manufacturing Day.

This is all well-intentioned, but, in my view, it is not enough.

These four challenges are weak public relations goals that really do not support the commitment and hard work needed to make manufacturing a preferred career choice by the end of the decade.

Here is what I think it's going to take.

Modified Challenges to Make the NAM Goal Happen:

- To the President of the United States:
  The challenge has to go beyond the President making manufacturing a national priority. He needs to say clearly and forcefully that manufacturing is so important that its demise would deal a mortal blow to our economy. He should suggest a program to achieve the NAM goal equivalent to sending a man to the moon within ten years.

- To the United States Congress:

There is hardly a representative that does not have some manufacturing in his or her district. They should also acknowledge that manufacturing is important enough to warrant this kind of attention. They should approve the funding to achieve the goal.

- To educators, parents, teachers and counselors in the U.S.:
Bringing your students, teachers, and guidance counselors to a manufacturing shop is only the first step. We need to urge you to look hard at the good opportunities for making a living that manufacturing can offer.

- To large manufacturers in the U.S.:
The National Association of Manufacturers represents most of the giant manufacturers as the chief lobbying group in Washington D.C. These manufacturers and their associations are key to making this happen. There is no doubt that if we really want to achieve the goal, these groups have the power, money, and connections with the administration and Congress to do it. As a group, they are the companies who will have to lead the charge in making these programs happen at all levels.

- To the government agencies in the U.S.:
We don't need another ineffective and money-wasting Workers Investment Act run by bureaucrats. It should be up to the manufacturers to decide who gets the training, how they are trained, and who will do that training. The best role for government is as the funding agency that gets industry, education, parents, counselors, and students together into collaboration driven and led by industry.

Key Points

If America is going to have a chance of reversing the decline of manufacturing, we will have to hire and train the 10 million workers needed by 2020. This is an issue where government can provide money, support, and facilities, and can play a key role in training and education.

The training and education that will save American manufacturing will require:

- Educating parents, teachers, and counselors
- Government and industry collaboration
- Reinventing the apprenticeship programs
- Improvements in K–12 education, including offering practical courses that will help students get jobs
- Better funding of vocational schools and community college vocational programs
- Offering practical courses in four-year colleges
- A commitment by the federal government to make saving manufacturing as important as putting a man on the moon
- A change in the attitudes and policies of large manufacturers who have helped make a career in manufacturing a poor choice in the eyes of parents, teachers, and students.

Suggested Action

By all means, open your plants and facilities to young people, teachers and parents at all times. But, more importantly, volunteer the money, time, and expertise to design and teach the new training programs.

Notes:

1. National Association of Manufacturers, "Keeping America Competitive: How a Talent Shortage Threatens U.S. Manufacturing," Washington, DC: National Association of Manufacturers, 2003.

2. National Association of Manufacturers, "The Skills Gap 2001: Manufacturers Confront Persistent Skills Shortages in an Uncertain Economy," Washington, DC: National Association of Manufacturers, 2001.

3. National Association of Manufacturers and Deloitte & Touche, 2002, Baccus Research San Francisco, CA.

4. David Stamps, "Blue Collar Blues," *Training* (May 1998): 34.

5. See Note 1.

6. "Caught in a Retraining Trap," *Oregonian*, Business, May 2, 2004.

7. Richard Walker, National tooling and Machining Association, 2003.

8. See Note 2.

9. Craig Barrett, CEO of Intel, *Wall Street Journal*, January 6, 2004.

10. National Center for Education Statistics, Digest of Education Statistics, 2001, Post secondary Education.

11. Ibid.

12. See Note 1.

13. "Baccalaureate and Beyond: A Descriptive Summary of 1999-2000 Bachelor's Degree Recipients, 1 Year Later," NCES, US Department of Education, 2003:165.

14. Victor Davis Hanson, "Topsy-turvy: American Universities Are Places Of Dizzying Unreality – And This Does Considerable Harm," *National Review*, October 13, 2003.

15. Pat Panchak, "Reversing U.S. Manufacturing's Skilled Worker Challenge," *Industry Week*, August 2004.

16. Occupational Outlook Handbook, 2002-2003 editions, bureau of Labor Statistics, U.S. Department of Labor.

17. Precision Metal forming Association .

18. Ibid.

19. Ibid.

20. "Career Update: Apprenticeships Help Companies Nurture Skilled Workforce," *Control Engineering*, Reed Business Information, May 1998, 21.

21. Betsy Hammond, "Lackluster Scores Disappoint," *Oregonian*, August 5, 2004.

22. Todd Openhiemer, "The Computer Delusion," *Atlantic Monthly*, July 1997.

23. Manufacturers Association of Northwest Pennsylvania, A Professional Employer Resource, Training Programs, March-August 2004.

24. Robert Reich, *The Work of Nations* (New York: Random House, 1991).

25. CamTech, Course Catalog 2003/2004, P,M01/03

26. See Note 1.

27. See Note 1.

Chapter 9

Developing a Growth Plan or a Turnaround Plan

A New Approach to Planning for Manufacturers

All businesses need some kind of a business plan – even if it is only a sales forecast and budget – with a few goals and a simply defined strategy. But wait – planning in today's economy has become a different animal.

Finding a way to grow when customers are shifting their business to other suppliers and relentlessly demanding price reductions is a totally new environment for small and midsize manufacturers (SMMs). Not surprisingly, it is forcing many manufacturers into a crisis situation.

The crisis is usually about manufacturers who have one or more of the following problems:

- Have lost some of their MVC (high volume) accounts
- Need to find new customers and markets
- Need to get rid of unprofitable customers
- In stagnant or declining industries with too many competitors
- Have lost market share and are not growing
- Have been losing money and need to get back in the black.

These kinds of problems suggest SMMs may have to find new customers and markets if they want future growth. As we discussed earlier in this book, finding new customers and markets may require:

- Developing new products
- Offering new services
- Changing sales channels
- Transforming the company to a Prospector organization.

You need a plan to implement change. Changing from a Defender-type organization to a Prospector organization that is ready to go on the attack in the marketplace requires a special type of plan – a Growth Plan.

If lost customers and volume have already put the company into financial crisis, you need more than a business plan, you need a "Turnaround Plan." Simply put, a "Turnaround Plan" is a business plan designed to be accomplished during a crisis. It is driven by the need to quickly find ways to replace lost sales.

These plans are about re-focusing in the marketplace and then restructuring and redefining your business to match the new customer needs. In short, it is about adapting your manufacturing company to the new market realities.

What about Strategic Plans?

The buzzword answer to a plan for all seasons has been the "strategic plan." Strategic planning has been a popular method of business planning for defender type companies (see Chapter 6) who could depend on steady growth and stable markets.

But with globalization the days of stable markets and steady growth may be gone. And this has made strategic planning less effective as a management process.

Strategic planning, for all practical purposes, simply has not produced the results that are implied by the name. It has been a failure for large, publicly held manufacturers in terms of accurate forecasting and predicting the future. And it certainly has been a failure for small and mid-size manufacturing companies who really need "breakthrough" performance or a plan that will transform or turn around the company.

Professor Henry Mintzburg wrote a book titled the "The Rise and fall of Strategic Planning"[1] which reveals why it was a failure for so many companies. He makes the point that the process of doing strategic planning became more important than the results. People who like quantification and processes loved strategic planning because the process itself makes them feel they have really accomplished something.

Professor Brian Quinn of Dartmouth College summarized the problem best when he said "A great deal of corporate planning is like a ritual rain dance. It has no effect on the weather that follows but those who engage in the dance think it does."

The problem is that strategic planning has not been "strategic."

Before discussing a practical planning process that can be tailored to the size and resources of SMMs, it is useful to spend a little time examining the weak points of the strategic planning process – from the perspective of SMMs.

1. **Mission/Vision/Values Trap** – The idea of defining the company's mission, vision, and values is a noble idea. But, too often, more time is spent on these definitions than in gathering the strategic information needed to plan the future.

   In many cases, defining the mission, vision, values, and core competencies of the company simply leads to well-intentioned generalizations that are not actionable. Statements about global leadership, valuing trust and integrity, and providing superior quality and service are simply platitudes that make people feel good. But all too often, they only lead to long flowery mission statements that are hung in the foyer of the manufacturer's office.

   What is missing are short goal statements that set the direction for the company and give managers the specific direction they need to do their part of the plan. You need statements that define growth, sales, new customers, market share, cost reduction, new products, and profitability; and exactly what is needed to turn around the manufacturing company and get back to growth.

2. **SWOT Analysis** – The strategic planning process always begins with the popular SWOT Analysis. SWOT means defining the strengths, weaknesses, opportunities, and threats. The term originally was to include both internal and external information.

   SWOT was supposed to include information on customers, markets, and competitors gathered by external research methods. But, more often than not, SWOT became an internally driven exercise. It is based on the manager's perception of customers, markets, and competitors and uses historical and internal information – not real, external data. It is usually subjective, and seldom an accurate picture of what is going on in the market.

It is this author's opinion that most SWOT analysis is not really based on up-to-date external research and does not realistically assess the external environment – much less the company's true position in the marketplace.

So why has SWOT analysis been so popular? Because it is much easier than gathering up-to-date market data and competitive intelligence. And it's an enjoyable mental exercise.

But when the primary problems of the manufacturer have to do with the loss of customers, changing markets, and erratic growth, external data on customers, competitors, and markets is much more important than internal analysis and opinion.

Strategic planners tend to focus on the hard data that is available rather than the soft data that describes customers, markets, and competitors. Mintzberg makes this observation: "While hard data might inform the intellect, it is the soft data that creates wisdom. They may be difficult to analyze but they are indispensable for synthesis – the key to making strategy." In fact, external information on competitors, markets, and customers, and using this information to develop new strategies is the most important and abused part of planning.

3. **Financial and Internal Information** – Reviewing historical financial information in the income statement and balance sheet can be very helpful but it is not enough.

   In my view, the problem is that there don't seem to be minimum standards against which financial information must be examined. For example, what if a cursory review reveals that sales are declining, profit is declining, and cash flow is awful. Should the plan be stopped until the reasons for these symptoms are totally explained? Planners often proceed hoping that somehow the process will cure these critical problems.

   A second often-overlooked issue is cost and margin information. This point cannot be emphasized enough because smaller manufacturers often do not have good cost and margin information.

This problem will automatically affect pricing strategies and finding new customers and markets. Too often, strategic planners will accept the financials that are available without digging into the implications

That said, I should note that many CPAs and marketing planners can be quite good at identifying and analyzing these issues. Use my comments as a checklist. If these issues are being addressed, well and good. If not, you need to get a better handle on your financial information.

The third issue related to financial information is knowing why the company is losing orders. Understanding why a company is losing customers or orders is obviously strategic to any Growth Plan. However, a "Lost Order Analysis" is seldom used as a strategic planning tool.

If the primary objective of a Growth Plan is to increase sales by finding new customers and markets, or creating new products, manufacturers must know where and why they are making or losing money on current customers, jobs, and products. It is dangerous to pursue new customers and projects without having a true understanding of costs and prices. In fact, if costs and margins are not adequately understood, sales success can lead to accelerated cash flow problems

4. **Top Down Planning** – Many Strategic Plans are developed by top management. They are top down processes. Top management decides the major goals, the specific business objectives and often the strategies.

Professor Mintzburg talks about the problems of detachment as fundamental to the downfall of strategic planning. He notes that "It is this disassociation of thinking from acting that lies close to the root of strategic planning problems."

It is as if there is an assumption that once you have done the thinking and have written a report, the plan is complete and will somehow be executed. The reality is that at this stage, the real planning that will lead to implementation of the plan should just begin. This detachment of top management from bottom and middle management and the necessary transition from thinking to doing is what has killed off many good plans.

When the top people design the plan and the strategies, you don't always get "buy-in" from the people who have to execute it.

5. **Developing Strategies** – Before you can decide on new strategies for sales channels, new products, pricing, promotion, etc., it is wise to first ask each department what obstacles or problems they must overcome before they can achieve those sales, profit, new product, and other company goals.

   As obvious as this sounds, many strategic planners decide the strategies first and ask the managers last. As an example, top management may decide that a sales increase is needed in a specific product line or that there must be an increase in market share. But the reality is the sales manager may need additional sales people, more funding for promotion, or special products developed for new markets in order to achieve these objectives

   Mintzberg thinks the primary rule of modern planning should be finding strategies in "unexpected pockets of the organization" rather then relying on top people to choose or define them.

   This extremely important point is often overlooked. Strategy is not a magic wand that management can wave. From many years of experience, I believe that finding the right strategies is best accomplished by the managers and people who control specific functions of the company. They must have a chance to think through all of the problems and obstacles first before deciding on the solutions that will lead to specific strategies. (Bear with me. You'll see a process that does this in just a little bit.)

6. **Implementation and Defining Tasks** – Implementation is the step where even well conceived plans break down. Most Strategic Plans are devoted to "what" the company wants to happen and not to the details of "how" it will happen. Implementation requires that

the plan be shared and known throughout the company and that problems and solutions are broken down to the specific tasks – it's "what" will we do and "who" will do it.

7. **Plans are Written Reports** – Another serious weakness of most strategic plans is that they are written in narrative form – like a college thesis. For those who are the products of an MBA program, or who have a background with a relatively sophisticated marketing organization, this may seem like the way things should be done.

The fact is that there has been far too much emphasis on process and paper work in planning, particularly in the world of SMMs. Process and paperwork can strangle the planning process and limit the company's ability to react to changes.

Even though this may sound minor, it is a huge problem. Some of it is cultural. But, within SMMs, the simple fact is plans that are 50 to 100 pages of even the best written narrative are not going to get implemented – no matter how good the information is.

People in industrial manufacturing companies do not generally communicate with long narrative reports or plans. In fact, technical people often communicate in spreadsheets, board drawings, and e-mails – not on word processors. Suffice it to say that the more succinct the plan is and the fewer paragraphs there are the better chance you will have of communicating and implementing the planning ideas.

A Growth Plan for Small and Midsize Manufacturers

Now let's work through a process that was designed for SMMs.

Based on quite a bit of experience, I know that SMMs do not like to do business plans. There are a lot of reasons for this. Not the least of them is that most SMM managers consider planning an academic exercise that leads to generalizations and no real results. Manufacturers are action oriented. They like to do things that lead to tangible and believable results.

I've tried numerous approaches to this problem in trying to come up with a workable planning format that would be accepted by SMMs. The following outline describes a planning process that was designed specifically for SMMs who manufacture industrial products. It is based on real life experiences in manufacturing turnaround situations and was implemented during the fires of combat to survive.

The plan is accomplished in five steps. It can be tailored to the resources and understanding of the owners and employees of any small manufacturing company.

Here's how it works.

Step A – **Internal Analysis:** Show Me The Money.
Step B – **External Analysis:** Where Will We Grow?
Step C – **Analysis:** Putting It All Together.
Step D – **Implementation:** Quad Planning.
Step E – **Strategic Renewal:** Changing The Organization.

These five steps are explained by a hypothetical manufacturer that we shall call General Material Handling. The specifics and background for this hypothetical but typical company are as follows:

General Material Handling (GMH)

Founded – 1960
Ownership – One family
Size – Annual sales of $10–11 million
Products – Material-handling machines used in warehouses
Employees – 100+
Type 3 – product manufacturer
Costing information – excellent
Growth – Erratic. Since 1995 has had a few good profitable years but market share has declined in a mature industry.
Financial Health – Industry growth became stagnant in 1998 and more competitors have come into the industry. General broke even in 1998, 1999, and 2000. From 2000 on the company has been losing money and has not been able to push through price increases.

Step A: Internal Information – Show Me the Money

Here, the purpose is simply to gather the most important financial information that is needed to develop the plan.

Since this is a Growth Plan, the obvious first question is how much growth? The next questions are how do we know if the company is healthy and does it have the resources to grow? Another closely associated question is does the company have accurate cost and margin information on customers, jobs, products, and services? A final question is does the company know why it is losing customers and orders?

Before embarking on a Growth Plan, the manufacturer must know where they are making or losing money – and why. The more you know about the answers to these questions the better chance you will have of choosing strategies that will lead to growth.

You do not have to be a CPA or financial analyst to do this step. The objective is to identify the problem areas that may hinder growth. If you find in a preliminary examination that there are a lot of "red flag" answers, then you may have to call in a financial expert.

Let's look at our example company, GMH, and how they answered 11 questions.

How Much Growth Do You Want?

1. What is your objective for increasing sales volume in the current fiscal year?
   _10%_ increase over previous fiscal year

2. What is your objective for increasing net profit in the current fiscal year?
   _10%_ increase over previous fiscal year

3. Given your firm's capabilities as well as customer and market conditions, how likely are you to reach the sales and profit objectives given above?

	Sales Goal	Profit Goal
Highly probable		
Very probable	X	
Somewhat probable		
Not very probable		X
Highly unlikely		

How Good Are Current Sales, Profits And Cashflow?

4. What have been your firm's total sales for the last three years? (Sales refer to dollar revenues actually received by your firm in each fiscal year.)

   $5 million year-to-date; enter the number of months _6_

   $10 million most recent fiscal year (year ending date 12/31/99)

   $11 million Next most recent year

   $10 million Next most recent year

Sales are declining for a number of reasons:
- some of GMH's customers are switching to buying foreign products
- some customers have relocated their plants to other countries
- some of their markets are declining
- several of their primary product lines are not selling.

5. Profitability (sales minus total expenses) during the past three years has been...
   __ Increasing   _X_ Flat   __ Decreasing

Profitability is flat, but has been slowly eroding because of some of the largest MVC customers have forced price discounts. In addition, GMH's costs have increased 5–6% per year for five years and they have not been able to raise prices.

6. Do you consider your current cash flow to be?
   __ Excellent   _X_ Good   __ Fair
   __ Awful (Why do you think this has occurred?)

Fortunately, cash flow is still good. GMH has a strong balance sheet with very little debt and a good cash reserve. They are not behind on their accounts payable and are doing okay collecting their receivables.

Worst Case Scenario – If a manufacturer answered sales are declining, profits are decreasing, and cash flow is awful, it is a "worst case" scenario. Then, they might be in a turnaround situation where immediate objectives should be to get costs down and cash flow straightened out. In this scenario, it is dangerous to work on any plan to increase sales unless you completely understand and can document the reasons for each problem.

Costs. Margins, And Prices

7. Does your firm maintain current information on of any of the following? (Check all that apply.)

Customers: __ Profitability   X Unit Sales
X Dollar Sales   __ N/A

Products/product lines: X Profitability   X Unit Sales
X Dollar Sales   __ N/A

Individual models: X Profitability   X Unit Sales
X Dollar Sales   __ N/A

Individual jobs: X Profitability   X Unit Sales
X Dollar Sales   __ N/A

Work orders: X Profitability   __ Unit Sales
__ Dollar Sales   __ N/A

8. Which of the following cost data information is used in developing prices or quotations? (Check all that apply)

Material Costs: X Actual costs   __ Standard costs
__ Estimated costs

Labor Costs: X Actual costs   __ Standard costs
__ Estimated costs

Overhead Costs: __ Actual costs   X Standard costs
__ Estimated costs
__ No cost data is used

9. Do you routinely compare estimated costs to actual costs after each job?

__X__ Yes

_____ No, we don't routinely compare estimated costs to actual costs after each job

_____ No, we don't compare estimated costs to actual costs after each job

10. Are the high volume, MVC customers profitable?

___ Yes   __X__ Some are   ___ No   ___ Don't know

GMH's answers to most of these questions are "best practice" answers. They have excellent costing and pricing systems and know exactly where they are making and losing money. However, there is a "red flag" answer. Do you see it? It's their answer that some of their largest MVC customers are not profitable. That's a "red flag" answer. This MVC customer problem must be carefully evaluated before they develop strategies to grow.

You have to dig a little deeper, but at least you know where to dig. A careful analysis of cost records and the lost order analysis showed that the margins on two product lines were poor. Aggregating costs by customer account showed that two large customers have squeezed the margins down so low that it is not worth seeking future orders. The manufacturing costs had also been increasing steadily at a 5-6% per year pace. Indirect costs had been climbing at an even higher rate in recent years Here are the results.

- **Conclusion** – Two of the products will have to be redesigned.
- **Conclusion** – Raise prices to the two large customers and begin looking for replacements.
- **Conclusion** – The increase in indirect costs forced the company to re-evaluate the contribution of the indirect departments such as IT, accounting and human resources.
- **Conclusions** – Immediately begin a cost reduction program based on Lean Manufacturing principals and evaluate each overhead department in terms of costs vs. benefits.

If, on the other hand, a manufacturer answered "no" to most of these questions, instead of just one, all the answers would be considered "red flag" answers. This would be the worst case scenario because they don't have the cost data to know where they are financially or set accurate prices. In that case, it would be dangerous to pursue a growth strategy because sales growth might accelerate cash flow problems or further decrease profitability. I am not arguing against growth. In fact, growth is *critical* for virtually every manufacturer. But, in today's environment, you must have profitable growth – and that starts with good internal information.

11. Do you know specific reasons you're losing orders to competitors?
   __ Yes   <u>X</u> No   __ Don't know

GMH had not been tracking lost orders, so they decided to do a Lost Order Analysis. The lost order Information was gathered for a three-year period and collected in a spreadsheet with tables. The analysis revealed that there was not one, but many problems that would have to be solved for GMH to survive. The most important findings were as follows:

- **Competitors** – The analysis revealed that 50% of the known lost orders were against 3 out of 29 competitors. The products of these three key competitors would have to be evaluated first using competitor matrices.
- **Models** – When the data was displayed by model it showed that two models were no longer saleable. They would probably have to be completely redesigned
- **By Rep Group** – This table showed that three rep firms were consistently being beaten by the competition and that lost sales exceeded orders by four to one.
- **Reasons** – The primary reasons for the lost orders are summarized as follows :
  - 40%   Price
  - 30%   Machines didn't meet spec
  - 15%   Sales reps are weak
  - 5%   Customer already owns competitor model
  - 5%   Service and support problems
  - 5%   Delivery

- **Conclusion** – Focus on competing against the top 3 competitors where the company is losing 50% of the orders.

Note: Find complete lost order tables in the Growth Planning Handbook.

Step B: External Analysis – Where Will We Grow

- **Profiling Customers** – Can you identify the best customers to sell – now and in the future?

Once costs/margins information and lost orders information were known it was possible to develop a list of the best potential customers using the + and – exercise covered in Chapter Two.

This, unfortunately, revealed that two of their largest customers were losing them money. Both of these customers were forcing price discounts, which resulted in very low margins. In addition, four other customers had become difficult to work with. These customers required heavy service costs.

Conclusion – GMH was going to have to face up to the fact that they needed to find new customers to replace these customers.

Are there new customers out there? Maybe. A careful examination of all customers produced a Best Customer Profile that they could use in finding more customers.

Note: An example of the table showing the + and – exercise is shown in Figures 2-3 and 2-4 in Chapter 2.

- **Customer Wants and Needs** – Do you know what kinds of products and services the best customers want?

The Need for More and Better Information

Even though GMH had an excellent customer database and very good financial information on each customer account they really did not know what their customers wanted and needed. So, they finally buckled down and hired an outside firm to find out. They conducted a customer satisfaction audit using both a survey and follow-up phone interviews. The audit form they used is shown in the following Figure 9-1.

Management was shocked at the results. Many customers felt that GMH's product designs were old-fashioned and not competitive. Quality was measured as poor to mediocre, and prices were too high compared to other competitor products and services. In addition, most customers thought GMH's overall response time to customer needs was poor.

Figure 9-1: Customer Satisfaction Audit

This is the summary of the Customer Satisfaction Audit. The scores are averages of all customer scores. Customers were asked to evaluate General Machine in seven major categories and to score each question with a report card grade.

A = THE BEST
B = ABOVE AVERAGE
C = SAME AS COMPETITION
D = NEEDS IMPROVEMENT
F = AWFUL

Consistent Product Quality

Does their equipment arrive tested?	C
Is their equipment reliable and durable?	D
Do they provide regular programming updates?	D
Do they provide factory demonstration tests?	C
Is their warranty program fair and adequate?	B

Reliable Delivery

Are delivery promises accurate & on time?	C
Is packaging and shipping a pleasant surprise?	C

Competitor Models

Do their designs (models) match up well with competitor models?	F
Do they use and offer the latest technology	F

Dependable Service

Do they resolve service problems quickly?	F

Is there fast response to downtime problems?	D
Do they provide adequate customer training	B
Are operation & parts manuals accurate & readable?	C

Competitive Pricing

Are equipment prices competitive?	F
Is credit terms fair?	C

Dependable Parts Support

Are parts shipments accurate and on time?	B
Are parts prices competitive?	D

Response Time

Do GMH's employees respond quickly and efficiently to your needs? D

- **Identifying Markets** – Do you know which market niches (customer groups) to focus on now and in the future?

  This step began with assigning NAICS codes to all customers and then grouping them into market niches that can be prioritized to determine target markets. (An example is explained in Chapter 2 in Figure 2-5).

  By using the other information gathered on lost order analysis, competitors, and margins, it was determined that GMH was only competitive in 50% of the markets they were in and would have to develop a program to find new markets. They proceeded to prioritize the markets where they thought they still had an advantage.

  Conclusion – With the customer profiles, NAICS codes, and priority markets it was actually fairly easy to buy a list of prospects for each market segment and begin the job of prospecting. However, it also became obvious that depending on only ten markets would not be enough.

  GMH would need to find and diversify into many new markets to have any kind of security in the future

- **Assessing Competitors** – Can you compare your products to the competitor's products in terms of price, delivery, and key features – model by model?

When GMH's seven product lines were compared to direct competitors (model by model) it was found that two of the product lines were no longer competitive and would have to be redesigned.

It was also found that sell prices on most models were 5-10% higher than most competitors in "apples to apples" matrix comparisons. To gain market share would require the development of two new product lines and a cost reduction program for the rest of the models. This was going to be a major investment for the company.

Conclusion – There was a considerable amount of competitive and market intelligence done in the first year (besides what is shown in the competitor matrix). External intelligence information was gathered on 51 market segments, MVC customers, competitor strengths and weaknesses, and the growth of the industry (as well as market shares by competitor). The new intelligence information showed that the company was ten years behind in product development. It also revealed that the company would have to increase market share in a declining industry. To increase market share would require a heavy investment in product development and promotion over a five-year period.

It is common with mature manufacturing operations to suddenly find that major products have become way out of date. This is just a sample of the type of competitive disadvantage that our hypothetical company faced.

Step C: Analysis – Putting It All Together
Master Plan Summary and Pro forma Forecast.

All of the internal and external information gathered was carefully analyzed and summarized on a one-page chart called a Master Summary Quad Chart. This chart provides all of the basic information and goals of the company, which will form the basis for all department plans. The Master Quad Chart is then presented to the team for debate.

Gathering external information on markets, competitors, customers, and lost orders is the most difficult and most important part of any plan. This foundation information is the basis for doing the rest of the plan.

The analysis included:

> The major problems facing the company
> The major solutions to these problems
> Hard mission goals in $
> Critical success factors
> Master Summary Quad Sheet
> Preliminary pro forma budget and forecast

Major Problems – Internal and external information was analyzed and the major problems were summarized in one-sentence statements. They are shown in the upper left-hand corner of the Master Quad Sheet, shown as Figure 9-2.

Solutions and strategies – The team reviewed and debated the problems until they agreed upon the general solutions to these problems. The solutions were written as single-sentence statements. They became the Corporate Strategies that would drive the rest of the Growth Plan. The solutions/strategies are shown in the lower left-hand quadrant of the Master Quad Sheet and the strategies marked with an X will either increase the costs of the specific department or require investment.

Measurable Objectives – The upper right hand corner of the Quad Sheet is the measurable objectives or hard mission goals. These will drive the plan and become the basis for the pro forma budget and sales forecast.

Critical Success Factors – The fourth quadrant is a review of the Critical Success Factors. These must be achieved to give the plan a chance of success and to insure growth. These factors should be reviewed carefully and debated when the plan is presented to the owners.

Pro Forma Budget and Forecast – Once the Master Quad Chart is developed showing the general problems and solutions, it is also a good idea

Figure 9-2: GMH Master Quad Sheet – The New Mission

Major Problems / Obstacles / Threats

1. Quality of machines is mediocre.
2. Reaction time of company is poor.
3. There has been no new product development for 10 years and some models are no longer saleable.
4. There is not enough money left to develop the new products and produce a net profit to the shareholders of 7%.
5. We are limited in budget to generate the leads that it will take to find new markets and expand market share.
6. Some major customers are forcing price discounting and we can't make a decent margin.
7. Customer support services are not offering the service customers demand.
8. Our manufacturing costs have been rising 6% a year and there is no program to reduce costs.
9. Many of our independent sales reps can not sell to specific customers and want the factory to help them sell every job.
10. We do not have the sales organization or sales channels to sell 4 customer types.

Hard Mission Goals

1. Improve gross margins by achieving a cost reduction of 5% per year on cost of goods.
2. Sales – 10% increase in sales volume every year.
3. Increase units shipped per year by 5 units per year.
4. Net profitability – Loss year 1, 2% year 2, 8% year 3, 9% year 4.
5. Market share – go from number 5 to number 2 within the 5-year period.
6. Market share – this means improving overall share of the industry from 12 to 20%.
7. Find 20 new market niches that can be dominated by new products.
8. Introduce 1 major new product per year for 5 years.
9. Look for acquisitions of individual product lines that will let the company access new market segments.
10. Replace unprofitable customers with 3–4 new major accounts.

Solutions / Strategies

X 1. Develop a new quality program measured by customers at installation.
2. We will improve the number of quotes completed per week by working the overtime it will take in all departments to respond to customers.
X 3. We intend to develop 1 major machine per year and all of the options that go with the new model to gain a competitive advantage in the marketplace.
4. All product development must come from internally generated funds and the first two years will be losses.
X 5. We will spend a minimum of $250,000 per year for 5 years on lead generation.
6. We will raise prices to these customers and launch a program to replace them with new major accounts that are partners rather than adversaries.
7. We will launch a new 10-point service program called SUPPORT 100.
X 8. We will immediately launch a Lean Manufacturing Program to reduce manufacturing costs.
9. We must find or develop at least 3 new rep firms or begin a factory sales effort in 3 areas of the country.
10. We will launch a multiple sales channel approach that includes a major account sales dept., 3 types of reps, specialized distributors, and some integrators.

Critical Success Factors

1. Must achieve an average of 70% cost of goods an average 30% gross margin to survive.
2. Must achieve cost reduction goals in manufacturing every year.
3. Must reduce indirect costs and find ways to work with fewer people in all of the support departments.
4. Must retain the key people with 10–20 years of service that are hard to replace.
5. We must spend at least $250,000 in lead generation per year to have a chance of finding the new markets and customers needed for growth.
6. We must spend at least $400,000 in product development to have a chance to get back into some markets and customers.
7. Growth is based on the assumption that the industry will have a 2-year recession and then bounce back with growth of 5–10% per year for 3 years.

to develop a preliminary pro forma budget and forecast that shows:

- A tentative sales forecast
- A tentative budget
- The preliminary net income by year.

The pro forma sales forecast/budget is necessary to give the managers and departments a projection of what they must prepare for and to test some preliminary cost benefit suggestions. This will provide enough information to play "what if" during the next step of the planning process. The pro forma forecast and budget is simply a tool to test various sales and expense scenarios.

The following chart (Figure 9-3) is designed for four years. If this type of forecast and budget is new to your company, begin with a single-year plan. More information on how to do pro forma forecasts is shown in the Growth Planning Handbook.

GMH's pro forma forecast and budget will continue to be modified until it is formally approved as part of the Growth Plan at the very end of the planning process.

Figure 9-3: Preliminary Pro forma Example

	1999		2000		2001		2002	
MAJOR SALES	8,000,000		10,000,000		11,000,000		12,000,000	
Parts	2,000,000		2,500,000		3,000,000		3,500,000	
Other Sales	1,200,000		1,700,000		2,000,000		2,500,000	
TOTAL SALES	11,201,999	100	14,202,000	100	16,002,001	100	18,002,002	100
Majors COG	5,920,000		7,000,000		7,480,000		8,160,000	
PARTS COG	1,000,000		1,250,000		1,500,000		1,750,000	
Other COG	720,000		1,020,000		1,200,000		1,500,000	
Under/Over	994,043		900,300		600,000		250,000	
TOTAL COG	8,634,043	0.77	10,170,300	0.716	10,780,000	0.674	11,660,000	0.648
GROSS PROFIT	2,567,956.00		4,031,700.00	0.74	5,222,001.00		6,342,002.00	
Commission	720000		900000	0.28	990000		1080000	
Other sales exp.	661,409		690,000		700,000		980000	
Wages/taxes/ins	560,766		604,600		704,600		804,500	
Advertising Exp.	250,000		300,000		300,000		300,000	
Total Expenses	2,192,175		2,494,600		2,694,600		3,164,500	
Net Margin	375,781		1,537,100		2,527,401		3,177,502	
G AND A	700000		750000		750,000		750000	
R & D Expend.	400,000		450,000		500,000		500,000	
TOTAL GA/RD	1,100,000		1,200,000		1,250,000		1,250,000	
NET INCOME	-724,219	-6%	337,100	2%	1,277,401	8%	1,927,502	11%

Step D: Implementation – The Magical Step

The fourth step of the planning process is where actual planning begins to lead to implementation. It involves a team that includes all the key people – those who will have to do the work to make the plan a success.

Step D Implementation includes:

10 department problems
10 department solutions
Measurable objectives for the department
The tasks
Presentation of all Quad sheets once year
Control and evaluation system
The finalization of the pro forma budget and forecast
A complete plan in 1–15 pages.

This step is a collective planning process. It is absolutely necessary that the people who are going to make the plan work participate in the this part of the process. This promotes "buy-in" and it develops understanding and empathy for other departments or functions. There is something magic about the collective process that welds the people together. In a simple, powerful way it makes the plan their plan.

In my earlier critique of strategic planning I emphasized the problems of "top-down" planning and the critical issue of detachment. In strategic planning and other types of plans this detachment can be explained as a dichotomy between:

• Dreaming and doing
• Process and results
• Thinking and action
• Planning and implementation
• Illusion and reality.

It seemed to me that this disconnect was a huge impediment to successful implementation. To truly succeed, you must focus on helping the people who have to implement the plan understand exactly what they are supposed to do. And, in some cases, help them do it – particularly the first time.

From my experience as a general manager and consultant, it seems to make the most sense to develop a simple action plan for each department or function. The idea is to push the authority down to the people who must do or supervise the work. Since they and their staffs are the people who will make the plan work or not work, it is important to use a process where they can systematically examine the problems and solutions – once they know exactly what the mission change is in the Master Quad sheet.

In our GMH example, the following departments each developed a one-page action plan: Mechanical Engineering, Electrical Engineering, Sales, Sales Channels, Advertising and Promotion, National Accounts Service, Parts, and Used Machines.

Department Quad Plans

In addition there were one-page Quad Sheets for functions such as current products, new products, pricing, and export sales.

The action plan for each department or function will describe the problems, solutions, objectives, and tasks in one page divided into four quadrants just like the Master Quad Sheet.

GMH's Quad Plan for their Sales Department is shown as an example in Figure 9-4. Sales is only one of eight departments – each has its own Quad Plan.

The process for developing departmental Quad Sheets is the same as the Master Summary Quad Sheet except that department plans have a quadrant for Tasks instead of Critical Success Factors. There are always specific tasks to be accomplished in each department and it is important that they are listed separate from the problems and solutions. During the planning meeting, tasks are suggested which must be completed to support the solutions. All tasks are written into the lower right hand quadrant of the Department Quad Plan (See Figure 9-4).

At this stage, the Quad Plan starts to really take hold. Remember, SMMs tend to be cultures where people like to get things done. The specifics of how to develop a Quad Sheet for each department and function are

Figure 9-4: GMH 1999 Sales Department Quad Plan

Mission: Increased Market Share; Sustainable Sales Growth

MAJOR PROBLEMS / OBSTACLES / THREATS	MEASURABLE OBJECTIVES
1. Independent reps spend little time on prospecting	1. Rep Sales = $5,000,000
2. Most reps can't handle requirements of large corporate accounts	2. National Acct.Sales = $6,000,000
3. Turnaround time on factory quotes is 10 days	3. Minimum sales in each major rep territory – 10 units
4. Sales in territories like CA, TX, VA, AZ, OK, IA are poor	4. Develop a new commission schedule by Dec.1999
5. Most reps do not have good product knowledge	5. Conduct the basic and intermediate training by July 200
6. Many reps need factory assistance finalizing sales	6. Reduce quote turnaround time to 3-5 days by Dec. 2000
7. The commission schedule penalizes the good reps	7. Hire a new sales manager by Dec. 2000
• Reps do not want to make cold calls on new markets or products	
• There is no objective method of evaluating rep performance	
• Order processing at the factory is slow and inefficient	

STRATEGIES	TASKS
1. Factory will invest in a lead generation to help with sales prospecting	1. Redefine all reps into 2 Classes-–Oct 2000
2. Factory must create a special sales dept. to deal with large accounts	2. Develop new contracts for each Classification – Oct 2000
3. Commit to developing a quote system to turnaround quotes in 3-5 days	3. Develop a certified Basic Training program for all new reps – Nov. 2000
4. Declare these territories as non-exclusive and find new reps	4. Develop an intermediate training program for – Dec. 2000
5. Create 3 levels of factory training	5. Develop an advanced training program – Dec. 2000
6. Hire a sales manager who can spend 50% of his time in the field.	6. Send out target account list to each sales territory –Sept 2000
7. Change the commission schedule to pay for sales tasks completed	7. Develop a list of all target markets and prioritize them for lead generation budget
8. Factory will invest in developing the leads for new markets and products	8. Design new system to evaluate all rep firms Sept 2000
9. Develop an evaluation system to fairly grade each rep in terms of 20 tasks	
• Reorganize the inside Sales Departments as part of the Division re-organization into a prospector-type organization	

detailed in the Growth Planning Handbook (Section VII).

All Quad plans are finalized and submitted to the general manager or facilitator for approval or recommended changes. A final meeting is held where each manager or supervisor presents his or her Quad Plan to the group for a final review and to insure that each plan coordinates with the other department plans.

The biggest benefit from the Quad Plan approach is the entire company plan is summarized in less that 15 pages including the Master Summary and pro forma. All department and function Quad Plans are "nested" under the Master Summary Quad Plan

Figure 9-5 shows how the whole Quad Plan process fits together and how many individual department and function plans GMH used for the entire company plan.

Implementation is a difficult step. It means getting into the minds of the team and developing an understanding of their problems and limitations. This step has a lot of logic and definable tasks, but what makes it work are the psychological dynamics of the team. I'm still not sure what happens in this part of the process when you get a team of professionals listening to each other's problems and offering input. It is difficult to describe the empathy, understanding, and trust that grows into a new type of thinking. I seem to see renewal at work – with a life all its own.

I think that the structure of the process sets the template for these changes to occur. But, it is the freedom to explain and share departmental problems and solutions that welds the whole effort into something that leads to results. Part of the success of Quad planning is turning the hard mission goals of the company into achievable strategies that can be implemented. Another important factor is that the Quad Plans give managers both the responsibility and authority to implement their plans. The plan won't be changed until the next year and they are free to carry out their strategies. From my experience in using this system, I've found that 90% of the strategies and tasks are implemented every year.

Remember that our hypothetical company is based on real experiences and real companies. Here are the last two steps in the Growth process.

Step E: Strategic Renewal – Changing the Organization to Fit the New Customers and Markets

GMH found that capturing new customers and markets required changes in the organization once the Growth Plan was executed. First, they found their reaction time to customer requests for quotations, service,

Figure 9-5: Quad Plan Process Flow Chart

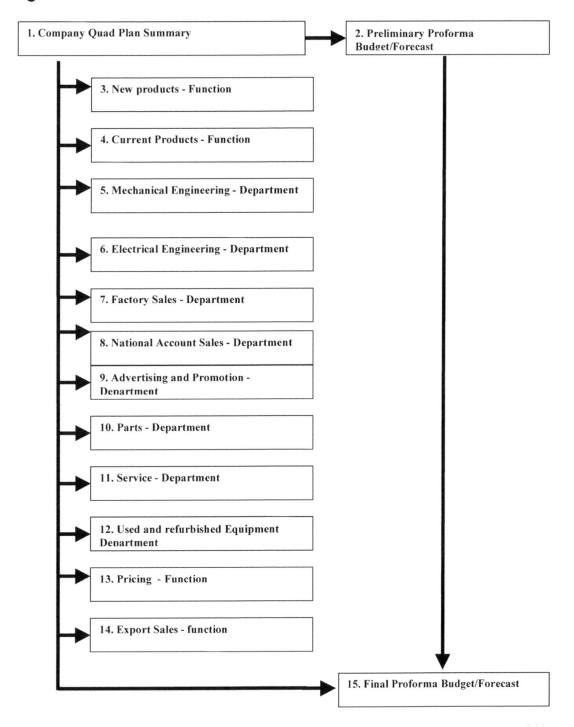

order-processing, etc., was too slow. In addition, decision making within the company was too slow and solutions to customer problems required too many approvals.

Changing the Organization

In short, GMH had to face up to the fact that the organization that had served them so well for so long was now too slow, too bureaucratic, and too inflexible to keep up with customer and market demands. They needed to re-design their organization if they were going to survive.

These are the key factors that describe a Prospector-type organization – and what GMH needed to consider before they made changes to their organization

- **Multiple Markets** – GMH could no longer make it by efficiently servicing a few markets. They had to find and exploit new product and market opportunities.

- **Market and Competitor Intelligence** – Prospector organizations maintain the capacity to monitor a wide range of environmental conditions, trends, and events. GMH had to consider hiring individuals who had the ability to scan the environment for potential opportunities.

- **New Products** – GMH needed to reorganize themselves and provide the resources needed to research develop, produce and market a new group of products.

- **Formalization and Administration** – "Prospectors develop only a low degree of structural organization, since it would not be economically feasible to codify job descriptions and operating procedures in an organization whose tasks change frequently."[2] This is a scary prospect, but GMH could not afford to invest in the new Prospector organization and carry the overhead of their current indirect departments. They had to make a choice.

- **Deviancy Tolerant** – Formalization is a means of reducing the probability that deviant behavior will occur. On the other hand the company was going to have to recruit "hunters" into the new organization who could go on the attack. These are highly motivated individuals who often have strange behavior but who are the kind of people needed in a turnaround situation. GMH management was going to have to take a chance on people who could perform and get rid of some of their conformers.

- **Centralized Command and Control** – Faster response and flexibility meant that GMH had to give up on a lot of command and control. They were faced with decentralizing the organization because the information needed to assess current performance and to take the appropriate corrective action had to be located in the operating departments themselves, not in the upper echelons of management. GMH was faced with decentralizing into a flat organization with many units, cells and teams

- **Decentralized Decision Making and Communication** – GMH could no longer afford the luxury of channeling all decisions to higher management for action. They had to find ways of pushing responsibility and authority down to the people who do the work. This new type of organization gives them the ability to quickly respond to customer demands

Other Questions – After careful review, GMH's management concluded that the Defender (Functional) organization that had worked until now was not going to work in the future. They decided to change to some kind of Prospector organization. This began with questions like these:

- How many new people will be needed in the next year?
- In the next five years?
- How will the addition of these people affect the organization?
- What do we do with the underachievers?
- Can we afford to maintain the staff we use in accounting, human resources, IT and other indirect departments?
- How can we eliminate bureaucratic functions that are unnecessary or do not bring value to the customer?
- What will the new organization chart look like?
- What should we do with jobs or functions that do not bring value to the customer?

- Where do we place our most skilled people and managers?
- How do we recruit hunters who can prospect for markets?

Note – If and when you do decide to change your organization, be sure to review the Methodology questions in Chapter 6: Changing Manufacturing to Reduce Costs.

As part of their strategic renewal, GMH also had to re-evaluate their manufacturing processes. They knew they had to reduce their manufacturing costs by 10% just to remain in the game.

In addition, their quality was mediocre and they needed to both lower warranty costs and improve customer satisfaction.

Finally, they needed to develop a better system of production control and replace existing production software with something simpler and easier to use. The major questions they had to answer were:

- What should we do to lower our indirect costs in the support departments?
- Which parts of the manufacturing process should we subcontract?
- How will we meet the customer's definition for the minimum quality needed to compete?
- How can we shorten order-processing time?
- How do we develop long-term suppliers and strategic alliances?
- Will Lean Manufacturing methods work for a custom machine manufacturer?
- If so, which parts of the Lean process apply?
- Is our cost accounting system adequate for the new mission of finding new customers and markets?
- Do production control methods adequately answer all customer requirements?
- Should we look for foreign vendors to outsource high-volume, simple-to-manufacture parts?
- Can we simplify our computer and software systems to make them easier to use by the decision-makers in each department?
- Do the current computer and software systems help us respond quicker to the new demands of our customers?

As you can see, they were faced with a lot of tough questions. They are, frankly, questions that many SMMs face. So even though the example might be hypothetical, the challenges are quite real. They didn't solve ten out of ten problems in each department, but they usually solved all the small problems and enough of the big ones to be able to keep going. Most important, they realized how they had to change as an organization – they all committed to organizational renewal and doing their best to make the turnaround a reality.

Conclusions – Investing for the Long Term

It is interesting to point out that this plan is the reverse order of how things normally happen in manufacturing companies.

Generally, people start with changes to manufacturing processes instead of changes in response to customers, competitors and the market. Or, they spend most of their time arguing about mission vision and values rather than "hard dollar goals".

The other unique idea in this planning process is "Bottom Up Planning." It took me many years to understand that change is not something you think or plan into existence. Change takes action – action by the very people who must make most of the changes. So, once you've developed the critical internal and external information, why not let the people who must make the changes collectively develop the plan?

Yes, there are many different ways to do these steps, but this chapter makes the point that growth or turnaround planning for small and mid-size manufacturers of industrial products requires a very different approach from most other business

This may sound like an old idea, but it is really unique for SMMs. Combining "bottom up" collective planning with the Quad Sheet process is not only unique. In some respects it is magical. I can't yet explain the bonding and empathy that goes on during this collective process, but I watched it work in two turnarounds. Since many SMMs are faced with transforming their companies to adapt to the new economy and some have to make the changes in a turnaround type crisis, the introduction of this new type of planning process is timely and necessary.

The focus of this type of planning is to help the company systematically find new customers and new markets for growth in the new economy. Once the manufacturer is focused on what they are going to do in the market, it will drive changes in new products, services, organization, manufacturing, etc. It is a long-range plan that answers the question "where is the company going and how will we grow and be prosperous in the new economy despite all of the changes."

There are many progressive small and midsize manufacturers who are finding opportunities in these times of great change. I call them the "New Stars of American Manufacturing." A profile of these Stars and how they compete is the subject of the last chapter.

Key Points

Understanding customers, markets, and competitors should be the first step in any program or plan that is focused on growth or profit. In fact, it is the author's opinion that gathering the necessary external information and having accurate cost/margin data are the two critical pieces of information that will make or break the Growth Plan.

This growth plan process is designed specifically for SMMs of industrial products and services. There are basically 5 steps

1. Show Me The Money – Step 1 finds out where the company is making or losing money and whether there will be enough money to invest in growth strategies
2. External analysis – This step gathers the vital information on customers, markets, and competitors
3. Putting the data all together – This analysis is done in one page
4. Implementation – The implementation is called Quad Planning and provides an action plan for each department or function with the top 10 problems, 10 solutions, measurable objectives and tasks
5. Strategic Renewal – The last part of the plan changes the organization and manufacturing.

Suggested Action

Do the "show me the money" test, by answering all 11 questions described in the first step. Your answers will give you a quick read on whether you have the financial information necessary to begin a growth plan.

Note:

1. Rise and Fall of Strategic Planning, Henry Mintzberg, The Free Press, 1994, NY NY.

Chapter 10
Conclusions – We Can Compete

During a workshop I was conducting during the last recession, a manufacturing owner stood up to vent his emotions on how badly the supplier manufacturers were being treated in supply chains.

He was mad and he decided to let everyone in the workshop know his feelings. He then proceeded to list all of the unfair changes that had happened in the '90s. I will paraphrase what became a long soliloquy.

- He despised globalization – it was as if it was a new form of communism spreading around the world.
- He described the large companies outsourcing to China and closing U.S. plants as un-American.
- He berated the government for not stepping in to protect U.S. manufacturers from floating currencies and unfair trade.
- He bemoaned the fact that his larger customers had not allowed any price increases and, in fact, were asking for contractual discounts for future work.

He was very frightened by a road to the future that seemed to be littered with unknown land mines. Out of frustration, he finally said that all he wanted was for the economy and manufacturing to return to the way they were in the early '90s.

He directed his impassioned speech at me and seemed to be looking for some kind of absolutist answer. I told him that while I could not offer prognostications about the future economy, I could answer one thing with great certainty. I told him that I was absolutely sure that we would never return to the 'good old days' of manufacturing.

I've reflected on this encounter many times since, and I've decided that worrying or complaining about how unfair things have become simply won't help SMMs survive in the future. In fact, I believe we have to quit worrying about high-volume parts going to low-cost countries and focus all of our energies on adapting to the demands of the new economy in ways that will work for us.

In addition, I don't think we should count on government help or any sympathy from the Fortune 500 companies.

The New Stars of Manufacturing

The manufacturers who are succeeding understand that it's a new world.

Harry Brown of EBC Industries understands this. He says, "it is not possible to reverse the tide of globalization. Harry is typical of a new breed of industrial manufacturers in the United States. In sharp contrast to the old Defender organizations of the past, these new breeds are SMMs who are market-driven and know how to prospect for opportunities.

There are many examples of SMMs who are not only surviving but are flourishing in this era of change. These companies stand out because they are usually innovative, good at monitoring customers, quick to adapt to the market changes, and more profitable than their competition.

They do not rely on a few customers or a few products. And they've learned to live with change. They eat change for breakfast. Change isn't a threat, it's nourishment. These companies are building a portfolio of market niches and a diverse customer base to insulate them from the changing demands of customers. They are niche marketers who know how to find new customers and market to those niches on an ongoing basis.

The new stars emerging in this economy are SMMs who are not afraid of foreign competitors and who are organized to "turn on a dime" when required. They prefer high margins and low volume and operate with excellent cost information. In fact, they absorb all kinds of information. I think they have that for breakfast, too. It's information that allows them to continuously prospect for new opportunities.

They accept the changes brought on by globalization and they don't waste their time and energy hoping or waiting to return to the "good old days." These new manufacturers are transforming their companies to fit the changes in their markets and they differ from the typical SMM in many ways. They are competing – and they are succeeding.

How are these companies different? In Figure 10-1 I've listed what I believe to be the key success factors for SMMs that are competing (and winning) in today's economy.

Figure 10-1: The New SMM Profile

1. Are very good at monitoring customers.
2. Focus on customer diversity and market portfolios.
3. Provide specialized services.
4. Use a system to develop new products.
5. Emphasize customization and short product runs.
6. Are decentralizing their organizations.
7. Focus on lowering corporate overhead.
8. Are using lean manufacturing methods.
9. Are willing to subcontract and outsource to lower costs.
10. Focus on margins and accurate costing.
11. Are active in workforce education and training.

Let's look at these factors one by one.

1. **Monitoring Customers** – This is the first of the Six Essentials we covered in Chapter 1. It simply means being close enough to and having the kind of trust with customers that allows you to know what they like and dislike quick enough to make a change. Remember that your customers are dealing with fast-moving change and globalization, too. Monitoring customers and their challenges helps make your company "part of the solution."

   Monitoring customers does require empathy, interviewing (and listening) skills, and visiting customers on their turf. Many Type 1 and Type 2 manufacturers (particularly job shops) have never had to do this and they may not even have people who are able to interview customers. But the hard fact is monitoring customer likes and dislikes is one of the keys to survival.

   D8 is a small manufacturer of custom-built molds in Potlatch, Idaho. The tooling and mold industry has been severely hurt by foreign-built, low-price tools and molds. It is no longer possible to compete against foreign mold makers simply on price. Even progressive U.S. manufacturers are struggling to find ways to compete.

Barry Ramsay of D8 is one of the new breed of small manufacturers who understands that the answers for competing in the new economy are found by monitoring customers. Barry makes it a point to visit all of his good customers on a regular basis to discover their problems and needs. He believes it is important to visit customers as if he is on a specific mission with well thought out goals, objectives, and strategies.

Barry says, "I look at these as missions where I visit customers and know my targets, planning my attack differently for each individual or group. I often visit the 'tooling manager' who is being beat-up by his boss to get the lowest tool price.

"I listen very carefully to his message and try to understand his motives, his environment, and his world. If I can, I then try to meet with the 'production manager' and try to listen to his pressures of meeting production goals, quality requirements, pressure to reduce scrap, use less energy, etc.

"If I am reasonably successful I can get both the tooling purchaser and the tooling user (production) talking about the common enemy – waste. I can then start to ask them strategic questions like; 'if you could have a mold that cycled parts with 20% more throughput, or 20% faster (cycle time), would that be of value?' Hell yes, of course it would!

"Then I have to prove it (which D8 can). Eventually I have to turn that discussion around from 'the price of the mold' to 'the cost of a mold running in their plant.' If I can do that I can show how D8's molds are more valuable at the end of the month or the quarter."

Here's another "new star" in action.

Alliance Equipment is a manufacturer of material handling equipment. They are very good at monitoring their customers' needs, particularly the special needs of the lift truck operators. Special design teams are formed that include both engineering and marketing specialists. These teams go into the field and interview lift truck customers and operators about their likes and dislikes.

They place a very high value on "trust-based" customer relationships and make every effort to talk to their customers in the customer's environment.

It is this market feedback that drives all of their new designs and customer support.

Monitoring customer likes and dislikes is a "face-to-face" field research approach, and the key to their design achievements. Alliance does not depend on phone research, secondhand opinions, or internal assumptions about what customers want. They go and see them on the job.

2. **Customer and Market Diversity** – For most SMMs, developing a strategy of customer and market diversity is vital. The only way to avoid the problems of losing high-volume customers, price discounting, margin erosion, or simply being the victim of an industry cycle, is to diversify your customer base.

   This means you must become a Prospector – you must be finding and developing new customers and markets on an ongoing basis.

   The problems of devoting your company to one industry or a few MVC customers are becoming more obvious every day. Two good (or bad) examples are what is happening to vendors in the auto and aerospace industries. These industries are dominated by Type 4 manufacturers like Ford. GM, Boeing, Lockheed etc. When they decide to source a product from overseas, or dictate price discounts, the small manufacturers who depend on them have nowhere to go and no security

   Minster Machine, of Minster, Ohio, figured this out a long time ago and made a conscious decision both to diversify their customer base and to avoid customers that did not want to form partnering relationships. Perhaps that's why Minster Machine is the only supplier in its industry that has survived.

Columbia Machine is another example. They used to sell a line of palletizing systems to a few large customers and to three or four major industries. In 1999, they changed to an aggressive strategy of customer diversity and a portfolio of markets. They now sell into twelve industries and sixty different market segments. When an industry like paper is in a down-cycle, other industries, like food, may be in an up-cycle. This strategy helps offset the ups and downs of capital goods purchasing

3. **Specialized Services** – Innovation is not just about new products – it is also about providing new services. These new services can be radical, such as Harry Brown's Rapid Response Manufacturing at EBC Industries – which changed the whole focus and organization of his machining business. Or, it can be good old common sense.

   New services can come from strong relationships with customers that will make it easy and natural for them to slowly outsource functions, products, and services that they may traditionally have done inside. This was the case at Ashfield Industries. The addition of these services has allowed the company to grow in an industry that has been moving offshore for many years.

   D8, the mold maker in Idaho, is another SMM that realized the wisdom of offering special value added services to solve customers' internal problems. The value-added services that D8 is marketing are an extension of the work they have done in digging into their customers' production processes.

   Barry Ramsay of D8 says, "We had to study our customers and learn what makes molds run faster and use less energy. We are now in a position to share that knowledge to help our customers. We offer 'free' production audits where we will do a brief preliminary analysis of a customer's production operation and make recommendations where they can improve their processes to save time, energy, reduce scrap, and increase throughput."

Customers view this as a trusting partnership. After all, they know that D8's primary business and motives are to sell more tooling. They know D8 wants them to be highly productive so the customer will have available press time and need additional tooling to maximize their capacity

Barry goes on to say, "I am much closer to a Midwest molder than my competitors in China and it costs me relatively little to visit the customer and help them by recommending operational improvements. I am offsetting my higher purchase price by supplying more than a mold; I am supplying tooling solutions, processing advice, and a periodic fresh look at their systems. And I can speak the language of their upper management, as well as the language of the guy on the shop floor. I am providing trust and confidence."

4. **Use a System to Develop New Products** – Michael C. LaRocco, of American Made LLC in Ambridge, Pennsylvania, is another terrific example of the new, innovative breed of small and midsize manufacturers. His system for developing successful new products can be viewed in terms of three different skill sets:

   1. First, the ability to envision a good idea as a solution to a specific customer problem.

   2. Second, the ability to find a solution by using a new or developing technology

   3. Third, knowing how to gather enough market, customer, and competitor information to help make sure the product will have enough of a meaningful competitive advantage to sell in the marketplace.

Michael C. LaRocco is one of the rare manufacturers who does all three things very well. So well, in fact, that his company is the fastest growing manufacturer in the Pittsburgh area. In less than 10 years, Michael developed three new products for the truck industry:

- the Final Lube solid grease plate

- the RE-Pro heavy duty truck bed liner
- BULITEX composite panels.

At a time when only one of seven new product ideas reaches successful commercialization, Mike is three for three. One reason for this success is knowing how to gather the "non-technical" market information. Remember this is 70% of the reason for most product failures.

5. **Customization and Short Product Runs** – It is the high-volume standardized products that are being outsourced. It is hard to compete against high-volume, low-cost suppliers. On the other hand, being able to gain a competitive advantage through customization and short production runs is something that is very difficult for foreign manufactures to emulate.

   Jacquart Fabrics in Ironwood, Michigan, is a good example of a small manufacturer that has employed customization as a survival strategy in an industry that is rapidly moving offshore.

   As you may recall, Jacquart is a "cut and sew" operation that manufacturers customized products from doggy beds to special outdoor hats. They have been successful because they offer customized products to targeted market niches with overnight delivery. Speed, organization and proximity to their market are all factors that have helped them to compete and prosper.

   Sexton Can Company of Martinsburg, West Virginia, has been very successful in developing specialized products for niche markets where they could gain a competitive advantage and maintain profitability. Sexton Can's primary competitive advantage is that they can manufacture a huge range of sizes in small lots and meet accelerated delivery requirements. They can't compete with low-cost countries for the cheap, high-volume orders, but they have been ingenious in designing their own proprietary hydraulic presses and processes. As a result, they can produce very high quality steel containers at very competitive prices.

6. **Decentralize** – Chapter Six explains why decentralization and mov-

ing away from the traditional functional manufacturing organization are necessary. The pressures to change to a decentralized organization that is more flexible and responsive are relentless. Sometimes the changes begin slowly. That's the case with Minster Machine who have spun off their foundry and parts businesses into separate profit centers.

Other times, decentralization can take place overnight – as in the case of SEMCO. Ricardo Semler decided to force all decisions down to the lowest levels and empower his employees. He realized that there was no way to achieve empowerment in a centralized, functional organization. He wanted fewer levels of management and faster response in decision making.

So he scrapped the pyramid shape of his organization and broke the company down into smaller units. Semler says "even the most cynical observers were astonished to find that things were better off once we got rid of the pyramid and all its rungs and roles."[1]

7. **Lowering Corporate Overhead** – As part of their ongoing efforts at cost reduction, many manufacturing companies are carefully evaluating any department or function that does not bring value to the customer. Progressive manufacturers are carefully scrutinizing corporate overhead departments for two reasons.

The first reason is that many SMMs find that they simply must reduce overhead to compete. There is no choice. To remain competitive, they simply will not be able to afford the corporate overhead they now carry.

The second reason is that, in many organizations, corporate departments have contributed to bureaucracy and a centralized command-and-control structure and behavior that runs counter to the need for a decentralized organization. Stoner Inc, a Malcolm Baldridge winner from Pennsylvania eliminated its Human Resources department and gave those responsibilities to their team leaders.[2]

EBC Industries intuitively saw the handwriting on the wall and eliminated employee handbooks to insure that supervisors and employees would work out their problems. Harry Brown observes that "you can never write enough pages in the handbook to cover all situations and, if you do have a handbook, you then must hire someone to enforce it. All of this runs counter to our commitment to get the decision making down to the right people in a decentralized organization."

Ricardo Semler's company, SEMCO, went even further by eliminating all types of structures, rules, manuals, and top down policies. They felt the overhead departments were too bureaucratic, too expensive and diverted attention from the company's real objectives.

Ricardo fired the entire Information Technology department when they found out it had become a priesthood of people who made systems more complex and harder to use, and was very expensive to boot. Semler also eliminated job descriptions because they limited workers potential and constrained the possibility of job enrichment.[3]

Radical? Maybe. But it worked.

8. **Cost Reduction and Lean Manufacturing Methods** – The companies we've discussed, Sexton Can, EBC Industries, Minster Machine, Epson Portland, and Jacquart Fabrics, have all employed some version of Lean Manufacturing.

   Each of them works at cost reduction and continuous improvement as a way of life. Many do business in industries where there is no chance of a price increase. The only way they can maintain their margins is through cost reduction.

   Here are some examples you might find useful.

   Sexton Can Company, Martinsburg, West Virginia – In recent years, pressures from foreign suppliers and powerful customers have made life a lot tougher. It was obvious to company management that their plants needed to step up efforts to reduce cost and waste through a program of Lean Manufacturing.

Yurij Wowczuk was assigned as the new plant manager in 2004 to begin the process of Lean Manufacturing. He selected a cross-functional team consisting of production, maintenance, engineering, and continuous improvement.

The team began by identifying the "low hanging fruit" in areas that required the most attention (in this case it was clean up) and could yield the quickest results. They went on to tackle the problems of changeover time, which were complex. In the beginning, it could take 6-8 hours to make a changeover. They also focused on downtime on the production lines using a Kaizen Event.

All progressive manufacturers are now using some kind of Lean Manufacturing methods to do something about cost reduction and waste. Sexton Can is only at the beginning of their Lean journey. They are among the thousands of SMMs who are on similar paths.

Epson Portland Inc, Hillsboro, Oregon – Dave Graham of the Epson Portland plant in Hillsboro, Oregon, had to find a way to keep their printer cartridge business from being outsourced to Asia. He reasoned that he could offset the low costs of labor in Asia by focusing on automation, throughput, and production efficiency. Epson's people studied the Lean Manufacturing methods used in the Toyota Production System, and began to implement their own system of continuous improvement that would reduce defects, lower costs, and improve quality

Under Graham, the defect rate plunged to 300 per million. The cartridges per employee increased about 40% (slightly better than other plants in the world). The Portland operation now manufactures about 50 kinds of cartridges and the production is up 200% from 2001 levels.

U.S. manufacturers shouldn't just look at estimated unit costs in Asia. These unit costs are not the whole picture. There are many hidden costs involved in sourcing from Asia and manufacturers should work hard to assess the total costs of manufacturing a product overseas. Increasing throughput and reducing scrap and quality problems can often result in a more efficient production operation and a better alternative than pursuing outsourcing to low cost countries.

9. **Subcontract and Outsource** – When all Lean Manufacturing practices have been tried and all internal cost reduction efforts have been implemented – but your company still cannot meet the price demands of certain customers – there are two options:

- You can fire the customer and try to find different customers to replace them. Remember, not every customer is worth keeping. The techniques covered in Chapter Two will show you how to determine the good from the bad customers.

- You can sub-contract part of your work to smaller manufacturers in the U.S. or overseas. Part of saving American manufacturing is figuring out what parts you can keep and what parts you must outsource to stay in business.

10. **Focus on Margins and Accurate Costing** – This tenth point is also the Sixth Essential covered in Chapter One. Although many, if not most, SMMs have been able to get by with poor cost/margin information in the past, I believe that investing in a system that gives accurate cost information is as important as developing a quality or Lean Manufacturing Program.

The logic is simple. Customers in the supply chain will continue to compare your prices to foreign supplier's prices or will demand discounts for volume orders. Often, both. The pressure for lower prices and discounting is not going to go away. After all, it's key to their survival, too. So having a cost system that produces accurate margins by product, job, and customer has become an absolute necessity.

In the specialized fastener industry, Harry Brown of EBC has many customers who regularly compare his prices to those of foreign competitors. He says, "you must know costs and margins to know when not to bid or when to walk away from an order." He adds this advice. "Today, all small manufacturers must have good enough costing systems to protect themselves."

Accurate cost information isn't limited to Type 3 manufacturers with accounting departments. Many progressive small manufacturers have also developed accurate cost systems. A good example is The Plastics Group (TPG), in Lawrenceville, Georgia. It was founded by Sam Brockway in 1992 as a high-tech injection molding shop specializing in the development and manufacture of critical plastic products and components.

The small company seemed to be operating profitably for three years. But, in 1995, they began having financial problems. Following an attempt to "grow" the business, the company was faced with a serious loss on nearly $1 million in sales. This was further complicated by the fact that the company did not have a cost accounting system and did not know if jobs or customer accounts were profitable.

However, Sam did have a work order system that allowed him to recover labor and materials costs. Sam and his son Buzz decided to manually cost all of their jobs to determine which customer accounts were profitable. To their surprise, they found that TPG's largest customer, who accounted for 40% of their sales, was not profitable when overhead was taken into account.

Sam, Buzz, and their sales manager, Dave Flood, went on to develop an accurate cost system using spreadsheets that would show them their contribution margin, breakeven sales, and accurate cost and margin information on each job and customer account. It also helped them to develop a realistic pricing strategy and better quotations.

Knowing which jobs to quote and not quote is an absolute necessity in the competitive plastics industry – because there are now so many foreign competitors.

11. **Active in Workforce Education and Training** – Most progressive manufacturers are investing heavily in training their workers and

some manufacturers are also involved in developing education and training programs in their communities. A terrific example of what a large manufacturer can do if they are really committed to closing the skills gap is what Siemens Energy and Automation had been doing in the U.S. to nurture a skilled workforce.

Since U.S. educational programs do not instill many of the skills required for his workers, Mr. Thomas Malott (Siemens CEO in 1998) suggests that manufacturers establish their own apprenticeship programs to train their own workers. Siemens current apprentice program is based on the company's 100-year-old program for funneling people from school to skilled jobs in industry.

Siemens now has 13,000 apprentices in 20 countries including 25 separate training programs at 13 U.S. sites.[4]

Structured around the basic educational needs, Siemens youth and adult apprenticeship programs provide specific work related skills through hands-on training, community college learning, and advanced manufacturing training.

Some manufacturers are also working on new solutions for traditional education. One example we mentioned is the Pennsylvania Global Academy Charter School. It was formed by a group of manufacturers and business people who got together in Erie, Pennsylvania, to try to come up with an alternative approach to K–12 education. The focus of this innovative program is to help students find a career.

The idea of this alternative school is a blend of academic classes and job skill or technical training. This alternative school is dedicated to educating children who can't or don't want to go to a four-year college. The alternative school approach is simple and essentially based on the concept that kids can acquire career skills along with a basic education.

The people who operate the Global Academy allow students to take classes in all kinds of technical or "hands-on" classes along with their usual courses in science, math, reading, and writing.

The idea is not to drag every kid through the "college prep knot-hole" whether they want it or not. It is to provide an education while preparing them to get a job and have a career

In the same part of Western Pennsylvania is CamTech, the Center for Advanced Manufacturing Technology, established in 2001 as a private, non-profit educational institution. It was designed to build and rebuild the regional workforce. CamTech's unusual goal is to "help provide qualified workers who can adapt to constant changes in the work environment."[5]

CamTech is a premier technical college providing technical courses and education designed to help people get jobs in the new economy. Their curriculum combines technical education and training with general education. It is a combination of education, hands-on training, and work experience that will prepare students for long-term success in the workplace.

These are examples of progressive manufacturers who are not just complaining about education and training. They are doing something about it.

Wanted: New Types of Leaders

One of the most difficult issues in making any changes in American manufacturing companies will be leadership. A key question is, "Can the current company owner or CEO act as the change agent or will he or she have to hire someone to play the role of change agent?"

For many leaders, owners, and managers, shifting from an internal operations focus to an external customer focus may involve a huge leap of faith.

There are many highly trained and experienced executives who did well managing Defender companies ten years ago. But many of them are now having trouble in leading their company through the 21st Century battlefields of globalization. They seem to be frozen in the headlights, continuing to rely on the skills and experiences that worked for them in the past.

With these once successful leaders seemingly no longer able to keep their companies competitive, an obvious question is "What kind of leader is needed to guide a manufacturing company through the problems of finding new customers and markets, changing the organization, reducing costs, and finding the opportunities in the new economy?"

The best research I have found that identifies a profile of what we need for new leadership is by Daniel Coleman, author of a book titled *Emotional Intelligence.* Coleman's research makes the case that "emotional intelligence" is the most important factor differentiating a typical leader from a great leader. Coleman says, "To be sure, intellect is a driver of outstanding performance. Cognitive skills such as big picture thinking and long-term vision are important. But when I calculated that ratio of technical skills, IQ, and emotional intelligence as ingredients of excellent performance, emotional intelligence proved to be twice as important as the others for jobs at all levels."[6]

Coleman measures five different components of emotional intelligence at work.[7] Here they are.

Figure 10-2: The Five Components of Emotional Intelligence at Work

	Definition	Hallmarks
Self-Awareness	The ability to recognize your moods, emotions, and drives, as well as their effect on others.	Self-confidence. Realistic self-assessment. Self-deprecating sense of humor.
Self-Regulation	The ability to control or redirect disruptive impulses. The propensity to suspend judgement, to think before acting.	Trustworthiness and integrity. Comfort with ambiguity. Openness to change.

Motivation	A passion to work for reasons that go beyond money or status. A propensity to pursue goals with energy and persistence.	Strong drive to achieve. Optimism, even in the face of failure. Organizational commitment.
Empathy	The ability to understand the emotional makeup of other people. Skill in treating people according to their emotional reactions.	Expertise in retaining talent. Cross-cultural sensitivity. Service to both clients and customers.
Social Skill	Proficiency in managing relationships and building networks. An ability to find common ground and build rapport.	Effectiveness in leading change. Persuasiveness. Expertise in building and leading teams.

We are now in a completely different era – one driven by customers and external forces. The problem now is adapting the manufacturing company to the marketplace and the changing demands of customers.

This new scenario means manufacturers must become "market driven" and focus on external forces. This will require skills in understanding and managing people rather than processes. In Coleman's research, the most successful leaders had the skills to understand customers, communicate, motivate, and persuade people to follow them.

Simply put, these are people who have the Five Components of Emotional Intelligence. It's worth reviewing one more time before you go get the book.

- **Self-Awareness** – This is the ability to understand your limitations and to handle constructive criticism. Any leader who can't or won't accept criticism sends a signal that criticizing their style, decisions, or policies is off limits. As soon as that happens, employees are forced to stylize the truth or modify the facts to fit the leader. The leader is then put in the position of not getting all of the hard facts and truth necessary to adapt the company to the changing marketplace. It takes a strong and open-minded individual to be aware of their weaknesses and to be strong enough and open enough to accept constructive criticism.

- **Self-Regulation** – The ability to control disruptive emotions, moods, and biases is also an important factor in Emotional Intelligence. One of the central tenants of critical thinking is the ability to be able to rise above your moods, biases, emotions, and prejudices to make the best decision. Coleman describes this ability as Self-Regulation. Self-Regulation is the key factor in making the right decision during a time of great change. It is the ability to suspend judgement – to think before acting.

- **Motivation** – There are many executives who are driven to succeed because of monetary rewards, status, or stock prices. But Coleman's research shows that the new leaders are motivated by a "desire to achieve for the sake of achievement".

These people have a passion for new challenges. They like work that is new and interesting and requires fast learning.

It is hard to describe the type of motivation required, but I think a story about Colonel John Boyd gets to the heart of the issue. John Boyd was one of the most influential but least known American military thinkers of the Twentieth Century. He created the strategy called the OODA loop and developed energy theories that greatly affected the design of modern fighter aircraft.

Boyd was a maverick and a genius. His personal credo was "to be or to do." In advising younger officers who had bright futures in the Air Force, Boyd said, "There are two career paths in front of you, and you have to choose which path you will follow. One path leads to promotions, titles, and positions of distinction. To achieve success down this path you have to conduct yourself a certain way. You must go along with the system and show that you are a better team player than your competitors."[8]

"The other path leads to doing things that are truly significant for the Air Force, but the rewards will quite often be a kick in the stomach because you may have to cross swords with the party line on occasion. You can't go down both paths. You have to choose. So do you want to be a man of distinction or do you want to do things that really influence the shape of the Air Force?"

To be or to do.

Coleman describes this type of motivated leader as someone with a "passion to work for reasons that go beyond money or status." I think he is describing leaders who want "to do" rather than "to be." These people are rare, but they are out there. And, the new challenges in manufacturing may be just the right match.

It is the motivated and self-confident leader who also sets the example for risk-taking. Many SMMs are going to have to take more risks – not fewer – to survive in the new economy. You can't issue proclamations about risk to the employees. Here, your walk must match your talk. If you want employees to take risks, the leader must set the example.

To change companies from Defender to Prospector culture is not going to be easy. It will take a leader who takes risks and wants "to do" things that really make a difference.

- **Empathy** – This characteristic is defined by Coleman as the ability to understand the emotional makeup of other people. It is also an absolutely necessary part of interviewing, something every leader must do everyday. Empathy is important for building teams, which are an essential part of the decentralized organization.

Teams are always composed of people with different agendas, emotions, needs, and views. But they still have to work together and make consensus decisions. It is essential that leaders understand the emotional make-up of the people to achieve team goals.

Empathy is also necessary to retain the talented people I call "hunters." These are the people who get things done and are very difficult to replace. Retaining hunters must be a high priority of the leader because it costs too much to replace them. It takes skills in coaching, mentoring, and empathy to be able to retain hunters and get them to follow you.

- **Social Skills** – This final component is about proficiency in managing relationships, building networks, and building rapport with people. Often, surviving in the new economy has more to do with people than with things.

  For example, building strong relationships with customers that can achieve a real partnership is one of the primary objectives of Prospector companies. By this, I mean the type of leader who can personally build strong relationships with customers and not rely on the sales department to do it. Today's SMM leader must also be able to build networks with vendors and find common ground with a wide variety of people if he or she is to succeed. The necessary social skills may also include persuasion – knowing how to make emotional pleas and how to use your persuasion abilities to influence other people.

Discussing empathy and social skills may sound like business psychiatry, but they are used as skill sets by the most successful of today's business leaders. These new leaders have the special social skills that allow them to deal with customers, customer groups, employees, unions, vendors, governments, competitors and people problems in general. They have another dimension to them that is beyond the administrative, analytical and data side of the business. They are the types of leaders who can manage a Prospector organization.

If you evaluate the characteristics of the successful Prospector company described in Table 6-1, you will quickly see that succeeding in new markets, with new products, and in a decentralized organization will require a different kind of leader – one who understands what drives people.

The data suggests that the best leaders to manage manufacturing companies in the future may be people who are comfortable with the challenges of people, the ambiguities of satisfying customers, and the intangibles of business. This is particularly true for those companies who are going to have to change their organizations from the traditional Defender model to a Prospector model.

A study in England by the Cranfield School of Management also came to a similar conclusion. The study found that "The picture that emerges from an analysis of these results is that the manager of the future will need to have a high level of marketing skills to be effective.

"Technical competence alone will be insufficient as managers will also need credibility and personal standing. The ideal future manager will be prepared to take risks and to use his or her influencing and interpersonal skills to convince and motivate colleagues."[9]

Discovering Opportunities in Change

As other manufacturers decry the effects of foreign competition and globalization, the new breed of manufacturers are relatively optimistic about the future and their growth potential. They intuitively know that where there is great change and chaos there are also always opportunities. It is a matter of getting out and looking for those opportunities.

They're there.
They may not be obvious.
They may not be easy.
But they are waiting to be discovered.
It's up to you to find them.

The Promise of New and Growing Industries

Certainly there will be many industries that continue to decline and perhaps some, like semi-conductors, apparel, and shipbuilding, will never come back. But there are other industries emerging and evolving that will provide new opportunities for manufacturers in the future:

In 1980, the personal computer arrived in our economy. Ten years later, the Internet was born. Nobody predicted the huge industries, thousands of market niches, or millions of applications that were created by these two technologies.

As some of our traditional industries die, they will be replaced by new and emerging high growth industries. Among those industries will be many technology industries – areas like biomedical devices, nano-technology, nano-manufacturing, informatics, biotechnology, pervasive computing, analytical instrumentation, and optic electronics. There is a good chance that one of these technologies might also blossom into a number of high growth industries. The technology will also "spillover" into many new products that will be invented and made by SMMs.

Of course, we can't forget that the huge traditional industries are not going to go away. See Figure 2-1 in Chapter 2 for a list of some of these traditional industries that have experienced reasonable, if not consider-able, growth in recent years.

Other reasons for optimism

The Asian Countries Are Not Invincible. You might remember that from 1980 to 1985 many manufacturers began believing that the Japanese were invincible. They were higher quality, lower priced, and seemed to be taking market after market away from us. We began studying books written about their management and quality systems and everyone in manufacturing thought we should start learning Japanese as a second language. Then they got into economic trouble and suddenly they were less than the powerhouse we had envisioned.

Now we are all living in fear of the new Chinese juggernaut and they are taking products and markets away from American manufacturers. But they already have problems with energy, resources, banking, and litigation – intellectual property issues are part of a long (and growing) list. They are a hot economy that might implode and end up slipping like the Japanese economy.

My point is this. Let's quit worrying about work going to low-cost countries and focus on what kind of work we do best here in America and where we have competitive advantage.

New Services Will Be Needed. Along with all of the opportunities for inno-vative new products, there will be a demand for new services. Remember that customers are also struggling to compete. They must continuously look for ways to increase productivity, improve product quality, improve performance, lower maintenance and service costs, improve their pro-duction capacity, and work with fewer employees. They need more than new products, they need new services from small manufacturers.

There are opportunities to sell new services, such as design, start-up, training and education, on-site maintenance, repair, emergency, financial, trade-in, dismantling, consignment, and a host of other services. But you must visit customers to find these opportunities. The new breed of manufacturers we've discussed, like D8, EBC, and Ashfield Industries, are on the cutting edge of figuring out what services customers will need, and pay for, in the future.

International Markets. Everyone, including the high-priced Europeans are coming to our markets. But American manufacturers, on the whole, don't seem to be either interested or ready to compete in International markets. The fact is that many small manufacturers have found market niches in foreign countries and they have proven we can compete.

Globalization can be a two-way street. This is all about marketing again and having the wherewithal to find out about foreign markets. We have been spoiled for a long time by doing business in this giant U.S. economy and we haven't had to market internationally. Well, the time has come and we need to look for international opportunities.

Products Coming Back to America. The Epson story in Chapter 7 shows that some products are coming back from overseas and that it is not just foreign unit costs but the total cost of manufacturing overseas that companies must examine carefully. I am sure that once the smoke clears on the stampede to China, many companies will find out that quality, delivery, and legal problems will make the total cost of outsourcing to Asia not worth it. We may find more than a little bit of business coming back our way. At a minimum, large companies will find it wiser to split production between U.S. and foreign suppliers – just in case the foreign supplier can't deliver what was promised.

Market Proximity. Companies will also find out that close proximity to the customer is more important than unit costs. This is a partial reason that Japanese and other nations build manufacturing plants in the U.S. to serve our markets. We have a proximity advantage.

The Giant Manufacturers Might Change. Although many large manufacturer have contributed to the woes of SMMs through relentless price concessions and many see suppliers as expendable – this may change. Some enlightened large manufacturers are beginning to see that continued reduction in the U.S. supplier base is not in their long-term best interests. They are beginning to see that many supplier manufacturers are also buyers of their products and the employees of these companies are domestic consumers.

Bob Johns, Director of Marketing for the sheet metal group at Nucor Steel says "We are all in the same boat, whether a manufacturer is large or small. We are going to fight the decline of U.S. manufacturing tooth and nail." He adds, "If small and midsize firms go down the tubes, the direct impact will be that volume will go down for large companies, and we'll all eventually disappear down the sewer."[10]

Opportunity Abounds

There are tremendous opportunities for those manufacturers who can adapt to the new customer demands. In fact, even with the overall decline of U.S. manufacturing there are still many opportunities to grow, create new products, access new markets, and create jobs.

However, we are now faced with our greatest challenge – halting the decline of U.S. manufacturing with new growth from new opportunities. Manufacturing has dropped from 26% of GDP down to 12%. It seems clear that we must prevent the decline from going below the critical mass or it will affect the entire economy. Big questions remain. What percentage is critical mass? Can we halt the decline? Can we grow in the future? No one knows, but I am optimistic that manufacturing will grow again in a number of ways if it can adapt itself effectively to its customers' new demands.

This adaptation process will not be easy. It will mean converting manufacturing companies from an operation-driven mind-set (Defender companies) to a market-driven mind-set (Prospector companies).

In 1970, Charles Ames wrote a landmark article in the Harvard Business Review titled "Trappings vs. Substance in Industrial Marketing." In the article, Ames predicted that American manufacturing companies were going to be faced with more competition in all markets and competing in a much tougher environment. He stressed the importance of manufacturing companies adopting a market orientation but said it would be a hard task to convert an "operations-oriented" company to one that is "market-oriented."

For 30 years, it appeared that Ames was wrong. During that time many operations-oriented manufacturers did pretty well. But in this new century, as globalization and foreign competitors continue to progress, Mr. Ames's predictions are coming true.

U.S. manufacturers can compete in the new economy. We can compete against foreign competitors, but not as we competed in the past. To become market oriented, we must change the culture of our companies and go on the attack. The most fundamental change will be for each company to adapt to the unique new demands of their unique niche in the marketplace. This is not a matter of simply hiring a few extra sales people or spending more money on promotion.

This kind of change involves monitoring customer needs, finding new customers, exploring emerging market niches, offering new products and services and generally experimenting with many methods that may be new and scary. Becoming market oriented means changing the company from an order taker to an order maker. It is about creating a new type of organization – a Prospector organization

American manufacturers have always been unique in the world. We have more than our share of entrepreneurs who are not afraid of risks. American manufacturing has proven itself very resilient and has always bounced back from recessions, depressions, world wars, and the threats of foreign competitors. I am optimistic that American manufacturing can do it again. It will be different. More challenging. More exciting. More a part of today's new global marketplace. But now, more than ever, there's a place for hard work and new ideas. This book is an attempt to show small and midsize manufacturers how we can make it happen.

Notes:

1. Ricardo Semler, *Maverick: The Story Behind the World's Most Unusual Workplace* (New York: Warner Books, 1995).

2. Traci Purdum, "Leadership at All Levels: Best Practices," *Industry Week*, July 2004, 66.

3. See Note 1.

4. Reed Business Information, "Career Update: Apprenticeships Help Companies Nurture Skilled Workforce," *Control Engineering*, May 1998, 21.

5. CamTech is a private non-profit corporation created under a contract with the Pennsylvania Department of Labor and Industry as well as local Northwestern Pennsylvania employers.

6. Daniel Coleman, "What Makes a Leader," *Harvard Business Review*, November/December 1998.

7. Ibid., 95.

8. Robert Coram, *Boyd: The Fighter Pilot Who Changed the Art of War* (New York: Time Warner Books, 2002).

9. Roger Palmer and Mike Meldrum, *The Future of Marketing in Industrial and Technological Organizations* (Bedford, England: Cranfield School of Management, 1998).

10. Doug Bartholomew, "Manufacturing in Crisis: A House Divided," *Industry Week*, November 2005.

11. Charles Ames, "Trappings vs. Substance in Industrial Marketing," *Harvard Business Review*, July/August 1990, 102.